The United States
and International Organization:
The Changing Setting

Edited by Lawrence S. Finkelstein

The M.I.T. Press
CAMBRIDGE, MASSACHUSETTS, AND LONDON, ENGLAND

Preface

IF one had to choose a single word to describe the present moment in world affairs, that word would surely be "indeterminate." No one can doubt that convulsive forces are at work reordering the familiar in our postwar international patterns. Nor can there be question that the issues have been broached, the struggles over their resolution begun, and vast consequences assured. The period is one of transition, and while one can say "from where," no one can tell "to where."

The great issues are in suspense wherever one turns. What is implied for world peace and order by Communist China, armed with nuclear weapons, rent by internal schism over dogma and power, contesting the ascendancy over world Communism, and soon to confront an inevitable leadership succession? Will the promise of the 1968 Treaty on the Nonproliferation of Nuclear Weapons be fulfilled? Or are we trapped on the nuclear escalator with a competition between the Great Powers for assured destruction capability and who knows how many races between the less powerful nations for superiority or deterrence against each other or even for places at the table of the great? What does current tension in the Middle East portend, not only for the countries of the area but also for relations between Great Powers? What direction will be taken in the organization of Europe and what will be the implications for the Atlantic nexus? At the heart of Europe's future lies a divided Germany. Will the schism be stabilized, perhaps even formally acknowledged, or will pressures for unification be renewed?

This short catalog suggests that it is overdrawn to say, as some do, that North-South issues have replaced the more familiar confrontations of the postwar period in the forefront of concern. Nevertheless, they will surely be on the international agenda for some time to come. The confrontation between the white-dominated bastions of southern Africa and the independent nations to the north is in suspense. More generally, there is the campaign of the poorer, less developed nations for a greater share of the world's riches, for new conceptions of respect for human rights, and for more leverage in the making of decisions.

What of the implications of exploding technology? Will the spoliation of the earth's environment and the competition to exploit untapped resources go

iii

on without restraint? Or will controls be accepted? Will innovations in transportation and communication help in "harmonizing the actions of nations in
the attainment of ... [the] common ends"[1] of the United Nations Charter, or
will they serve as instruments of competition in Cold Wars, by whatever name
we may henceforward know them?

These uncertainties describe the changing international context for the pursuit of United States purposes in the world. Change is not confined to the
external world. War weariness, the rediscovery of major problems at home,
and a new Administration in Washington combine to raise questions of a
kind not heard since before World War II about the constancy of American
commitment to an active international role.

This volume seeks to illuminate the implications of these changes for one
aspect of United States foreign policy, its participation in multilateral organizations. It had its origin in a lecture I gave in the spring of 1967 before a seminar conducted by Professor Harold Jacobson at the University of Michigan. It
then appeared that the assurance of United States commitment to the multilateral mode of conducting its foreign policy was already under growing strain.
While the sources of the strain were many—among them the shifting mood
of the American people, the frustrating complexities of "internal wars" that
proved difficult to cope with through intergovernmental instrumentalities, the
resistance of poverty to the campaigns mounted against it through international means—they could all be viewed in terms of the changes that had taken
place and were continuing in the environment for international cooperation
since World War II. In that lecture I sketched the broad outlines of these
changes and their implications for United States purpose. This volume is the
result of the conclusion I then reached that the changes should be described
and analyzed more fully.

The volume is limited in purpose. It does not seek to add to the freshet of
recent scholarship looking toward a more quantitatively scientific discipline
of international organization study. It does not seek to add to the growing
lore concerning international development—economic and political. The recent special issue of *International Organization*[2] devoted to this subject would
make such a focus for this volume redundant in any case. It does not purport
to represent a worldview of international organization today; it focuses specifically on the setting as it affects United States policy in international organizations. It is policy-oriented in the sense that it is concerned with the
environment for policy. It does not seek to prescribe policy although individual authors were free to express their own views as to desirable future policy.
Moreover, the volume does not pretend to be comprehensive; an early deci-

[1] Article 1, paragraph 4, of the UN Charter.

[2] Richard N. Gardner and Max F. Millikan (ed.), "The Global Partnership: International Agencies
and Economic Development," *International Organization*, Winter 1968 (Vol. 22, No. 1).

sion was made to keep the volume short even at the cost of omitting to cover thoroughly such topics as economic development, population, or human rights. Critics may well point to gaps in the coverage; there can be no doubt that they exist and their justification lies in the volume's success in avoiding the mammoth proportions of too many compendia.

The volume owes much to many and my thanks go to: the contributors who cooperated mightily, meeting onerous deadlines or missing them only slightly; others who advised and criticized, especially those who joined the authors at a review session in New York on March 14-15, 1969; the Board of Trustees of the World Peace Foundation who have sanctioned and supported the project; and the World Peace Foundation staff who have supplied encouragement and technical assistance and whose editorial skills are apparent in the succeeding pages. Miss Claire Gilbert, particularly, has served beyond the normal call of duty. Finally, a word of thanks is due to my wife and daughter for their kindly tolerance of the idiosyncratic behavior of a beleaguered editor fighting the printer's deadline.

APRIL 1969   LAWRENCE S. FINKELSTEIN

TABLE OF CONTENTS

vii

International Cooperation in a Changing World:

A Challenge to United States Foreign Policy

LAWRENCE S. FINKELSTEIN

IT was above all to avoid the recurrence after World War II of threats to world peace and order that the United States set out to design and bring into being the United Nations and the congeries of related agencies. "From the very beginning," says the report of the American delegation to the United Nations Conference on International Organization at San Francisco, "the problems of post-war peace and security were paramount."[1] This seemingly obvious observation is not as trivial as it may sound, for it is a benchmark by which to measure the transformation that has occurred in the character, emphases, and achievements of the United Nations. It will no longer do to say, as was once possible, that the UN's value can be judged solely by its success in avoiding international conflict. Today, the United Nations very likely would command American attention and participation even if it had no utility in the realm of peace and security.

MAINTENANCE OF PEACE THROUGH THE UNITED NATIONS

Even with respect to the peace and security functions properly so called—the problems dealt with in Chapters VI, VII, and VIII of the UN Charter—dramatic shifts of emphasis have occurred. They have been too often described

LAWRENCE S. FINKELSTEIN, a member of the Board of Editors of *International Organization*, is Secretary and a Research Associate of the Center for International Affairs, Harvard University, Cambridge, Mass.

[1] *Charter of the United Nations: Report to the President on the Results of the San Francisco Conference by the Chairman of the United States Delegation, the Secretary of State, June 26, 1945* (Department of State Publication 2349, Conference Series 71) (Washington: U.S. Government Printing Office, 1945), p. 21.

I

to require lengthy exposition here.[2] For our present purpose what is important about that evolution is the altered environment it has brought about and the new issues it poses for the United States.

The Role of the Russians

There has always been a close interaction between our relations with the Union of Soviet Socialist Republics outside the UN and within it. In the post-war days of rapidly mounting hostility and the desperate effort to stabilize Europe and limit the extension of Soviet power the United States turned to the UN as an instrument to mobilize political and material support and to record moral opprobrium against Communist violations of political independence and human rights.[3] Conditions favored success by the United States in seeking endorsement of its purpose to prevent expansion of Communist power and to stabilize territorial arrangements after World War II. It turned to the UN to legitimize the contingent threat to apply American force, as in Iran in 1946–1947, or its actual use, as in Korea in 1950. The United States also succeeded in mobilizing, and for some period maintaining, a substantial majority in support of its approach to arms control, especially the control of nuclear weapons. In those days United States leadership profited from the crude heavy-handedness of Soviet policy under Joseph Stalin and from the composition of the Organization which assured an essentially friendly constituency for most American positions on important matters.[4] The Uniting for Peace Resolution of 1950[5] reflected the hope that majority will could be substituted for the unanimity of the Great Powers anticipated in the Charter as the basis for action to maintain or restore peace.

Even in the early days there were limits to the extent to which the Soviet Union was ready to carry its hostility.[6] It did not hesitate to persist in its opposition to the majority. But, faced with a United States monopoly and later its great preponderance of atomic military power and confronted by an unsympathetic voting majority in the United Nations, the capacity of the Soviet

[2] See, among others, Marina S. Finkelstein and Lawrence S. Finkelstein, "The Future and Collective Security: An Essay," in Marina S. Finkelstein and Lawrence S. Finkelstein (ed.), *Collective Security* (San Francisco, Calif: Chandler Publishing Co., 1966), pp. 255–265; Leland M. Goodrich, "The Maintenance of International Peace and Security," in Norman J. Padelford and Leland M. Goodrich (ed.), *The United Nations in the Balance: Accomplishments and Prospects* (New York: Frederick A. Praeger, 1965), pp. 65ff; Leland M. Goodrich and Anne P. Simons, *The United Nations and the Maintenance of International Peace and Security* (Washington: Brookings Institution, 1955).

[3] Although it did so cautiously and not without misgiving. See Lawrence D. Weiler and Anne Patricia Simons, *The United States and the United Nations: The Search for International Peace and Security* (National Studies on International Organization) (New York: Manhattan Publishing Company [for the Carnegie Endowment for International Peace], 1967), pp. 124–128.

[4] For a table showing the facts of membership change in the Organization until 1965 see the author's "The United Nations: Then and Now" in Padelford and Goodrich (ed.), pp. 13–16.

[5] General Assembly Resolution 377 (V) of November 3, 1950.

[6] Philip E. Mosely has commented on this. See his "The Soviet Union and the United Nations" in Padelford and Goodrich (ed.), pp. 303–304.

Union to influence UN outcomes was limited. Nevertheless, it did not quit the forum[7] even when the United States led the Organization in the major military action against aggression in Korea by Soviet allies. It may be said that the Soviet Union cooperated with the majority at least to the extent of tolerating that majority's exploitation of the United Nations for its own ends.

Even during this early period, moreover, there were issues which, with hindsight, may be said to have foreshadowed the later era of "peacekeeping." In some cases in which the Soviet Union was either directly involved, such as the Iranian case, or indirectly concerned because of the involvement of its allies, such as the Greek border affair, the Corfu Channel case, and the charges against Bulgaria, Rumania, and Hungary of having violated the terms of the peace treaties, the UN was one instrument for conducting the Cold War. In these cases the Soviet Union submitted to the victories of the majority, at least to the extent of not withdrawing from the UN. In other situations, however, such as the Palestine and the Kashmir cases, there was a degree of Soviet cooperation with the peacekeeping aims of the majority; this included, in some cases, voting with the United States and the majority or, at least, acquiescing in the decisions reached. Soviet tolerance was further tested during this period by the universal practice of excluding Soviet participation in UN bodies sent to the field while other permanent members of the Security Council were not excluded.[8]

Beginning with Suez, however, in the post-Stalin period of "peacekeeping," the basis shifted. While the Russians could not participate, neither could the United States.[9] This development was a response to important changes in the world setting as reflected in the UN environment. The Soviet Union had, for one thing, demonstrated a nuclear capability beginning in 1949. The evolving mutuality of nuclear threat between the Soviet Union and the United States made it seem prudent that the two countries should be shielded to the extent possible against the risk that they might slip into nuclear confrontation with each other through involvement in peacekeeping operations.

With the influx of new Members after 1955 the importance of nonalignment grew. The voting odds shifted in a direction unfavorable to the United States. In part this was because the Soviet Union was able to exploit the colonial experiences and memories of the new countries, something the United States

---

[7] Except, of course, for the famous "walkout" from the Security Council over the Iranian issue in 1946 and the "boycott" of the Security Council because of the continued seating of the Republic of China (Nationalist China) in 1950.

[8] See Weiler and Simons, p. 223.

[9] Indeed, with the exception of United Kingdom forces in the Cyprus operation, forces of all permanent members of the Security Council have been excluded. On the United Nations Emergency Force (UNEF) decision see William R. Frye's dramatic account in *A United Nations Peace Force* (New York: Oceana Publications [under the auspices of the Carnegie Endowment for International Peace], 1957), p. 12; and Gabriella Rosner, *The United Nations Emergency Force* (New York: Columbia University Press, 1963), pp. 118–119.

with its alliance ties to the colonial nations of Western Europe could not do.

It was in this context that peacekeeping operations were mounted in the Middle East, the Congo, Cyprus, Yemen, and New Guinea. In each case the Soviet Union, for different reasons to be sure, either agreed to or acquiesced in the UN decision to intervene. In the Congo it was possible after initial Soviet agreement to carry on a complex operation in the face of Soviet opposition. But the price was heavy because this experience no doubt strengthened Soviet unwillingness to pay the peacekeeping assessments levied by the General Assembly under Article 17 of the Charter. The resulting "Article 19 crisis" in 1964–1965[10] made it abundantly clear that future peacekeeping decisions will be unlikely unless the Soviet Union and the United States can agree, together with a sufficient number of other members of the Security Council to constitute the requisite majority. At the very least it seems that future peacekeeping decisions will depend on Soviet agreement to voluntary financing by others. That has been the pattern of peacekeeping operations since the crisis over financing.

The UN's peacekeeping successes in the years after Suez have depended on Soviet and American willingness to limit pursuit of national advantage in crises occurring in parts of the world that were not of direct vital concern to them in order to limit the risks that they might become embroiled with each other. The balance of benefit was not, however, entirely symmetrical. Thus, for a host of reasons which cannot be examined here United States purposes were better served by the UN operation in the Congo than were the Soviet Union's.[11] The Article 19 experience makes it appear unlikely in the extreme that the Soviet Union will hereafter wish, or find it necessary, to agree to operations that do not meet its requirements. The United States thus cannot count on future operations serving its interests in competition with the Soviet Union's. The question then is squarely whether the interests and policies of the United States and the Soviet Union are likely to coincide sufficiently to permit peacekeeping to go forward, with mutual support, with one acquiescing in an operation supported by the other, or with both acquiescing in an operation from which they both abstain.

What are the prospects for such agreement? Much depends on whether the two powers build upon the recent relative détente in their relationship.[12] The evidence is ambiguous. We may, or may not, be at a new turning point

10 See Norman J. Padelford, "Financing Peacekeeping: Politics and Crisis," in Padelford and Goodrich (ed.), pp. 80–98; John G. Stoessinger and associates, *Financing the United Nations System* (Washington: Brookings Institution, 1964); and Ruth B. Russell, "United Nations Financing and 'The Law of the Charter,'" *Canadian Journal of Transnational Law*, 1966 (Vol. 5, No. 1), pp. 68–95.

11 See Inis L. Claude, Jr., "United Nations Use of Military Force," *Journal of Conflict Resolution*, June 1963 (Vol. 7, No. 2), pp. 128–129; and Ernest W. Lefever, *Crisis in the Congo: A United Nations Force in Action* (Studies of U.S. Policy and the U.N.) (Washington: Brookings Institution, 1965), *passim* but especially p. 180.

12 For arguments as to the unlikelihood of this occurring see Stanley Hoffmann, *Gulliver's Troubles,*

in our relations with the Soviet Union. There is hope of a better future in the apparent Russian retreat from the ideologically motivated campaign Ambassador Charles Yost has aptly termed its "evangelical Diaspora."[13]

We know that a high degree of tacit collaboration occurred in 1965 when the United States in subtle but important ways supported the Soviet Union's successful intervention to end the Indo-Pakistani war. No doubt an important factor was a shared interest in preventing gains by Communist China which might have resulted from growing Pakistani dependence on Chinese support had the war continued. In the future if active hostilities continue on the Soviet-Chinese Far Eastern frontier or if Chinese strength should extend along the southern edges of Soviet Central Asia, the Soviet Union may well find that its interest lies in collaborating with the United States in avoiding threats to the peace in less vital areas. We know also that both superpowers backed away from becoming irrevocably committed in the Middle East war of June 1967. The success of Israeli arms may well have spared the United States the painful decision whether to intervene more actively than it did. The Soviet Union certainly preferred the humiliation of seeing its Arab clients defeated to the risks of intervening further to prevent that result. The evidence is at least not inconsistent with the hypothesis that both shied away from any form of involvement that might have enhanced the risk that they would confront each other.

The evidence is far from conclusive and it is only prudent to assume, with Vernon Aspaturian,[14] that the future course of Soviet behavior is uncertain. Among the uncertainties are the influence of China and of Sino–United States relations on Soviet behavior. If the Soviet Union seeks, as Aspaturian suggests may be implied by recent Russian emphasis on long-legged conventional military capabilities, to play a competitive role on a global scale, whatever the risk, the United States will have to decide whether its own interest in particular cases or in the general inhibition of Soviet gains requires it to accept the risk of stepping in, unilaterally or in concert with others, to counter the Russians. In such circumstances, it bears repeating, UN intervention is not likely to be feasible. Moreover, continued active competition between the two Great Powers in the "third world" would make a mockery of the idea of "guarantees" to safeguard nonnuclear states in Africa and Asia against nuclear threats. By removing one incentive for restraint in acquiring nuclear weapons on the part of the "threshold" countries, competitive great-power behavior might

Or the Setting of American Foreign Policy (Atlantic Policy Studies) (New York: McGraw-Hill [for the Council on Foreign Relations], 1968), pp. 350–352; and Zbigniew Brzezinski, "Peace and Power," *Survival*, December 1968 (Vol. 10, No. 12), pp. 390–392, reprinted from *Encounter*, November 1968 (Vol. 31, No. 3). The uncertainties in the sphere of arms relationships are dealt with in Professor Lincoln Bloomfield's article later in this volume.

[13] Charles Yost, *The Insecurity of Nations: International Relations in the Twentieth Century* (New York: Frederick A. Praeger [for the Council on Foreign Relations], 1968), p. 15.

[14] In his contribution later in this volume.

further complicate problems of maintaining peace in the "third world."

If, on the other hand, the Soviet Union and the United States conclude, as Aspaturian considers possible but by no means certain, that their highest interests lie in avoiding confrontation with each other, then two broad possibilities will exist with respect to threats to peace that may arise in the great in-between zone beyond the areas of their direct and vital concern. When, whether because of the ominous shadow of China or for other reasons, the two share an interest in preventing or suppressing threats to the peace and toward that end are able to forego competitive efforts to benefit from chaos, as it is by no means clear that they will do in the Middle East today, then effective UN peacekeeping can take place. There will no doubt be resistance to Soviet-American "duopoly" or "condominium" but it is reasonable to anticipate that if the two are persuaded that the risks of not controlling crisis are too great, enough others will agree to make action possible. In these circumstances even more far-reaching collective peace maintenance activities are not excluded.[15] Even should mainland China become a UN participant and complicate the decision processes, it is possible to visualize something like the history of the 1940's being repeated with the limits on the UN's role being set by the effective limits of Chinese power and vital concern.

A second possibility is suggested by a hypothesis that does not seem inconsistent with the record since 1956. There is some reason to wonder whether nuclear superpowers reliant on their own strength for defense of their vital interests may not be shielded against the consequences of peace breaking down in parts of the world that are not vital to them. If the national security of a Great Power can be seriously threatened only by another Great Power, what risk is posed to them if there is warfare in Biafra? Collective intervention to prevent the worsening of situations that threaten peace has rested in good part on the concept that peace is indivisible—that a threat to peace anywhere threatens peace everywhere. If threats to the superpowers are in fact arrested at their nuclear frontiers—and the consequence of guessing wrong imposes caution in testing where they lie—may not the Soviet Union and the United States become relatively indifferent to threats to local order arising in areas remote from their vital concerns? If so, may they not be able to acquiesce in peacekeeping by others?[16]

Even if the two giants, shielded by their nuclear defenses, have not suppressed the competitive impulses of the past, they may still be driven to con-

[15] For an imaginative essay on such possibilities, written in 1957 by Paul H. Nitze, subsequently Secretary of the Navy and Deputy Secretary of Defense, see "Where and Under What Circumstances Might a United Nations Force Be Useful in the Future?", appendix in Frye, pp. 111ff., especially pp. 119 and 121. See also Finkelstein and Finkelstein (ed.), pp. 266–269.

[16] If the Great Powers sit benignly on the sidelines, the burdens for others may increase. As Inis Claude points out in his contribution later in this volume, the history of UN peace maintenance activities does not lend much comfort to the belief that successful UN intervention can be mounted without material and political leadership by the United States.

clude that the risks of intervention exceed the risks of abstention. Even if the two do not agree enough to make them wish to collaborate to suppress threats to peace, they may nevertheless symmetrically conclude that peace is not totally indivisible, that threats to the peace and their national involvement in some parts of the world are more divisible than in others, and that in such cases they can, perhaps must, allow events to take their course.[17] The Middle East crisis will be a revealing indicator of whether the two powers will: pursue competitive ends, whatever the risks; collaborate to contain threats to the peace; or frighten each other into the status of bystanders.[18]

The Role of Communist China

In some important ways Communist China in recent years has been the ghost dominating the banquet. China's behavior will no doubt influence Soviet incentives to join or resist efforts to control threats to peace. It is perhaps overly mechanistic to suggest that balance-of-power considerations might persuade the Soviet Union and the United States that they have an interest, in which they might be joined by other powers, to mobilize restraining power to contain China if it threatens. Offhand, it might appear to the contrary that the United States has no direct interest—except perhaps to fish in troubled waters—in the kind of threat posed to the Soviet Union by border violence in the Far East. Similarly, the Soviet Union might see no special reason for concern over threats China might pose to the United States or, more to the point, American allies or friends in the Far East. Yet, can the United States remain entirely indifferent if the question should prove to be who commands the Asian accesses to the North Pacific and the Bering Sea?[19] More broadly, a high United States official, now on the White House staff, called attention to United States interest in the maintenance of "a balance of power in Asia so that no single nation can gain sufficient control of the area to directly threaten the American homeland."[20]

If such a "reversal of alliances" should come to pass, the bases of Soviet-American cooperation would no doubt be laid outside the UN. But the UN might be the vehicle through which Soviet-American understandings might

[17] Carl Kaysen has recently written along these lines. See his "American Military Policy" in Survival, February 1969 (Vol. 11, No. 2), pp. 51–56, reprinted from Carl Kaysen, "Military Strategy, Military Forces, and Arms Control," in Kermit Gordon (ed.), Agenda for the Nation (Washington: Brookings Institution, 1968), pp. 549–584.

[18] As this is written in April 1969, Moscow and Washington seem to be searching for the bases of collaboration. It remains to be seen whether this purpose or their competitive objectives will prevail.

[19] Although China's capacity for aggressive military action is limited. See, for example, Kaysen in Survival, Vol. 11, No. 2, p. 54.

[20] Morton H. Halperin, "After Vietnam," Survival, December 1968 (Vol. 10, No. 12), p. 404, reprinted from Morton H. Halperin, "After Vietnam: Security and Intervention in Asia," Journal of International Affairs, 1968 (Vol. 22, No. 2), pp. 236–246. See also Hans J. Morgenthau, A New Foreign Policy for the United States (New York: Frederick A. Praeger [for the Council on Foreign Relations], 1969), p. 193.

be expressed. The obligations undertaken in connection with the 1968 Treaty on the Nonproliferation of Nuclear Weapons with respect to threats by nuclear armed states (read "China"?) against states not having nuclear weapons are a step in that direction.[21] The fact that that agreement took the form of an acknowledgement of obligation to turn to the Security Council may be understood, correctly, as a means of limiting commitment in view of the protective veto in that body. It might also be said, however, that there is no better forum than the Security Council in which to explore and reveal the convergence of interests and the nature and limits of agreement. It might well serve as an outlet for Soviet-American leadership in instances when the two powers are agreed.[22] This would be true even if mainland China should be seated in the Security Council and thus be able to veto decisions it opposes.

Nothing especially significant remains unsaid about the issue of China's place in the UN. The arguments for and against seating mainland China in the Organization have been rehearsed time and time again.[23] One point perhaps deserves emphasis. The analysis in the preceding paragraphs does not pretend to predict the course of Chinese behavior. There is a chain of thoughtful and respectable analysis that emphasizes Chinese caution and the limits to Chinese risk-taking.[24] Others point to the hostile assumptions of China's ideology, the harsh and aggressive tone of its propaganda, its widespread support of insurrectionary activities, and the series of events in which Chinese military force has been threatened or used in Asia starting with the intervention against the United Nations in Korea in 1950. The fact that uncertainty dominates consideration of future plans affected by China points to the desirability of engaging China's representatives in a forum in which there will be both opportunity and need to present and rationalize China's position in the world and to submit to the testing processes of public and private exchange.

Tension with China there will be. To the extent that military power is relevant that power will be largely in the hands of other Great Powers applying it unilaterally or in concert, perhaps through less than global collective agencies. This was true of the tense period of confrontation with the Soviet Union. That experience offers a relevant lesson. Contained by countervailing power outside the UN, the Soviet Union found it useful to seek a hearing for its views and support for its positions in United Nations forums. In so doing

[21] Security Council Resolution 255 (1968), June 19, 1968.

[22] See Professor Aspaturian's interesting observation later in this volume about Soviet resort to the Security Council when its "policy is oriented toward accommodation and détente with the United States."

[23] See, e.g., *China, the United Nations and United States Policy: An Analysis of the Issues and Principal Alternatives with Recommendations for U.S. Policy,* a report of a National Policy Panel established by the United Nations Association of the United States of America (New York: United Nations Association of the United States of America, 1966).

[24] Going back at least to Alice Langley Hsieh's early work at the RAND Corporation. See her *Communist China's Strategy in the Nuclear Era* (Englewood Cliffs, N.J: Prentice-Hall, 1962).

it submitted itself to the processes of bargaining and compromise of those organs. The result of this mixture, reinforced, of course, by internal change, has been a desirable attenuation of Soviet militancy. It is not unreasonable to speculate that similar processes might work if China was in the UN. At the least Chinese participation would provide useful and much-needed information about Chinese purpose and policy. It would also directly confront China with the mediating, hopefully moderating, influence of a UN majority eager to seek peaceful accommodation of issues in contention between potentially hostile states. The United States faces the question whether it wishes to take advantage of these mediating potentialities or whether it fears resorting to them because their influence on the outcome of issues in dispute is unpredictable and not certain to favor American objectives.

The Role of the Newer Members

The effect of the character and distribution of the UN's membership on its deliberations and decisions in the realm of peace maintenance has, since 1945, altered in many ways.[25] Attention has already been given to the evolving role of the Soviet Union. In what might loosely be termed the Western camp the early postwar dependence of Western Europe on the United States and the relative harmony of aims that characterized United States relations with its Latin American neighbors have given way—in varying degrees and depending on the issues—to vigorous, often fractious, independence. France, in particular, shows a determined will and demonstrates that it has the ability to pursue its own course in foreign affairs. Its course, for example, paralleled the Soviet Union's in the events leading to the crisis of 1964–1965 over financing UN peacekeeping. The transition in United States relations with Latin America is reflected in the fact that the Latin American nations which before and at the 1945 San Francisco Conference insisted that the inter-American system be insulated against intervention by the UN have in recent years on occasion sought to invoke UN intervention to counter United States influence in the hemisphere. The Old World is called in to right the balance of the New. Even Canada, long thought to be most intimately dependent on the United States for reasons of geography and history, has for some years been carving out an independent role, welcome to the United States when it enabled Canada to contribute constructively to UN peacekeeping ventures, less welcome when it takes the form of flagging Canadian support for the North Atlantic Treaty Organization (NATO). In short, the United States is more and more compelled to bargain intensively in its own camp for the support it needs to succeed in UN initiatives.[26]

[25] See the recent article by Leon Gordenker, "The 'New Nationalism' and International Organizations," *International Studies Quarterly*, March 1969 (Vol. 13, No. 1), pp. 31–45.

[26] This is obviously a very truncated synopsis of—even an allusion to—a very complicated history of change. A complete analysis would have to deal with such questions as: the effects of colonial issues

What is true for the countries to the west of the rusting iron curtain is also in some degree true to its east. Symptoms of diversity have existed at least since 1948 when the Soviet Union had to forbid Czech and Polish participation in the conference to organize European response to the United States' Marshall Plan initiative. The Stalin-Tito split in 1948 set in motion the fissiparous tendencies in the Communist world that have developed into sharp Sino-Soviet hostility and strivings for forms of autonomy by Rumania, Poland, Hungary, and, most recently, Czechoslovakia.

This weakening of what might be termed the polar magnetism of the two greatest powers has been accompanied by the enlargement, invigoration, and diversification of the "in-between" forces. Beginning with the membership "breakthrough" of 1955 which saw the admission of Jordan, Libya, Ceylon, Nepal, Cambodia, and Laos, in addition to the European nations caught in the membership logjam of the preceding period, the UN's rolls have been enlarged by the spate of newly independent countries. The result is a "generation gap" between the older nations, of whatever political complexion, and the newer ones. Naturally enough, the latter share neither the historical experience in which the UN was rooted, the political outlooks, nor the schemes of priorities of older Members. Nonalignment became a pervasive force in the UN with the accretion of new Members. As a consequence the United States has met increasing difficulty in finding support for its view of priorities[27] and of proper UN approaches to problems of peace and security. The crisis over UN financing ended as it did not just because of Russian and French resistance to compulsory payment for voluntary peacekeeping activities but because a substantial number of the newer countries were not willing to take a stand against the Soviet position or to subject themselves to the financial burdens of a compulsory system. There was also an element of reluctance by the United States to commit itself to pay for future peacekeeping operations decided upon by unpredictable majorities.

There is some ambiguity as to the significance of these facts for United States leadership in the UN.[28] On the whole the superficial conclusion is also the correct one. It is and will be much more difficult for the United States to have its way in an organization so much more diversely populated and motivated than it used to be in the "good old days" when on issues of major im-

on United States relations with its Western European allies and the changes in the "postcolonial" era; the proposed Nordic alliance which led to Norway and Denmark joining NATO and Sweden continuing its "neutrality"; the imbroglio with the United Kingdom leading to the Suez crisis of 1956, the *Skybolt* misunderstanding, and the continuing "special relationship"; the episodes over Guatemala, Cuba, the Dominican Republic, and the controversies over peacekeeping arrangements in the Americas; etc.

[27] In the 1967 General Assembly session the question of South West Africa (Namibia) was dealt with in plenary session while the Nonproliferation Treaty was "relegated to the First Committee." See "Issues Before the 23rd General Assembly," *International Conciliation*, September 1968 (No. 569), p. 68.

[28] For a recent interesting study of voting patterns see Edward T. Rowe, "Changing Patterns in the Voting Success of Member States in the United Nations General Assembly: 1945–1966," *International Organization*, Spring 1969 (Vol. 23, No. 2), pp. 231–253.

portance to this country the membership was effectively divided between "us" and "them" with "us" in a substantial majority. There is no reason to believe that the trend toward what has been termed a "multi-hierarchical" system[29] will be arrested. Particularly if nuclear power proliferates, but even if it does not, the levers of control will be more difficult to manipulate in an increasingly complex international system.

Paralleling this development in the UN balances, the United States has decided to go it alone in a number of cases it has considered of importance. Unilateral American actions in the Lebanon crisis of 1958 and in Vietnam reflect growing doubts on the part of the United States about the desirability of submitting its policies to the uncertain consensus of the UN processes. The contrast with Korea in 1950 is marked. In that case the United States did, to be sure, move alone out of a sense of military urgency but it also quickly sought and obtained UN endorsement and participation through the Security Council. Resort by the United States to the organs of the Organization of American States (OAS) and of the UN in the Cuban missile crisis may suggest certain parallels. The clear external threat to the hemisphere speedily carried the day in the OAS. The clarity and firmness of the American purpose to have the missiles withdrawn, the risk of major confrontation between Great Powers, and the clear evidence of Soviet duplicity in denying that the missiles were in Cuba won political support for the United States position in the UN although the Secretary-General sought to dispense evenhanded justice by urging both the withdrawal of the missiles and a suspension of the American quarantine.[30] In other cases close to home, the Guatemala intervention of 1954, the Bay of Pigs debacle in 1961, and the intervention in the Dominican Republic in 1965, the United States may have been moved by uncertainty as to the consensus in the OAS[31] paralleling its uncertainties about the UN.

Not only have the shifting balances in the Organization raised far-reaching questions about the ability of the United States to win support for its preferred policies and courses of action; they also pose new questions as to the ability of the United States to resist policies and courses of action to which it is opposed. Finally, of course, the United States can refuse to commit its national resources to UN ventures it does not find congenial. It can veto proposals in the Security Council, refuse to accept General Assembly resolutions as binding, and even, with the Article 19 outcome to rely on as a precedent, refuse to pay peacekeeping costs that the General Assembly might assess.[32]

29 By Stanley Hoffmann in *Gulliver's Troubles*, p. 356.

30 See Richard N. Gardner, *In Pursuit of World Order: U.S. Foreign Policy and International Organizations* (New York: Frederick A. Praeger, 1964), pp. 67–75, for an official argument for the utility of the UN in this crisis.

31 Although the United States sought and obtained agreement on an OAS force to make possible its own withdrawal from the Dominican Republic, success was achieved only by the narrowest of margins.

32 See an earlier suggestion that the United States might refuse to pay assessments going beyond the "proper bounds" of the General Assembly's "competence under Article 17" in "Budgetary and Financial

Particularly, it may be concerned to preserve the ground rule against intervention in matters that are essentially domestic. That the issue is not wholly irrelevant is suggested by the success the new Members have enjoyed, in alliance with others, in altering the balance of UN resolutions on colonialism,[33] racism, and, more particularly, on racial tensions in southern Africa.

The crucial turning point here was the Declaration on the Granting of Independence to Colonial Countries and Peoples[34] which led to creation of the Special Committee of Twenty-Four,[35] in the words of one critic "to harass the colonial Powers."[36] Since then the majority has achieved a formidable record of UN declaration of increasingly inflammatory tone and, more significantly, of decision in these realms.[37] Frustrated by the failure of the International Court of Justice (ICJ) to render a judgment on the substance of the South West Africa case brought by Liberia and Ethiopia[38] the majority moved the General Assembly, almost unanimously, to terminate the South African mandate over South West Africa (now Namibia), an action of dubious legality. A General Assembly resolution in 1967 requested the Security Council "to take all appropriate measures" to enable the Council it had set up to take over administration of the territory.[39] Stronger language referring specifically to Chapter VII[40] of the Charter and calling the Republic of South Africa an aggressor was not adopted. In 1968 the General Assembly went further, recommending that the Security Council "take all effective measures" to bring about South African withdrawal.[41]

The issues arising out of the confrontation between the United Kingdom

Problems of the United Nations," *Review of the United Nations Charter: Compilation of Staff Studies Prepared for the Use of the Sub-committee on the United Nations Charter of the Committee on Foreign Relations* (Pursuant to Senate Resolution 126, 83rd Congress) (Washington: U.S. Government Printing Office, 1955), p. 165.

[33] See Rupert Emerson, "Colonialism, Political Development, and the UN," in Padelford and Goodrich (ed.), pp. 129–136. See also his *Self-Determination Revisited in the Era of Decolonization* (Occasional Papers in International Affairs, No. 9) (Cambridge, Mass: Center for International Affairs, Harvard University, December 1964), pp. 1–24. For a comparison with the original balances with respect to colonial matters see Finkelstein in Padelford and Goodrich (ed.), pp. 11–13, 23; and Lawrence S. Finkelstein, "Colonial Activities," in L. Larry Leonard, *International Organization* (New York: McGraw-Hill, 1951), pp. 477–533.

[34] General Assembly Resolution 1514 (XV), December 14, 1960.

[35] Special Committee on the Situation with regard to the Implementation of the Declaration on the Granting of Independence to Colonial Countries and Peoples.

[36] Rupert Emerson, "Self-Determination," *Proceedings of the American Society of International Law*, 6oth annual meeting, Washington, April 28–30, 1966, p. 138.

[37] For good summaries see the annual numbers of *International Conciliation*, published by the Carnegie Endowment for International Peace on issues before the General Assembly, particularly the numbers for 1965–1968.

[38] For an interesting and insightful examination of the implications of this case and of the Court's decision see Milton Katz, *The Relevance of International Adjudication* (Cambridge, Mass: Harvard University Press, 1968), pp. 69–144.

[39] General Assembly Resolution 2325 (XXII), December 16, 1967.

[40] It is Chapter VII which provides for Security Council measures, including the use of force, to deal with threats to the peace, breaches of the peace, or acts of aggression.

[41] General Assembly Resolution 2403 (XXIII), December 16, 1968.

and Southern Rhodesia over the conditions of independence have led to even
more far-reaching decisions, including a series of Security Council resolutions
imposing increasingly severe economic sanctions against Southern Rhodesia.[42]
Even more extreme measures, involving use of force, have been advocated by
the General Assembly[43] and proposed in the Security Council.

The Western powers have been able to fend off the pressures for more
far-reaching enforcement measures in southern Africa, in good measure
because of the obvious impossibility thus far of conducting such operations
without their support. Yet there can be no doubt that there is a vigorous
determination on the part of a large number of UN Members to employ the
Organization as an instrument to change the status quo in southern Africa
and to resort to the enforcement powers of Chapter VII to that end.[44] They
have proved their ability to move the spectrum of acceptable choice far from
its starting point even for nations that do not share their priorities. The United
States, for example, felt it expedient to vote for the General Assembly resolution terminating the South African mandate which found only Portugal and
South Africa in outright opposition. The far-reaching sanctions against Southern Rhodesia imposed by the Security Council in May 1968 were unanimously
adopted.

As long as the participation or support of the United States or other Western powers is necessary for military measures in southern Africa, they will have
the power to prevent it. If military conditions change, if new Soviet conventional capabilities, for example, should become relevant and, unlikely though
it may seem, be put to the service of the activist majority, or if military capabilities should in time grow among the activist-inclined African nations, a
different situation would exist and the United States and others of like mind
would be up against the issue of whether to acquiesce or resist. Even in present
circumstances the issue is a painful one—how much sustenance to give the
majority's view of what should come first in the United Nations when the
issues are relatively remote from direct United States concerns, when the
remedies may involve costs to the United States in loss of trade and communication or even commitment of resources in support of enforcement measures,
and when the United Nations is to be used to change conditions which used
to be thought of as essentially matters of domestic concern. The alternative to
success for those who would change the status quo in Africa, there is much

[42] Security Council Resolution 232 (1966) of December 30, 1966, was the first clear imposition of
sanctions against a particular country under Chapter VII of the Charter. The expanded embargoes imposed in 1968 by Security Council Resolution 253 (1968) of May 29, 1968, have been described as
going beyond the sanctions imposed by the League of Nations against Italy in 1935–1936. See "Issues
Before the 23rd General Assembly," International Conciliation, No. 569, p. 71.

[43] See General Assembly Resolution 2383 (XXIII), November 7, 1968.

[44] On some implications of the use of collective measures to enforce change see Amelia C. Leiss (ed.),
Apartheid and United Nations Collective Measures: An Analysis (New York: Carnegie Endowment for
International Peace, 1965), pp. 74–79, 163.

reason to believe, may be a growing disenchantment with the usefulness of the Organization for any purpose. If it cannot deal, they may say, with the problem at the top of the list, why bother with it at all, especially if the uses to which it might be effectively put are of greater concern to others? If the United States wishes the UN to be strengthened for peacekeeping, as Professor Claude urges in his article hereafter, it may confront the issue of giving greater support for what some have termed the "peacebreaking" proclivities of black Africans frustrated by the continuance of racism and colonialism in southern Africa.

Altogether then, the likelihood that the United Nations can serve American interests in peace maintenance hereafter is highly problematic.

REGIONAL SECURITY ORGANIZATIONS

The preceding discussion of UN peacekeeping has focused on the UN's relevance to issues of peace and security which do not arise out of immediate and vital concerns of the Great Powers. Except on the margins the UN has not been directly relevant to such great issues as the stabilization of power in Europe, the division of Germany, the status of Berlin, changes in Soviet relations with other East European countries, the Austrian peace, the independence of Taiwan, and the peace with Japan. Essentially, there is no reason to expect the future to differ greatly from the past in this respect. The main function of defending vital interests against threats from Great Powers will continue to be performed by Great Powers. The structure of world order, even if it profits from a degree of comity and collaboration between Great Powers, will continue to be based on deterrence. The effective will and capacity will have to be great-power will and capacity. Thus in the foreseeable future as in the recent past, while the Great Powers may signal each other or even act via the United Nations, they will continue to rely on their own capacities, sometimes reinforced by the strengths of allied nations. Collaborative defensive arrangements will continue to take the form of less than global organizations which are inaccurately in some cases, but conveniently in all, labeled "regional."

For the United States, with its global commitments and interests, major issues of regional organization arise in widely separated areas. The twentieth anniversary of the North Atlantic Treaty in April 1969 has sharpened critical reexamination of the purpose, scope, and means of NATO and its relation to other collaborative institutions within the area of its concern. In the Far East there is the constant question whether some new form of regional association might not perform the dual purpose of strengthening the political resolution and capability of the countries of the area to deal with their common problems, including security, and of providing the basis for the legitimized projection of United States military power in case of need.[45] In the Americas the United States faces continuing tensions resulting from the size of the shadow it casts over its less powerful neighbors and leading to suggestions that Latin-Americanism might replace or parallel inter-Americanism.[46]

The North Atlantic Area

No brief summary can do justice to the complexity and the difficulty of the issues of organization among the countries that, by geography or by grace of definition, comprise the North Atlantic grouping.

Several major issues are at stake. First, there is the issue of defense organization and commitment. The fear of aggression from the East that inspired the original commitment of Article 5 of the North Atlantic Treaty has greatly diminished. The trend toward relaxed tensions continues despite the excitement of concern over Soviet intentions and capabilities resulting from the Soviet move into Czechoslovakia in 1968. Now a Soviet campaign of reassurance appears under way which, if it further anaesthetizes the Western powers, may also accentuate the placatory tendencies in the Warsaw camp. On both sides of the Atlantic the temptation to question the importance and relevance of major conventional force deployments in Europe stems from doctrinal doubts and controversies accentuated by economic considerations. Despite the fact that France's withdrawal from the decisionmaking organs of NATO made possible the formal adoption of the long-mooted strategy of flexible response the likelihood is that the conventional forces deployed in Europe to support the strategy will be reduced. The entire question of France's relation to the NATO forces and plans is left hanging.

Moreover, important issues remain unresolved as to the nature of participation by the allies in decisions concerning the acquisition, control, and use of nuclear weapons committed to the alliance. The issue has been a nagging and long-lived one. Allied nations naturally have concerns about the reliability of nuclear deterrence controlled by a United States which is itself increasingly vulnerable to nuclear attack,[47] despite the fact that as long as major American ground and tactical air forces remain deployed well forward they will constitute cogent collateral for the United States pledge to defend Europe. The United States has a natural concern and is in important respects bound by

---

[45] It is not intended to suggest that bilateral defense arrangements or even, in some circumstances, unilateral use of force are not legitimate. There is, however, a disposition to assume that the greater the number of participants in the arrangement on which the use of force is hinged, the more legitimate it is. The UN Charter, of course, heads the pecking order. Professor Claude deals with this point in his contribution hereinafter.

[46] For an early expression of this view see Jorge Castañeda, *Mexico and the United Nations* (National Studies in International Organization) (New York: Manhattan Publishing Company [for El Colegio de México and the Carnegie Endowment for International Peace], 1958), pp. 165–196.

[47] Zbigniew Brzezinski has referred to "parity in non-survivability." See his "Peace and Power," *Survival*, Vol. 10, No. 12, p. 390.

law and Congressional surveillance to maintain control over the most vital of national decisions—the projection, acquisition, deployment, and use of nuclear weapons. Recently progress toward accommodation of these irreconcilable interests has been made as a result of the American initiative leading to the Nuclear Planning Group—the so-called McNamara Committee—which serves as a forum for intensified information sharing and planning. Yet it is difficult to believe that as long as nuclear deterrent force remains as central as it has been to European stability, the issue can be thus easily resolved, particularly given the intensive pressures for autonomy and influence exerted by Gaullist France, itself committed to developing and maintaining its own deterrent forces.[48] Little contribution to management of the problem is made by the seemingly irrepressible United States tendency to make important decisions, such as the new rationale for the *Safeguard* antiballistic missile system, without adequate consultation with its allies.[49]

A second major issue is the question of relations with Eastern Europe. While all NATO members favor the idea of improved relations with the Soviet Union and of developing détente,[50] there is less agreement on purpose, strategy, and means.[51] Not only does each NATO member pursue a range of bilateral relationships with countries of Eastern Europe, but there are important differences on such central issues as how to deal with the Oder-Neisse frontier problem and whether to continue to seek to isolate the German Democratic Republic (East Germany) diplomatically and politically or to move toward recognition.

Additional complications result from the special position of the United States as the only global power in the alliance and particularly from its concern for the complex limited adversary relationship with the Soviet Union, especially in the realm of nuclear force stability. The Nonproliferation Treaty is the prime instance thus far of the United States and the Soviet Union being

[48] For a different view, based in good part on the diminishing importance of any force, see John W. Holmes, "Fearful Symmetry: The Dilemmas of Consultation and Coordination in the North Atlantic Treaty Organization," *International Organization*, Autumn 1968 (Vol. 22, No. 4), pp. 822–839.

[49] In his February 24th address to NATO President Richard Nixon paid special attention to this problem and pledged "full consultation" at least with respect to negotiations with the Soviet Union. (*The New York Times*, February 25, 1969.)

[50] The Federal Republic of Germany (West Germany), for example, has said:

> Its aim is an equitable European order on the basis of peaceful agreements, an order in which all nations can live together freely and as good neighbours. After all, the Soviet Union and the countries of Eastern Europe belong to Europe as well.

("Note from the Federal Republic of Germany to Other Governments" [March 25, 1966], reprinted in, e.g., *Documents on Disarmament: 1966* (United States Arms Control and Disarmament Agency Publication, No. 46) (Washington: United States Arms Control and Disarmament Agency, 1967), pp. 168–174. This significant statement, issued by the Ludwig Erhardt Government, marked an important step in the Federal Republic's progression of efforts toward more harmonious relations with Eastern European countries. The policy has been carried forward, indeed intensified, by the Kurt Georg Kiesinger Government. See the remarkable testimony by Vice Chancellor and Foreign Minister Willy Brandt, *A Peace Policy for Europe* (New York: Holt, Rinehart and Winston, 1969).

[51] For a perceptive analysis see Hoffmann, pp. 387–458.

drawn to a common program—in the case of the United States, at least, at considerable cost in terms of the reluctance of some of the NATO allies—by the characteristic they have in common, their responsibility as the premier nuclear powers of the world. If the lesson drawn by the allies is that United States support is qualified by its concern for developing comity with the Russians and by prudent self-interest arising out of nuclear exposure, the consequences for the cohesion of the alliance can be far-reaching indeed. On top of the inference that the United States defense commitment may be unreliable there is vigorous distaste for Soviet-American condominium in European affairs, shared, although for different reasons, by France and the Federal Republic of Germany.[52]

Third, there are the central questions about the scope and character of the organizational frameworks. Further progress in the supranational direction of the Monnet program for Europe seems most unlikely for the foreseeable future, given the interest in more autonomous forms of association inspired by General Charles de Gaulle. The recurrent issue of British membership in the European Economic Community (EEC), unresolved but by no means interred, encounters this dilemma. At least as centrally it runs into French resistance to a United States relationship to Europe via a Britain believed to be America's surrogate. France's resistance to the United Kingdom's entry has been a form of attack on the notion of an Atlantic relationship in which the United States predominates. Other manifestations, of course, were France's virtually complete withdrawal from the military and political organization of NATO and its insistence on withdrawal of American forces from French territory.

A mutually satisfactory solution of the problem of balance between European and American influence is not yet in sight and, indeed, may not exist so long as Europe—especially Germany—remains dependent on the American nuclear equalizer, control of which the United States cannot relinquish. Nor is there much promise in the oft-mooted idea of a European political-military counterweight based on the British and French nuclear forces. Those forces are hardly likely to prove an adequate substitute for the far more significant American strength. In reality independent use of these forces could be intended to do no more than invoke the latter rather than dispense with it. Moreover, France is hardly more likely than is the United States to share final control of its *force de dissuasion* with Germany, short of a political federation which is inconsistent with French goals.

Bearing on these issues is the long-term goal of an all-European Europe, in General de Gaulle's phrase "from the Atlantic to the Urals," which may be at odds with the objective of further tightening the organization of the Eu-

[52] Although, as John Holmes has pointed out, the European power to prevent duopoly is limited. (*International Organization*, Vol. 22, No. 4, p. 825.)

rope of sixes and sevens or of the Atlantic grouping. It is worth emphasizing, however, that unless those who seek an all-European reconciliation welcome greater freedom of action for the Federal Republic of Germany,[53] they will have to accommodate something like either or both the existing Western European and Atlantic arrangements with their long-term purpose.

There are no more important questions of foreign policy before the United States than these. They appear as issues of international organization because we have become so accustomed to having them fought out dramatically in and with reference to the existing international forums and because they are so often presented in terms of the prospects for the further development of this or that institution or the choice of this or that institutional alternative. Yet no issues more clearly demonstrate the intimate relationship between policy and institutional means. The issues for the United States are issues of purpose and strategy. Stanley Hoffmann[54] and others are surely correct in emphasizing the necessity for an ordering of goals and priorities as a first step toward untangling the institutional arrangements. That is by no means to underestimate the difficulty of the instrumental problems. The United States has to decide whether with respect to the large issues of European political accommodation and military security it needs to maintain its intimate participatory role through the Atlantic institutions. If so, it will have to find the means to accommodate the European desire for a more effective role in the decisionmaking of the alliance, including decisions with respect to Soviet relations and nuclear strategy and capabilities. Both spheres pose major difficulties for the United States, hinted at in the preceding analysis, and both will require major sacrifice by the United States with respect to its freedom of action. A way will also have to be found to bring about a more equitable sharing of the economic and technological benefits of weapons development and procurement. Again, major sacrifice will be required. Even so, it is by no means certain that the effort would succeed in the face of the European resistances alluded to unless a means is simultaneously found to enable the European members of the alliance to speak more powerfully to the United States. That would involve at least the loosening of the special ties to the United Kingdom and West Germany and a sophisticated strategy of support for the strengthening of Western European institutions of political and military consultation and planning. There would be no assurance that success in this respect would not lead to a more autonomous Western Europe anyway.

The alternative may well be a further fragmentation in the alliance. While that would be unlikely to force the elimination of the United States commitment to defend Europe, it might reduce its credibility by casting doubt on its

[53] Or a "special relationship" between the United States and the Federal Republic.
[54] In *Gulliver's Troubles*.

political basis. It would also, obviously, interfere with orderly processes of political accommodation with Eastern Europe.

The Far East

Whereas in the Atlantic area the question is whether it is desirable and feasible to preserve and build upon existing institutions, in the Far East it is rather whether new ones should be constructed. The unproductive career of the Southeast Asia Treaty Organization (SEATO) and the checkered experience of Asian efforts to cooperate[55] comprise a cautionary lesson as to the undesirability of seeking to substitute a legal and institutional framework for the political will and consensus that are lacking. In his chapter of this work Joseph Nye cautions about the danger of "telescoping of time"—that is, of taking the institution for the reality that requires much time to come about. In the case of SEATO not even the passage of time produced the reality to match the proud words of the Southeast Asia Collective Defense Treaty. SEATO has become essentially a framework for bilateral engagements between the United States and some of the other members, especially Thailand.[56] However, if the Vietnam war can be ended, conditions for regional development might be found in the combination of uncertainty about the intentions of Communist China, the People's Republic of Korea (North Korea), and the Democratic Republic of Vietnam (North Vietnam) and the reviving respectability of Japan coupled with its growing potential for economic and political leadership. Also significant may be the encouraging erosion of the conflict between the Republic of Korea (South Korea) and Japan, the ending of confrontation between Indonesia and Malaysia, and, hopefully, reduced tension over territorial issues in the area.

It is important to distinguish the purposes for which institution building might seem appropriate in the Far East. Different institutional responses might be appropriate to differently defined needs. To begin with there are encouraging signs of a movement toward regional treatment of potentialities for economic cooperation in Eastern Asia. The Ministerial Conferences for Economic Development of Southeast Asia are providing a vehicle both for Japanese engagement with and contribution to the other non-Communist nations of the area and for association of hitherto incompatible Southeast Asian nations. It is perhaps early to predict whether a continuing organization will come about. Surely, if the participating nations wish to develop an institutional framework for mutual help, the United States should be pleased and should respect the wish of the participants to avoid giving their collaboration a politi-

[55] See, e.g., Bernard K. Gordon, "Regionalism and Instability in Southeast Asia," in Joseph S. Nye, Jr. (ed.), *International Regionalism* (Boston, Mass: Little, Brown and Company, 1968), pp. 106–125.
[56] See Fred Greene, *U.S. Policy and The Security of Asia* (New York: McGraw-Hill [for the Council on Foreign Relations], 1968), pp. 102, 122.

cal anti-Communist orientation. The United States might even find it useful
to channel economic aid via the organization.[57]

In the political/security realm the prospects are muddier. The United States
already has defense treaties with South Korea, Japan, the Republic of China,
the Philippines, Australia, and New Zealand. In addition, Thailand and Pakistan come under the protective defense umbrella by way of the SEATO[58]
Treaty and Pakistan is also covered by a bilateral agreement related to the
Pact of the Central Treaty Organization (CENTO). The three Indochinese
states are covered by the Protocol to the Southeast Asia Treaty. This amounts
to a far-reaching set of defense commitments by the United States. While all
the countries concerned have military forces of their own, for the most part
the treaties provide the basis for the mobilization of American power to defend its partners.[59]

Superficially, it might seem desirable to find vehicles to enable the Asian
states to contribute to each other's defense and to encourage those with the
capability, especially Japan, to carry a greater share of the defense burden
themselves. In most cases, however, military capabilities cannot be significantly
increased, short of major crisis justifying exceptional effort, without severe
strain to national budgets and to civilian economies. Japan is a special case
because, while it is capable of a greater defense effort, it is constitutionally
prohibited from undertaking overseas commitments and the strong strain of
antimilitarist feeling makes military questions intensely political domestic
issues. As of now it is out of the question for Japan to participate in any regional defense schemes. Participation by Nationalist China is of dubious political benefit. Significantly increased contributions by the others are unlikely.
Moreover, it would be extremely difficult, given anti-American and antimilitarist tendencies in some of these countries, to find the political basis for
cooperative security arrangements. Countries such as India, Burma, and
Indonesia with which the United States does not have security treaties (and,
in substance, Pakistan, despite the security treaties) would be most unlikely
to abandon their nonalignment to join and the result would thus seem to be
another anti-Communist coalition, another factor inhibiting participation by
Japan and probably the Philippines. On the whole it seems therefore that any
attempt to generalize defense responsibilities in the area, with or without direct United States participation, is, to put it mildly, premature. To the extent
that an American defense commitment in this area is desirable it will have to
continue to rest on the existing treaty network and the UN Charter.

[57] The United States made an abortive effort to follow the model of the Organization for European
Economic Cooperation (OEEC) in Asia via the unsuccessful Simla Conference of 1955. See Hollis W.
Barber, *The United States in World Affairs, 1955* (New York: Harper & Row, 1957), pp. 108–109.

[58] Australia, New Zealand, and the Philippines are also SEATO members.

[59] For military strengths of the countries in the area see *The Military Balance, 1968–1969* (London:
Institute for Strategic Studies, 1968).

There is not much ground either for optimism about the likelihood of an organization for peaceful settlement functions within the area. Despite the post-World War II history of essays toward regionalism in Southeast Asia geography works against collaboration. Nearby countries tend to become embroiled in disputes and those farther away are geographically insulated and thus indifferent. There is some ground for optimism in recent third-party interventions to dampen disputes in the area.[60] Nevertheless, it seems doubtful that there is enough community of interest or agreement on disputed issues to sustain a regional framework for peaceful settlement. It is possible that Japanese leadership might provide the impetus that is now lacking toward regional association. There is not yet much evidence that Japan is prepared to play such a role despite its limited initiative in the realm of economic cooperation. Nor is it clear that the institutionalization of a Japanese role as peacemaker, acceptable though it may be in moments of crisis, will appeal to countries still insecure in their small-power relations with a great Asian power at whose hands they suffered greatly in recent history.

To sum up, the short-term promise of regionalism in Asia lies in the development of common interest in economic cooperation. The success thus far in establishing and employing the Asian Development Bank, the interest shown in the cooperative opportunities of the Mekong River development program, the invigorated resort to the UN's Economic Commission for Asia and the Far East (ECAFE), and the Ministerial Conferences referred to above are all hopeful signs that such common interest may come to pass. At the same time the distinct and overlapping constituencies of these ventures in cooperation suggest that it may be difficult to find a single framework that adequately represents the diverse interests of nations which range so far in geography and vary so greatly in their situations and needs.

Inter-American Regionalism

In the Americas the history of nearly a quarter century of postwar efforts at collaboration makes clear that the United States is the victim of its own predominant power. The early postwar comity, the consequence of the Good Neighbor policy, wartime collaboration, and the willingness of the United States to pay attention to Latin demands for special protection for the regional system of the Americas in the United Nations Charter, soon gave way to renewed fear of *Yanqui* interventionism. In part this was the result of vagaries in United States recognition policy, beginning with the imbroglio over the Juan Perón regime and, later, of erratic responses to the challenge of military juntas. More fundamentally, however, the United States has

---

[60] Japanese and Thai good offices toward ending confrontation between Indonesia and Malaysia and Thailand's role, in Maphilindo, in the Philippine-Malaysian dispute. See Gordon in Nye (ed.), pp. 113, 121.

evoked longstanding fears of interventionism through its efforts to avert Communist encroachments in the hemisphere. In doing so it was motivated both by the historic imperative of the Monroe Doctrine that

> we could not view any interposition for the purpose of oppressing them, or controlling in any other manner their destiny, by any European power in any other light than as the manifestation of an unfriendly disposition toward the United States

and by its view of Latin America as an important aspect of the global struggle with Soviet-inspired international Communism. Starting with the struggle over the Caracas Resolution of 1954[61] the record has been one of widespread resistance among the Latin American states to United States efforts to invoke collective intervention to exorcise "the domination or control of the political institutions of any American state by the international communist movement."[62]

Indirect intervention in Guatemala in 1954 and in Cuba in the Bay of Pigs disaster in 1961 and the overt invasion of the Dominican Republic in 1965 gave point to the Latin fears.[63] The United States campaign to give legitimacy to collective intervention and to create an inter-American peace force has thus far come to nought. The inter-American system is in disarray and doubts are expressed as to its capacity, at least for the time being, to play a useful role in the political and security sphere.[64] There can be little doubt that the United States faces stringent limits on its ability to lead the Organization in collective action, owing to the fears of American predominance. The Latin Americans are reluctant to go along with the development of instruments and precedents that might later provide the basis for further United States intervention. The dilemma for the United States is a pointed one. Without American leadership there is not likely to be enough momentum to produce effective action to deal with situations threatening peace. But attempts to lead evoke resistance that frustrates success or at least ensures bitter controversy. A consequence of this recent history is a growing Latin American susceptibility to Soviet blandishments—what Professor Aspaturian calls "reverse 'bridge building'"[65]—which may in turn exacerbate the difficulties of achieving consensus.

[61] See John C. Dreier, *The Organization of American States and the Hemisphere Crisis* (New York: Harper & Row [for the Council on Foreign Relations], 1962), pp. 50–53. The Caracas Resolution is Resolution 93 of the Tenth Inter-American Conference adopted on March 13, 1954.

[62] The quote is from the Caracas Resolution. In the words of the Resolution such "domination or control . . . would constitute a threat to the sovereignty and independence of the American States, endangering the peace of America." (*Ibid.*, p. 51.)

[63] Although American intervention in Dominican Republic affairs, in the form of a naval display of force, was applauded in November 1961 when it prevented the Trujillo family's return to power. Some interventions are more interventionist than others.

[64] See Jerome Slater, "The Limits of Legitimization in International Organizations: The Organization of American States and the Dominican Crisis," *International Organization*, Winter 1969 (Vol. 23, No. 1), especially p. 69.

[65] See his contribution later in this volume.

As Professor Nye points out, the several roles of regional agencies may be in conflict.[66] In the Americas it is clear that the United States effort to employ the inter-American mechanisms for interventions against Communist intrusion have had the unhappy consequence of reducing the relevance of those mechanisms to the old-fashioned kinds of issues—territorial disputes mainly— with respect to which the system had in the past attained no little success.

Some authors have suggested that an opposite process may work—that different functions may support each other through what is termed a "spillover effect."[67] The suggestion is that OAS effectiveness in the political and security realm may benefit from the legitimizing "spillover" produced by its achievement in other functions, such as protection and promotion of human rights and economic development. That suggestion, however, leads into the subject of the next section, the role of international agencies with respect to issues between "have" and "have-not" nations. Such issues are of central importance in the organizational framework of the Americas.

The "Haves" and the "Have-Nots"

The drive of the new nations to employ international instruments to speed elimination of noxious racial practices in southern Africa has already been described. More broadly, their voting strength of numbers has been mobilized to bring about adoption of a series of standard-setting resolutions, declarations, and conventions, the most important of them being the International Convention on the Elimination of All Forms of Racial Discrimination, adopted by the General Assembly in 1965. While domestic progress toward elimination of legal devices of racial discrimination enabled the United States to support this Convention on the substance, the provisions for implementation cause greater concern because of the call to signatories to "eradicate all incitement to, or acts of," racial discrimination, a requirement which not only plainly lies beyond the powers of the United States government in this federal system but also threatens constitutional guarantees under the First Amendment. The United States signed the Convention, but ratification seems more than unlikely.

This new emphasis on human rights questions in the United Nations reflects the basic shift in the orientation of the Organization described in the section of this article concerned with maintenance of peace. In the early days the United States established a claim to leadership associated with the name of Eleanor Roosevelt. It was able to turn to the UN for support in its opposition to Soviet violations of human rights. More recently it has usually found itself part of a beleaguered "fluid grouping of Western powers"[68] confronted

[66] See his contribution later in this volume.
[67] See Slater, *International Organization*, Vol. 23, No. 1, p. 70.
[68] "Issues before the 23rd General Assembly," *International Conciliation*, No. 569, p. 100.

with demands to outlaw racial injustice, especially in southern Africa.

If the United States wishes, in the image of a former Assistant Secretary of State for International Organization Affairs, to employ the UN searchlight to direct "sharp beams of international light . . . into the world's darkest recesses of reaction,"[69] it faces practical issues of leadership. They involve, first, its ability to accept the use of the searchlight by those moved not alone—or at all—by the traditional civil rights concern of "Western middle class liberalism" to protect the individual *against* the state but more significantly by the urge to obtain economic and social rights *from* the state.[70] Can the United States accept the standards not only of the UN's Covenant on Civil and Political Rights but of the Covenant on Economic, Social, and Cultural Rights as well?

They involve, second, the question of accommodating to our federal constitutional system the vigorously expressed international demand, which has taken the form of provisions in or attached to recently approved international human rights treaties, for international supervision of national performance of the standards established in the treaties. These provisions include in some cases a right of complaint to international forums by individuals feeling themselves the victims of national violations of the international standards.[71]

They involve, third, the challenge with which this section began, posed by the effort of a substantial number of UN Members, able to command required majorities, to use the international machinery to set standards aimed at noxious racialism. This effort is synchronized with the pressures for direct enforcement action in southern Africa. To what extent should the United States lend its support to this effort which, although it is directed at practices which the United States too regards as evil, invokes the specter of manipulation by a majority to which the Biblical query may apply: "Why beholdest thou the mote that is in thy brother's eye, but considerest not the beam that is in thine own eye?"

These are poignant issues if the United States remains, as the United States delegation to the San Francisco Conference said it was in 1945, "particularly interested in the promotion, through international means, of human rights

---

[69] Assistant Secretary of State Harlan Cleveland, "Switch on the Lights," Address Before the American Jewish Committee, April 30, 1964, Department of State Press Release No. 199 (Quoted in Gardner, p. 259.)

[70] The issue has been formulated this way by Morris B. Abram, a former United States representative to the UN Commission on Human Rights. The quotes are from his "United States and International Human Rights—Retrospect and Prospects" (mimeographed).

[71] For a good, brief treatment of some of the issues see "Issues before the 23rd General Assembly, *International Conciliation*, No. 569, pp. 96–99. For a fuller treatment see Commission to Study the Organization of Peace, *The United Nations and Human Rights* (Eighteenth Annual Report) (Dobbs Ferry, N.Y: Oceana Publications, 1968); and William Korey, "The Key to Human Rights—Implementation," *International Conciliation*, November 1968 (No. 570).

throughout the world."[72] It will be at best difficult to restore a proper balance between the voting power of the majority and minority rights. Unbridled majority rule in the United Nations is less frightening than in a domestic society only because in a world of sovereign states the majority's power to enforce its will is severely limited. In the prospect of a frustrated majority consistently striving but unable to impose its will on an uncooperative minority lie endless bitter controversy and the real possibility of fragmentation.

In the realm of economic welfare, too, the United States faces piercing dilemmas arising out of the demand of the new countries for more of the world's material benefits. Patricia Blair's essay in this volume dramatically presents the relationship between the "haves" and the "have-nots" as perhaps "the most fundamental long-term problem of international relations today."[73] Her emphasis on the demand of the clamant less developed countries for participation in the political processes by which their share of aid and the regulations governing trade are decided points up the issue for the United States—whether it wishes to participate with others in a process which puts the United States under pressures to make greater sacrifices in the interest of the poorer countries. We have come a long way since 1945, when the United States opposed reference to "full employment" in the United Nations Charter.

At one level the question is whether it is reasonable and efficient for the rich countries, the United States foremost among them, to submit to majority procedures limited only by the minority's ability not to do what the majority decides. It makes no sense for the majority to vote to create a Capital Development Fund, as was done in 1966, if the countries whose capital is essential do not go along. The conciliation procedures devised by the first UN Conference on Trade and Development (UNCTAD)[74] may point toward the kinds of parliamentary devices essential if the international forums are to remain hospitable to the donor countries. Somehow, procedures have to be devised which bridge the difference between the General Assembly in which the poor have voting dominance and the World Bank family[75] in which it is the rich who control. The procedures will have to meet the rough standard set by this author in 1965:

> It is the degree of tension that is all important. Too little, and nothing or not enough happens. Too much, and the binding ties may snap to the disadvantage of all.[76]

Issues have to be confronted also in the realm of strategy—by what com-

---

[72] *Charter of the United Nations: Report to the President on the Results of the San Francisco Conference,* pp. 110–111.

[73] See her essay later in this volume.

[74] See Richard N. Gardner, "The United Nations Conference on Trade and Development," *International Organization,* Winter 1968 (Vol. 22, No. 1), pp. 115–120.

[75] The International Bank for Reconstruction and Development (IBRD), the International Finance Corporation (IFC), and the International Development Association (IDA).

[76] Finkelstein in Padelford and Goodrich (ed.), p. 29.

bination of means to achieve the posited goals. Overlapping questions arise of some technical density: the balance of trade and aid; import substitution versus export promotion, both agricultural and industrial; the most effective instruments of trade regulation; the effects of inflation and stability on development; the relationship to development of exchange rates and monetary policy; the importance of exchange liquidity and the best means to provide it; and so forth.[77]

There are issues also as to the organization of aid programs. There is no need here to rehearse the familiar arguments about bilateral or multilateral programs.[78] One point may deserve emphasis. As the stimulus for competitive aid-giving by the Soviet Union and the United States diminishes, as it seems to be doing, one incentive for bilateralism may be reduced and multilateral channels may seem more appealing. At least as important are the issues raised by Mrs. Blair's allusions to the pressures for participation by the developing countries. It is by no means apparent that all the governments of developing countries are equally representative of their peoples. Nor is it certain that maximum participation by all those governments is the best way to ensure equitable development in the interest of their peoples.[79] The issue received legislative recognition in the injunction of Title IX of the 1966 AID bill to seek to build participatory democracy in developing countries.[80] There may be here an important argument between participation as the essential psychological ingredient of progress in development against external intervention to ensure most efficient and equitable use of externally supplied resources in the interest of development.

Important as are these issues, however, they merely overlie the fundamental question: Why should the United States share its wealth with the new, poorer countries? Mrs. Blair's analogy between the domestic and the international dimensions of poverty focuses attention where it belongs—on the question whether the historic institutions and boundaries of national sovereignty adequately describe or, better, prescribe for today's world. Mrs. Blair's essay does not create the issue; it merely dramatizes the question that is intrinsic to the

---

[77] These issues are dealt with in the recent work by Harry G. Johnson, *Economic Policies toward Less Developed Countries* (Washington: Brookings Institution, 1967).

[78] See Robert E. Asher, "Multilateral Versus Bilateral Aid: An Old Controversy Revisited," *International Organization*, Autumn 1962 (Vol. 16, No. 4), pp. 697–719; and Frank M. Coffin, "Multilateral Assistance: Possibilities and Prospects," *International Organization*, Winter 1968 (Vol. 22, No. 1), pp. 270–287.

[79] Richard Gardner recently recalled Senator Russell Long's pertinent observation in 1964 that he was "against taxing the poor people in the rich countries for the benefit of the rich people in the poor countries." (At a meeting of contributors to this volume and members of the Board of Editors, *International Organization*, March 14–15, 1969.)

[80] "Emphasis shall be placed on assuring maximum participation . . . of the people of the developing countries through the encouragement of democratic private and local governmental institutions." ("Foreign Assistance Act of 1966," in *United States Statutes at Large*, Vol. 80 [1966], Part 1 [Washington: U.S. Government Printing Office, 1967], p. 800.)

role of the United States in the world today. Since World War II the United States has been generous in its international giving, measured by all previous standards. It has participated in—in many cases took the initiative leading to—the army of international agencies concerned with the direction and distribution of aid and technical help and with the rules to govern trade and the regulation of relations between currencies. Often it has rationalized its involvement and its appropriations by standards of self-interest and quite often they have had the result that the well-being of others has been seen as instrumental in our competition with world Communism. That rationale is wearing thin. We have also learned to doubt whether there is a positive correlation between economic development and political stability and security, at least in the short term. Partly for these reasons we see a decline in the commitment to foreign aid programs. Mrs. Blair's essay asks us to consider whether we should help development of less developed countries because in some sense that is important to us we are part of a community with them.[81] Her assumption that this is so does not accord with the contemporary evidence of declining foreign aid appropriations and popular support for them. In 1969 the answer the American people seem to be giving is that the problems at home demand, if not exclusive, at least priority, attention. The conclusion may well be that just as peace may not be entirely indivisible, neither is welfare.

The Issues: Both Without and Within

When Hamlet faced his anguished dilemma, he saw about him the "slings and arrows of outrageous fortune." Yet his difficulty consisted equally of his own indecisiveness. So it is with the United States confronting the dilemmas sketched in the preceding pages.

Externally, there can be no doubt that the changes that have occurred since 1945 and that are reflected in multilateral institutions make it much harder for the United States to see clear benefit resulting from international commitment. During the period when American leadership was predominant this country was in a way spared confrontation with the issue of whether it was really prepared to engage the national interest in international processes because the international processes served the national interest. It always faced the necessity of compromising somewhat its short-term policy goals in order to maintain needed consensus in the international institutions; but the compromises were peripheral to the main objectives which were, by and large, served. There was a period when, if the United States knew what it wanted through the international processes, it was usually able to get it.

---

[81] In a recent article Frank M. Coffin emphasized the theme and referred to the Papal injunction, " 'the new name for peace is development.' " See Coffin, *International Organization*, Vol. 22, No. 1, p. 280.

For some time now that has been changing for the reasons explained above. Although the origins of the change can be traced backward many years in the history of multilateral institutions, at least as far as the tense negotiations over the ending of the Korean War and the status of the prisoners of war, the full impact did not make itself apparent until the 1960's. Two events were traumatic: General de Gaulle's famous press conference of January 14, 1963, announcing France's opposition to British entry into the Common Market and signalling his challenge to United States leadership in NATO; and the deadlock over the Article 19 crisis in the UN and the final capitulation of the United States on the issue in 1965.

Henceforward, there can be no doubt, commitment to international cooperation involves the likelihood that the United States will have to compromise—on the objectives of peacekeeping operations, on the goals and mechanisms of arms control agreements, on the principles of declarations in the sphere of human rights and racism, on the principles and limits of law in the regulation of state behavior,[82] on the nature and balances of decisionmaking mechanisms on these and other questions. While its control over its own resources and policies protects its ability to avoid paying prices that it finds absolutely intolerable—with respect to financial aid for development, commitments of force to international actions, arms limitations, the level of its tariffs—it can expect to be under unremitting pressure to make sacrifices in these and other realms.

International cooperation will go forward in a setting of great complexity with much flux in coalitions and balances of interest on different subjects and much uncertainty about the attainability of United States goals. This is not to say that the United States is at a disadvantage compared to other Great Powers in pursuing its national ends through multilateral means. Not at all. The United States is still the world's strongest and richest power. It has numerous staunch allies with which it shares interests and purpose. It is relatively free of doctrinal rigidity and can, therefore, adapt to changing needs. It is experienced in the conduct of multilateral relations and brings to the task a diplomatic apparatus of unrivaled scope and skill. The comparison is not with other nations but with the United States itself in past years. That comparison suggests that the future will produce a full measure of irritating issues and frustrating conclusions.

To these external reasons for reevaluating the nature, extent, and meaning of United States commitments to cooperate through multilateral means must be added the domestic stimuli to retrenchment. The national doubt over the wisdom of the involvement in Vietnam has produced some tendency to wonder whether involvement anywhere is necessary or desirable. The sublimated

---

[82] On the changing context of international law see Professor Louis Henkin's article later in this volume.

isolationist strain in the American polity shows some sign of revival under the dual stimulus of the enhanced risk of international involvement in the face of Soviet—and Chinese—nuclear strength and the temptation to believe that safety can be found in unilateral strength. The revived concern for unresolved domestic issues leads to doubts that the United States can afford to commit major energies and resources to foreign affairs. The burdens of military service inspire pressures to reduce military commitments.

These add up to a powerful set of forces for retrenchment. Even so hardy an optimist and internationalist as Ambassador Harlan Cleveland was obliged to take notice of them in a recent address entitled "The Irrelevance of Anti-Commitment."[83] The tendency toward autarchic nationalism which has been evident in Europe as an antidote to regionalism and in Africa as an antidote to tribalism may find an echo in the United States as an antidote to globalism.

But the inescapable fact is that the world will not permit the United States to withdraw. Neither the United States' self-interest nor its self-image will permit it to assume the pariah status that would result from an effort to disengage from the tangled web of international commitments into which it has entered. The point of no return has long since been reached in American acceptance of international responsibilities. For one thing economic interdependence is a reality.[84] Moreover, the rapidly advancing technology of transportation and communication ties the United States ever more closely and tightly to other countries (although there is potentiality for tension in the incongruity between this fact and the groundswell of nationalism around the world). Finally, even though there may be reason to believe that its vital interest may not always be involved, the United States has learned in the postwar era that it does have interests in almost everything that happens in the world. Given the uncertainties about Communist China's future course and about the degree of restraint that will govern Soviet behavior, it is more than likely that the United States will continue to discern potential or real threats to its interests or to those of its close allies in a variety of threats to peace, even in distant areas. The United States will not be able to be indifferent to all the turbulence we are likely to see in the next years. Nor can the United States be indifferent to the issues of development because in a certain elusive but nonetheless operative sense the world is the American neighborhood.

All this means that the question for the United States will not be whether it will continue to cooperate internationally but when and how and how much.

As the preceding pages have emphasized, two trends over the years have imposed obstacles to effective United States leadership in multilateral agen-

[83] Delivered to the 1968 annual meeting of the American Political Science Association, Washington, September 2–7, 1968.

[84] Peter Kenen's article later in this volume describes the irreversible ties with the rest of the world in monetary matters.

cies. The first has been the relative diminution in American dominance in the several ingredients of power, defined as the ability to induce others to agree with us. This trend is probably irreversible. There is, and, ineluctably, will be, a redistribution of power. The international agencies will be "centers for harmonizing the actions of nations"[85] which, singly and in groups, will have effective influence, not guaranteed to coincide with that of the United States, over the definition of the "common ends" to be sought and the method of their attainment.

The second trend, closely related to the first, has been the growing divergence of purpose among the constituencies of the international agencies. Not only is the United States relatively less powerful than it was; it also finds itself in a relatively smaller company of nations that believe as it does.

For both these reasons participating in multilateral agencies will demand of the United States increasing tolerance of, and ability to accommodate to, the views of others. The adjustment will be a difficult one for this country, newly come to international responsibility and accustomed to successful leadership.

The challenge is even more complex. For, if the United States, out of caution as to its involvements or as a result of domestic fatigue, fails to employ to the full its still great capacities for leadership in the international arenas, the consequence is likely to be even more diffusion of purpose and even greater departures from the United States view of the purposes and priorities to be pursued through the international mechanisms. The result might well be more, not less, frustration reinforcing domestic fatigue in a downward spiral of despair and withdrawal.

If that is to be avoided, the United States will have to find the ways to project more, not less, leadership in the increasingly complex environment described in the preceding pages. Caution in commitment, particularly if carried to excess, may prove to be the wrong style. Paradoxically in the circumstances, the United States may have to commit more, rather than less, to the collective processes.

---

[86] Article 1, paragraph 4, of the UN Charter.

Soviet Foreign Policy at the Crossroads:

Conflict and/or Collaboration?

Vernon V. Aspaturian

I. Introduction

THE decision of the Union of Soviet Socialist Republics to occupy Czechoslovakia in August 1968, while it represents a fundamental turning point in Soviet foreign policy, most of whose implications are ambiguous yet ominous, should not be permitted to obscure the fact that the Soviet regime remains confronted with a wide array of postponed internal and external problems that demand action and yet defy resolution. The decision to arrest forcibly the processes of liberalization in Czechoslovakia stands out as an uncharacteristic act of will on the part of a regime whose four years in power have been marked by drift, indecisiveness, vacillation, paralysis, and "muddling through." For five years the government of Leonid Brezhnev and Alexei Kosygin has postponed action on painful problems, has permitted events and situations to accumulate dangerously, and in general has allowed itself to be dominated by events rather than domesticating them. During its first two years in office the regime's inaction was perhaps inaccurately ascribed to prudence, caution, and calculated restraint. It now appears in retrospect that paralysis was confused with prudence, inertia was mistaken for caution, and factional indecisiveness was accepted as self-restraint.

The inaction of the Brezhnev-Kosygin government was viewed as a welcome respite from the erratic, contradictory, and irrational pattern of behavior during the decade of Nikita Khrushchev's rule[1] which contrasted unfavorably with what appeared to be the calm, controlled, and rational demeanor of his two principal successors whose bland, bureaucratic, and pragmatic personali-

VERNON V. ASPATURIAN is Director of the Slavic and Soviet Language and Area Center and is Research Professor of Political Science at Pennsylvania State University, University Park, Pennsylvania.

[1] Khrushchev held both the post of First Secretary of the Communist Party and that of Chairman of the Council of Ministers. Brezhnev succeeded to the former post and Kosygin to the latter.

ties seemed eminently to correlate with their behavior. It soon became apparent that the Brezhnev-Kosygin team represented not so much a new unified collective rationality as it did a latently explosive marriage of factional convenience in which the partisans of Khrushchev's policies joined forces with his detractors to topple the Soviet leader for divergent reasons.

Khrushchev's successors inherited not only his policies but also the problems his policies had created, and for at least a year it appeared that Moscow's policies indeed corresponded to what Peking labeled as "Khrushchevism without Khrushchev." The continuity in policy between the Brezhnev-Kosygin regime and its predecessor is indeed greater than the differences. It may be that this continuity represents more the automatic consequences of indecisiveness and drift than of conscious deliberation. The personalities and groups that supported Khrushchev's détente policies remain powerful forces within the Soviet hierarchy, but they may not possess sufficient power and leverage to exercise anything exceeding a veto over fundamental departures.

After more than five decades of revolution, civil war, social convulsion, and unprecedented destruction which witnessed the growth of the Soviet state from a near cipher in world affairs to a mighty modernized and industrialized global power second only to the United States in the magnitude of its influence and the scope of its interests the Soviet leaders are now faced with a series of fundamental questions which cannot be postponed indefinitely and whose resolution may be impossible without provoking a leadership crisis.

The Soviet leaders must first make a decision regarding the root problem of all their problems, the question of purpose. It is the loss of purpose and the search for a surrogate that has divided the Soviet leadership and undermined the Soviet will to act in the face of both new dangers and new opportunities. This is the fundamental cause for the malaise and indecision that grip this aggregation of mediocrities whose mandate is as obviously transitional as its passions are inferior to those of its predecessors. The Soviet leaders must decide whether they are directing a state or a movement; in the face of the Communist Chinese challenge and pressures from the United States the current transitional attempt to behave like a state while clinging to the rhetoric of revolution cannot be sustained indefinitely. If they choose to play out their role as a global power, the Soviet leaders must once again decide to challenge the United States for paramountcy, demand parity, or settle for second place as did Khrushchev when his bluff was called in the 1962 Cuban missile crisis. Furthermore, they must decide whether to postpone maximum utilization of scarce resources for internal growth in order to widen foreign policy options and achieve diplomatic goals. Moscow must also decide whether it will seek spheres of influence on four continents or retrench to the Eurasian land mass. No matter what the decisions, they will affect the delicate internal social equilibrium and cause renewed factional conflict.

There is substantial evidence to suggest that the Soviet leadership is seriously divided over the direction of its next major moves in foreign policy, just as it was probably divided over the occupation of Czechoslovakia and continues to be wrenched by factional controversy on how to deal with passive resistance. As a consequence most decisions are still being postponed rather than resolved. It would be a gross oversimplification to divide the Soviet ruling group into "hawks" and "doves" although the issues and options represented by these avian symbols are the focal points of controversy. The Soviet leadership appears to be gravely agitated over the allocation of resources and to be divided into two broad groupings: those advocating a greater relaxation of international tensions, a retreat from overcommitments in foreign policy, and a demand that marginal international disputes be resolved through compromise and mutual concessions; and those advocating a buildup in Soviet strategic capabilities, perhaps even to the point of challenging the United States for global primacy, greater assistance to allies under attack to which the Soviet Union is committed in one form or another, and the postponement of internal growth in the interests of national security and the exploitation of international opportunities.

It would be an overstatement to characterize the second group as being made up entirely of expansionist-minded or ideologically oriented leaders although both types are undoubtedly included. Rather, it is on the whole a grouping that feels that Khrushchev surrendered the initiative to the United States, overestimated its capabilities and staying power, overlooked its domestic contradictions, and allowed many opportunities to slip by. This group is skeptical of American intentions and is inclined to the view that the Administration of Lyndon Johnson used the détente to the detriment of Soviet interests and that international stability works to the advantage of the West not only because it preserves the Western status quo but also because it undermines the Soviet position in Eastern Europe and in the international Communist movement. Instead of a détente it envisions a continuous period of challenge and response between the two global powers with periodic respites in the form of *ad hoc* arrangements and *de facto* stalemates. It does not rule out the possibility of China becoming an object of attention from both sides, and hence this group would probably make more concessions to achieve an ultimate reconciliation with China in order to preclude the unpalatable prospect that Moscow might become the chief victim of a Sino-American understanding. Hence it might be willing to risk mending relations with China even if that should retard or reverse the détente with the United States.

The Arab-Israeli war in June 1967 and the occupation of Czechoslovakia a year later served to bring these contradictory currents in the Soviet leadership into sharp relief. Soviet policy in both instances seemed to veer from one extreme to another, as if some leaders were demanding a more vigorous response while others were counseling prudence.

Since most of the tendencies as well as the problems of Soviet foreign policy were inherited from the Khrushchev era, it might be useful to examine the conditioning factors which have shaped and continue to shape Soviet attitudes and behavior in international affairs. Three conditioning factors are of crucial significance. These are: 1) the erosion of ideology and the consequent loss of the sense of purpose and direction which has always been a strong point in Soviet decisionmaking; 2) the fragmentation of the decisionmaking process which has contributed to the erosion of ideology and which in turn has been accelerated by it; and 3) the globalization of Soviet foreign policy which has extended the range and scope of Soviet commitments in world affairs at a time when that country has suffered both a loss of purpose and a weakening of will.

The contemporary crises in Soviet foreign policy can thus be defined in terms of a divided leadership confronted with expanding obligations while being shorn of its purpose. This serves to create instability at the top, unpredictability in behavior, and diminished capability for the rational control and containment of dangerous situations.

II. THE EROSION OF IDEOLOGY: THE LOSS OF MISSION

One of the most conspicuous characteristics of Soviet foreign policy during the Khrushchev era was the increasingly agnostic character of its operative norms, to say nothing of its actual policy behavior. This feature has continued to distinguish the foreign policy of his successors. In fact, the erosion or waning of ideology as a motivating force in foreign policy has not only accelerated but has also assumed a variety of dimensions. The traditional ideological goals of "world revolution," "world Communism," and "proletarian internationalism" have lost much of their relevance for Soviet foreign policy although they continue to be intoned systematically for rhetorical effect and residual pragmatic value. This is not to say that the erosion of ideological commitment has progressed evenly in all sectors of the Soviet population, the Soviet elites, and the Soviet leadership. For some, of course, the waning of ideology is viewed as a catastrophe whereas for others it may appear as an unmitigated blessing.[2] Although the spectrum of views in the leadership is probably much narrower, it is this very difference of outlook which contributes to the erosion.

The concept that ideology is eroding in the Soviet Union has provoked

[2] *Cf.*, for example, the remarkable document, "Thoughts on Progress, Coexistence and Intellectual Freedom," by the celebrated Soviet scientist, Andrei D. Sakharov, which represents a virtual repudiation of ideology as a factor in Soviet foreign policy calculations. Although this document has restricted circulation inside the Soviet Union, it apparently represents the views of a significant number of Soviet scientists, artists, and other intellectuals. For the text see *The New York Times*, July 22, 1968.

considerable controversy and is subject to varying constructions. The erosion of ideology can mean the lessening of its intensity or value as a variable in foreign policy; it can mean the lessening or waning of both commitment and conviction on the part of the leadership, individually or collectively; it can mean a contraction in its scope or range of application; and finally it can mean its subversion by resort to purely pragmatic and opportunistic behavior which debases its character, undercuts its functionality in shaping policies or decisions, exhausts its potential as a source of innovation, and subverts its appeal and effectiveness for internal and external audiences.

The erosion of ideology in the Soviet Union has been characterized in varying degrees by all of these processes. With specific reference to foreign policy it would perhaps be more appropriate to refer to *de-ideologization* rather than the erosion of ideology to define the process whereby foreign policy goals have been progressively disengaged from ideological norms. The de-ideologization of Soviet foreign policy set in motion at the Twentieth Party Congress in 1956 and the repudiation of some sacrosanct ideological principles served to free foreign policy from Stalinist fetters, but it also shattered the myths of Soviet ideological infallibility and political omniscience. This in turn released disintegrative forces. Factional politics, having spread throughout the Communist world, has become increasingly institutionalized, making it virtually impossible to coordinate policy or resolve conflicts between Communist regimes and parties.

Viewed in historical perspective, ideology has not been a constant in shaping Soviet behavior but a relative factor whose relationship to other factors affecting Soviet behavior has fluctuated widely. This protean and variable characteristic has been a prime source of controversy in assessing the significance of ideology for Soviet policy. Soviet foreign policy has always been the product of ideology in combination with other variables: capabilities, perceived opportunities, personalities, internal group and factional interests, and extravolitional institutional and functional restraints. The long Stalinist era served to distort and dull the perception and analysis of Soviet behavior from abroad. Soviet policy was judged to be the product of two variables: ideological goals as interpreted by Josef Stalin and Soviet capabilities. Ideology determined long-range goals while short-range goals were limited by Soviet capabilities. An extremely complicated process of interaction and metamorphic development was thus reduced to an oversimplified two-factor analysis in the prediction of Soviet policy. Stalinist behavior was mistakenly assumed to be the immutable behavior of the Soviet state. The leader's personality and the internal political order were accepted as constants while ideology was viewed as an instrumental extension of Stalin's personality. Stalin's long-range ideological goals were no secret; it was his short-run intentions which were inscrutable. On the assumption that Stalin would take what he could get the most common method for predicting short-run Soviet behavior was to measure Soviet capabilities. While such an approach had its utility during the Stalin era, it unfortunately spilled over into the post-Stalin period when it served to obscure the influence of other important variables which had been largely mute or latent until then.

The relative influence of ideology as a motivating force in Soviet foreign policy cannot be properly separated from the utility of the world Communist movement as an instrument of Soviet policy: The disutility of the latter was bound to subvert the animating force of the former. Under Stalin the interests of the world movement fused with those of the Soviet state, and the interests of the state were largely merged with the personal and political interests of Stalin which were then conceptualized as "proletarian internationalism." World revolution, i.e., the extension of Communist power, became indistinguishable from Soviet expansion. This was largely a hypothetical relationship until 1939, but after the outbreak of World War II it became a practical matter which ultimately resulted not only in the territorial expansion of the Soviet Union but in the establishment of a system of vassal states which was first successfully challenged by Yugoslavia in 1948 and has been in a state of progressive dissolution since 1956.

While Stalin's death set the stage for the disintegration of the world Communist movement into its constituent states and national parties, the underlying cause for the divorcement of Soviet interests from those of other Communist parties was the rapid growth in Soviet capabilities. As Soviet power grew, so did the risks and costs of implementing a forward policy. As the risks and costs of a militant ideological foreign policy increased, the general tendency was for Soviet ideological goals to recede or to erode into ritualistic rhetoric while the growth in Soviet power created greater opportunities for the pursuit of traditional great-power goals.

In the fifteen years since Stalin's death the Soviet Union has been forced to adjust to changing configurations of interests and power at home, in the Communist interstate community, in the world Communist movement, and in the international community at large—changes which have resulted in a fundamental restructuring of priorities among the various interests and purposes which motivate Soviet foreign policy.

The progressive de-ideologization of Soviet foreign policy goals under Khrushchev took place more by inadvertence and as a consequence of his opportunism than by deliberate design. Once domestic pressures—for instance, in favor of raising the standard of living—were given equal legitimacy with ideological pressures, it was axiomatic that they would become a factor in internal politics and in turn impel Khrushchev to cater to them while spurning the simultaneous demands of foreign Communist states and parties. To assign higher priority to Communist China and the world Communist movement might have been necessary to preserve Soviet preeminence in the world of Communism, but it was bound to be of little value in preserving Khrushchev's authority at home which increasingly depended upon his ability to meet the demands of powerful domestic constituencies.

The loss of purpose, i.e., the loss of the sense of historic mission which has characterized Soviet foreign policy since the establishment of the Soviet state and which animated the Bolshevik Party long before it gained control of the state, created a vacuum which has been spontaneously filled by the traditional operational norms and assumptions of great-power behavior—national interest, security, survival, economic and material well-being, national pride, prestige, and power—which are increasingly displacing rather than supplementing the abstract goals of "world revolution" and "world Communism" in Soviet foreign policy behavior.

While the Soviet subjugation of Czechoslovakia in 1968 is not the first time the naked security and national interests of the Soviet Union have been given a higher priority in Soviet calculations than ideological considerations, the ideological rationalizations employed by Moscow to justify its intervention in Czechoslovakia were so patently transparent that they earned the scorn, ridicule, and condemnation of virtually every important Communist leader in the world. The flimsiness of Moscow's pretext was further exposed by the candid Polish admission that Warsaw cooperated in the venture on grounds of pure raison d'état. What makes this particular Soviet subordination of ideological norms to state interests unique and transcendentally significant is that the Soviet leaders were unable credibly to correlate and identify their state interests with ideological norms in a manner that persuaded the overwhelming majority of Communist leaders throughout the world. Even Fidel Castro felt called upon to recognize the action as contrary to basic communist precepts although he embraced it on grounds of Cuban self-interest.

In spite of the brazen enunciation of the so-called "Brezhnev" or "Socialist commonwealth" doctrine attempting to justify Soviet intervention in any "Socialist" country on grounds of higher ideological interests, the military occupation of Czechoslovakia signifies a Soviet determination to maintain a sphere of influence in the traditional great-power sense. Contrary to an impression in some quarters, the Soviet decision to intervene does not imply that Communism is once again "monolithic" but the exact opposite. Neither does it signify a militant resurgence of "world Communism" as a motive force in Soviet behavior. On the contrary, the Soviet occupation signifies the full flowering of the Soviet state as a traditional imperial power whose influence and role in the world is determined not by the attractiveness of its ideology or its social system but by the enormity of its power and the determination to employ it in its self-interest.

While the Soviet Union appears to have exhausted ideology as a motivating force in its foreign policy because it has become increasingly dysfunctional, ideology has not exhausted its utility in other dimensions. It continues to serve the Brezhnev-Kosygin regime as a valuable instrument of epistemological, political, and social analysis, i.e., as a theory of reality, as a repository of moral truths and standards of ethical conduct, as a medium of communication, as an effective and necessary vehicle for the rationalization and explanation of the Soviet social order, and as the indispensable foundation of legitimacy upon which the entire Soviet structure reposes. While ideology wanes as a motivating force, it may simultaneously wax in its other functions, much as religions have undergone similar functional metamorphoses.

In the process of gradually disentangling ideological norms from policy goals Soviet ideology has assumed a new function whose effects are not altogether an unmixed blessing. It now functions to legitimize Moscow's behavior as a *global power,* i.e., a power which asserts a right to intervene in any dispute or conflict in any part of the globe. While the Soviet leaders have abjured ideology as a norm-defining mechanism, they have by no means abdicated their self-appointed role as the guardian and spokesman of the oppressed masses of the world against international imperialism. Otherwise, Soviet global interventionism could be justified only in terms of raw power and naked self-interest, an impression which Moscow avidly desires to avoid. The spiritual emptiness of naked self-interest as the motivating force of a once great revolutionary power is nowhere more eloquently and pungently phrased than in Peking:

> The Soviet leaders seek only to preserve themselves and would leave other people to sink or swim. They have repeatedly said that so long as they themselves survive and develop the people of the world will be saved. The fact is they are selling out the fundamental interests of the people of the world in order to seek their own momentary ease.[3]

Correspondingly, however, and with considerable irony the residuary Soviet commitment to the transcendental normative goals of ideology serves simultaneously to legitimize the global behavior of the United States. For if the Soviet Union is the self-appointed defender of the weak and the oppressed from imperialist aggression and the "export of counterrevolution," the United States is the self-proclaimed defender of the weak, vulnerable, gullible, and unstable nations which are the natural prey of "international Communism" operating through the manipulation of "national liberation movements" and "popular uprisings" which are viewed as mere euphemisms for "export of revolution" and "subversion." Without the omnipresent threat of "international Communism" (now presumably to read "Asian Communism") the United States would find it difficult to explain and justify its behavior in terms other

---

[3] "Statement by the Spokesman of the Chinese Government—A Comment on the Soviet Government's Statement of August 3," *Peking Review,* August 16, 1963 (Vol. 6, No. 33), p. 14.

than might and self-interest which it too wishes to avoid. This is not to imply that without the presence of "international Communism" as a legitimizing instrument Moscow and Washington would halt or even limit their penchant for global interventionism but rather that they would have to contrive new legitimizing instruments for behavior that is essentially a natural function of their power and status in the international community and which is animated more by self-interest than by messianic fervor or purpose.

III. The Fragmentation of the Decisionmaking Process: The Paralysis of Will

Under Stalin policy formulation and decisionmaking were tightly centralized in Stalin's person: Thought and action were coordinated by a single personality. Under his successors, however, the inconclusive struggle for power resulted in the fragmentation of the decisionmaking structure, distributing power among various individuals and factions, each in command of parallel institutional power structures. Ideology was divorced from policy formulation which in turn was frequently out of phase with the administration and execution of policy as rival factions assumed control over policymaking bodies. The fragmentation of the decisionmaking structure was artlessly concealed by the figleaf of "collective leadership" as factional politics replaced one-man decisions in the Soviet leadership. Personalities, factions, and eventually sociofunctional and socioinstitutional groupings assumed a more variable role in the shaping of Soviet behavior, and a new fluid relationship was established among Soviet capabilities, ideology, personalities, and institutions in the decisionmaking process. While this made it even more difficult to judge Soviet intentions and predict Soviet behavior, it was compensated for by the corresponding inability of the Soviet Union to pursue the single-minded and precisely calibrated type of foreign policy which was characteristic of the Stalin era since Soviet leaders are apparently as uncertain as Western Kremlinologists in charting the course and outcome of internal factional conflict.

Factional conflict in the Soviet hierarchy has thus introduced a new and fortuitous element in Soviet behavior since it is by no means predictable that a given Soviet personality or faction will continue, repudiate, or modify the policies of its predecessors. Even more significantly, Soviet policy may fluctuate not only in accordance with obvious institutional and personality changes but with the changing equilibrium of factions within the hierarchy on a more or less continuing basis. As Soviet capabilities expand, these factional conflicts register changing and conflicting perceptions of risks involved in relation to possible returns; they represent shifting configurations of interest, both domestic and external; and finally they represent conflicting and changing sets of priorities as new choices and options proliferate out of expanded capabilities. In the absence of a stable consensus in the policymaking Politburo the tendency in post-Stalinist Russia has been for various factions to implement their own views and policies through Party or state institutions and organs under their direct administrative control, thus conveying the impression of contradictory, inconsistent, and ambivalent behavior in Soviet policy. While this is the net effect for the Soviet system as a whole, it is not necessarily true of individual groups, factions, or personalities whose own views may be consistent and firm but are simply unable to prevail over equally consistent and obdurate views held by other groups and individuals. The possibility of factional vacillation and ambivalence is, of course, not ruled out.

Whereas the United States has always been accustomed to self-restraint in the exercise of its power, the self-restraint introduced into Soviet behavior because of factional politics confronts Soviet leaders with a new and bewildering experience to which they have not completely adjusted. Accustomed to being guided in their behavior by the principle of "pushing to the limit," the Soviet leaders have in the past assumed that the American "ruling class" was guided by the identical principle and have behaved accordingly. It should be emphasized that Soviet behavior in this connection was encrusted in a conceptualized doctrine concerning the behavior of capitalist ruling classes which existed long before the advent of the Cold War and thus could not be explained as a spontaneous response to American behavior, except in concrete cases. Correspondingly, American decisionmakers have always assumed, on the basis of both Soviet doctrine and past behavior, that the Soviet leaders do not exercise self-restraint and will always "push to the limit," not recognizing that self-restraint is not entirely a subjective phenomenon but can be imposed upon decisionmakers objectively as well. Hence, American decisionmakers have yet to adjust completely to this new departure in Soviet behavior. This element of self-restraint is not necessarily deliberate or calculated in all intances but has also resulted from institutionalized factors such as internal power rivalries, conflicts of judgment, perception, and interests, and sheer bureaucratic inertia, i.e., the fragmentation of the decisionmaking process.

The fragmentation of the decisionmaking process combined with the erosion of Soviet ideology has produced a new element of both instability and uncertainty in Soviet behavior, an institutionalized irrationality, particularly in crisis situations.

Collective leadership, therefore, may not necessarily contribute to more rational or controlled action but may, under certain conditions, be even more dangerous and difficult to contend with than one-man rule. Under some circumstances collective leadership may turn out to be collective irresponsibility as decisions are made and unmade by shifting conditions or autonomous action is taken by powerful socioinstitutional bodies in the face of factional paralysis or bureaucratic inertia. The deliberations of a divided oligarchy are not only secret but anonymous as well and can yield many surprises. In the words of Professor Leo Mates of Yugoslavia in referring to Czechoslovakia:

> If it is possible for unprovoked military intervention to follow negotiations and agreement, then the danger to peace is transferred to the domain of the unpredictable, which can but leave deep traces on the general behavior of states in international relations.[4]

This suggests that if the Soviet Union could unleash massive military forces *after* tensions had been presumably dissipated, the Soviet leadership is capable of virtually any kind of rash and irresponsible behavior. The Soviet occupation of Czechoslovakia thus is bound once again to raise the entire question of the role of duplicity as a conscious and calculated instrument of Soviet diplomacy and conjure up the specter of a Soviet "Pearl Harbor" in the minds of the American public.[5] More than ever Soviet decisions in foreign policy may reflect the anxieties, fears, insecurities, and ambitions of individual factions and personalities involved in secret and faceless intrigue and maneuver. This cannot but tarnish the image of rationality, sobriety, and predictability which had emerged during the first years of the Brezhnev-Kosygin regime. We may, of course, be witnessing the disintegration of a hitherto stable equilibrium or consensus sustained by the lowest common denominator of factional interest, i.e., sheer inertia. Whether the assumption of mutual rationality which has formed the foundations of Soviet-American relations has been seriously undermined remains to be seen.

In the absence of crisis situations, whether acute or chronic, the assumption of Soviet rationality will continue to be valid. As personalities and as individual factions the Soviet leaders appear to be a sober and calculatingly rational group and in their separate capacities are determined, forceful, and animated by purpose. But in the absence of a stable majority or durable consensus and with the fluidity of the decisionmaking process characterized by rapidly dissolving and reconstituted majorities on various issues the behavior of the Soviet leadership as a collectivity is likely to be fluctuating and inconsistent. The multiplication of divergent rational inputs can thus produce a collective irrational output. It is in this restricted sense that the real possibility of institutionalized irrationality may come to characterize Soviet behavior.

[4] Cited by Anatole Shub, "Lessons of Czechoslovakia," *Foreign Affairs*, January 1969 (Vol. 47, No. 2), p. 267. *Cf.* also Vernon V. Aspaturian, "The Aftermath of the Czech Invasion," *Current History*, November 1968 (Vol. 55, No. 327), p. 263.

[5] *Cf.* Vernon V. Aspaturian, "Dialectics and Duplicity in Soviet Diplomacy," *Journal of International Affairs*, 1963 (Vol. 17, No. 1), pp. 42–60, and "Diplomacy in the Mirror of Soviet Scholarship" in John Keep and Liliana Brisby (ed.), *Contemporary History in the Soviet Mirror* (New York: Frederick A. Praeger, 1964), pp. 243–274.

IV. The Globalization of Soviet Foreign Policy:
The Expansion of Commitment

It was during the Khrushchev decade that the role of ideology underwent its most significant transformation although the process of erosion had already started during Stalin's last years as the risks of a militant ideological foreign policy escalated at a faster pace than the growth of Soviet power. Under Khrushchev ideological erosion was accelerated by the inadvertent de-ideologization of Soviet foreign policy in order to exploit new diplomatic opportunities. In the process Khrushchev abdicated Moscow's assured status as leader of the world Communist movement in return for the dubious status of acting on the world stage as a global power whose oyster was not only the world of Communism but the great globe itself.

There is a sharp distinction between a Great Power or even superpower and a global power, of which there are only two, the Soviet Union and the United States. Under Stalin the Soviet Union was transformed from a sprawling, rickety, and weak giant into an authentic Great Power—a superpower. Stalin not only created the technical-industrial base for the transformation, but he also presided over the conversion of the Soviet Union into a nuclear power and through skillful diplomacy and military conquest created a new territorial and hegemonial base for the further intensification and expansion of Soviet power and influence under his successors.

If it was Stalin who transformed the Soviet Union into a Great Power, it was under Khrushchev that Soviet Russia was transformed into a global power directly challenging the United States for paramountcy and unilaterally commanding the right to intervene in any part of the world to assert an interest and to influence developments. Stalin pursued essentially a cautious continental policy oriented toward the communization, first of the Soviet periphery and then of the new geographical periphery of the expanded Communist bloc, relying on direct physical contiguity and the concentrically radiating expansion of Communism from the Soviet base. He was loathe to overcommit the Soviet Union militarily, politically, or ideologically and was reluctant to burden himself with ideological obligations which he could not or preferred not to fulfill.

Khrushchev, on the other hand, broke out of the doctrinal shell in which Soviet diplomacy had been encapsulated and embarked upon a bold global strategy of reaching out over oceans, mountains, and continents in search not only of possible recruits to the Communist bloc but also of diplomatic client states in any part of the world.

Khrushchev's global strategy, pursued in the wake of Soviet space spectaculars which he tried to metamorphose into military power, was designed to breach the non-Communist world at its vulnerable points all along the "zone of peace"—in the Middle East, Southeast Asia, Africa, and even Latin America —irrespective of the strength of local Communist parties. In the process Soviet foreign policy was largely, but not entirely, de-ideologized since the maximization of possible diplomatic gains in the non-Communist world presupposed a minimization and dilution of the ideological content of Soviet foreign policy. Ultimately this was self-defeating although advantageous momentarily since it dictated the abandonment of certain foreign policy strategies associated with Moscow for decades. It meant, in some instances, sacrificing the future of local Communist parties in return for diplomatic gains in the third world; it also meant the diversion of scarce resources and funds from internal development and allied Communist countries to seduce the newly independent countries of Asia and Africa with economic bribes; it meant the assumption of new risks, costs, and burdens in areas far removed from the centers of Communist power and vulnerable to American sea and air power. For a time Khrushchev capitalized on the alleged "missile gap" to unfurl a protective nuclear-missile umbrella over the three continents of Asia, Africa, and Latin America in the mistaken conviction that the United States could be deterred or dissuaded from interfering with Soviet policy or intervening to arrest local revolutions promoted or encouraged by the Soviet Union.

While Khrushchev successfully transformed the Soviet Union into a global power, he did so at the expense of weakening Soviet control in its own sphere, alienating Moscow's strongest ally, China, overcommitting the power and resources of the Soviet Union, and maximizing the risks of thermonuclear war by persistently prodding and probing weak spots in the Western world and by forcing the United States into a series of confrontations in the hope that these confrontations would result in the settlement of outstanding issues on Soviet terms and would force the United States to withdraw from exposed positions. The Suez crisis of 1956, the spasmodic Berlin crisis of 1958–1961, and finally the Cuban missile crisis of 1962 were all grim consequences of Soviet risk-taking in foreign policy in pursuit of substantial diplomatic gains.

V. Soviet Options in Foreign Policy:
Condominium, Détente, Primacy, or Entente

Each of these conditioning processes will have an important impact on future trends in Soviet foreign policy, individually as well as in dynamic interaction with one another. To the degree that Marxist-Leninist ideology relies on the epistemological imperative of viewing conflict and contradiction as the mainsprings of progress, then to that degree will the progressive de-ideologization of Soviet foreign policy reduce the compulsion to turn to conflict and violence as inevitably fruitful sources of political and diplomatic gain. While this may sweep away certain dogmatic preconceptions that have interfered with Soviet perceptions of international stability as a desirable goal, at the same time it may incite the Soviet state to behave more in the fashion of a traditional imperialist power whose behavior will be shaped by the logic of its role in world affairs and the momentum of its capabilities. Ideologically calculated employment of violence to promote world Communism may thus be supplanted by opportunistic and expedient resort to force to promote Soviet power and prestige, irrespective of its relevance to world Communism.

Similarly, the fragmentation of the Soviet leadership into factional groupings will tend to institutionalize self-restraint in Soviet behavior. While this is a factor favoring international stability, at the same time it creates the possibility of instability in the leadership and an element of fortuity and unpredictability in its behavior which will tend to create further barriers to collaboration and international stability. Dealing with a divided oligarchy whose deliberations remain concealed and whose fluctuating dominant coalition remains essentially anonymous can induce irrational anxieties and provoke impulsive responses and overreactions in the behavior of other powers. Greater rather than less emphasis might be placed on external countervailing power as a restraining mechanism, and the result might be a spiral of rivalry and intense competition rather than collaboration.

On the whole, however, the globalization of Soviet foreign policy is a factor working in favor of international stability since global pretensions require that the Soviet leaders transcend their parochial responsibilities to the interests of Communist states and parties in order to cultivate an image of concern for the interests of a wide spectrum of states with variegated regimes and social systems. This would tend to encourage the Soviet leadership to develop a vested interest in the virtues of prestige, self-image, sensitivity to world opinion, and appreciation for outlooks and attitudes different from its own. At the same time, however, it weakens Moscow's role as the leader of an ideological coalition, sacrifices the interests of Communist parties, and creates openings for an ambitious ally like China to compete for the favor of neglected Communist states and parties. Global concerns will also run the risk of overextension and overcommitment that might divert scarce resources away from pressing domestic problems and thus contribute to internal unrest and discontent.

Furthermore, as a global power the Soviet Union will inevitably find itself in worldwide competition with the other global power, the United States, in areas remote from its vital interests in distant parts of the globe. This will increase the possibilities and risks of confrontation and will force the Soviet Union to assume positions for the sake of prestige and its standing as a global power. Since much of this rivalry will take place in an increasingly unstable third world, the danger of being sucked into the center of rapidly developing vacuums will be enhanced with the distinct possibility of the Soviet Union being maneuvered unwittingly and inadvertently into assuming explicit and implicit obligations forcing it to commit its power and prestige over relatively trivial issues. Soviet commitments to the Arab states illustrate what might happen in other parts of the world although the Soviet leaders have so far shown great prudence and caution in this regard by spurning a major effort in sub-Saharan Africa and in Latin America.

Only in the Indian subcontinent have the Soviet leaders undertaken commitments comparable to those to the Arab states and in this case the solicitude is motivated more by their preoccupation with the Chinese danger than anything else. Moscow is both displacing and supplementing American military assistance to both India and Pakistan in the interests of local stability which works in favor of Soviet interests. Hans Morgenthau's observation that the American policy of arming both India and Pakistan was an illogical exercise in that the United States was conducting an arms race with itself seems not to have persuaded the Soviet leaders of its perversity since Moscow is now similarly engaged in a race with itself in this vital region. Both Moscow and Washington apparently feel that it is the better part of wisdom, if not strict logic, to conduct an arms race with oneself in preference to one with the other global power since it can be more precisely calibrated and controlled.

It appears that the Soviet Union is irrevocably committed to function on the world stage as a global power irrespective of its problems of purpose and divided leadership, but the precise contours of that role have by no means been delineated. It is likely that the Soviet leaders will avoid pressing confrontations with the United States in peripheral areas and instead will utilize the United Nations as both a forum and an arena to either postpone decisions, induce stalemates, settle for provisional and *de facto* settlements, or work out mutually agreeable compromises. Neither the problem of purpose nor of divided leadership, however, can be settled by outside agencies or powers, for both must be resolved at home. Similarly, it is not likely that either Soviet-American relations or Sino-Soviet relations can be fruitfully ventilated in international bodies, and the Soviet Union will continue sedulously and relentlessly to treat its relations with Eastern European countries as internal rather than international problems in accordance with the "Socialist commonwealth" doctrine.

The decisive factor in international stability, of course, remains the state of relations between the United States and the Soviet Union. This will, in turn, depend in large measure upon the Soviet leadership's perceptions of Washington's intentions and capabilities as measured against its own purposes and power. The Soviet leadership appears sorely divided over the precise character that Soviet-American relations should assume. Some, apparently, like Kosygin, seem to favor a continuation and expansion of the détente ushered in by the 1963 Treaty Banning Nuclear Weapons Tests in Atmosphere, in Outer Space, and Under Water; others may wish to challenge the United States overtly for primacy in an increasingly hierarchically structured international system; still others, perhaps including Brezhnev, may perceive a limited or arrested détente as the best formula to assure the sanctity of the status quo where Moscow would like to preserve it while freeing the Soviet Union to alter it elsewhere. A fourth possibility, entente, may have attractiveness for sectors of the Soviet intelligentsia, for people like Andrei Sakharov, but it is not likely that the Soviet leaders conceive of it as a viable possibility at the present time. Therefore, the debate probably revolves around the three other alternatives enumerated above.

VI. The Khrushchev Option: Condominium

Khrushchev had opted for a policy of accommodation and détente with the United States in July 1963 but only after his vigorous attempt to overcome American strategic superiority had failed and the world was twice brought to the brink of thermonuclear war—once over Berlin and again over Cuba. The Soviet Union found itself politically overcommitted, financially overextended, militarily vulnerable, ideologically challenged by Peking, and economically on the verge of bankruptcy. In return for the respite gained by signing the test ban treaty, which was a tacit recognition and acceptance of American strategic superiority, Khrushchev elevated American-Soviet relations to the top-priority item in Soviet foreign policy since only an understanding between the two global powers could guarantee the avoidance of thermonuclear war. In addition, Khrushchev expected a long period of international stability and Soviet-American cooperation which he thought would strengthen his position at home and further Soviet interests abroad.

Khrushchev's détente policy assumed the faint but definite contours of a Soviet-American condominium or dyarchy in the international community whereby the two superpowers would demarcate their respective areas of vital interest, define their area of common interest, delineate the status quo which was to be preserved, and establish the guidelines which would govern their competition in areas marginal or peripheral to their vital interests.[6] It was Khrushchev's view that no problem of international relations could resist the imposition of a joint Soviet-American solution. Such a condominium would, in effect, ensure American nonintervention in such areas of Soviet vital interests as would be mutually agreed upon implicitly and explicitly. Thus Khrushchev on various occasions stressed that "history has imposed upon our two peoples a great responsibility for the destiny of the world"[7] and that

[6] Parts of this section are adapted from Vernon V. Aspaturian, "Foreign Policy Perspectives in the Sixties," in Alexander Dallin and Thomas B. Larson (ed.), Soviet Politics Since Khrushchev (Englewood Cliffs, N.J.: Prentice-Hall, 1968), pp. 141–144.

[7] Pravda, December 31, 1961.

"our interests do not clash directly anywhere, either territorially or economically."[8]

This condominium approach was most pungently described by Peking with its customary self-serving rhetoric of exaggeration, but it was also clearly discernible in the speeches of Soviet statesmen and in Soviet writings, especially in two books, the *Motive Forces of U.S. Foreign Policy* and *The U.S.S.R. and the U.S.A.—Their Political and Economic Relations,* which were published in 1965. Accordingly, the two books were pounced upon by Chinese critics as ample confirmation that the policy of the Brezhnev-Kosygin regime was indistinguishable from that of its predecessor although it is quite obvious that the two books can be more accurately described as expositions of the Khrushchev policy. Thus, according to a Chinese review published in *Hung Chi* the first book

> proclaims that "Soviet-American relations, the relations between the two greatest powers in the world, constitute the axis of world politics, the main foundation of international peace." Using the words of US Secretary of State Rusk, it preaches that "the two great powers—the USSR and the USA—bear special responsibility for the destiny of the world and of mankind." It says that the Soviet Union "strives for peace and co-operation with the United States, realizing that Soviet-American relations are the primary thing in contemporary world politics and in the question of war or peace."
>
> . . . .
>
> The book stresses that an "extremely important feature in Soviet-American relations" is the so-called "community of national interests of the two countries." It says, "Except for the black spot—the US participation in the military intervention against Soviet Russia from 1918 to 1920—Russian-American and Soviet-American relations have not been clouded by any military conflicts or wars." "At the present time, too, no territorial or economic disputes or conflicts exist between the two countries, and their national interests do not clash either on a world scale or on any regional scale."[9]

Hence, as *Hung Chi* correctly noted, Moscow and Washington could, in effect, shift the competitive aspects of their relations to the periphery of their vital interests:

> The book asserts that provided there is "peaceful coexistence" between the Soviet Union and the United States, "the competition between the two socioeconomic systems and the ideological struggle between the two main antagonists on the international arena will proceed within the confines of broad

[8] Khrushchev interview with Gardner Cowles, April 20, 1962, as quoted in "Confessions Concerning the Line of Soviet-US Collaboration Pursued By the New Leaders of the CPSU," (*Hung Chi* editorial, February 11, 1966) (Peking: Foreign Languages Press, 1966), p. 6.

[9] *Ibid.,* pp. 3–4. The two Soviet books were published by the Institute of World Economics and International Relations of the Soviet Academy of Sciences.

economic, diplomatic, scientific and cultural competition and co-operation, without sanguinary collisions and wars."[10]

All of this is rendered possible because the Soviet leaders have redefined the nature of the American "ruling class." "The book divides the US ruling circles into two groups, 'the sober and sensible' and 'the bellicose and aggressive.'" And

> it also speaks of "the struggle that has intensified to the extreme between the two tendencies in foreign policy, the two groups in American social life—i.e., on the one hand, the ultra-reactionary and wildly aggressive and, on the other, the moderate and sober who are inclined towards a reasonable assessment of the balance of power that has now taken shape, and towards peaceful coexistence."

> Who are "the moderate and sober who are inclined . . . towards peaceful coexistence"? According to this book, they are the chieftains of US imperialism, the successive US presidents since the war. It speaks of Eisenhower as representing "more moderate circles, which were not inclined to put into practice their adventuristic doctrines and go to the risk of a big war"; of Kennedy as "the president popular among the people," who had "breadth of vision and a sober approach to the burning problems of international life" and "understood the possibility and necessity of peaceful coexistence"; and of Johnson as "a cautious and moderate political figure" who is "not given to political risks" and as enjoying "an absolute mandate from the people to carry out a policy directed towards consolidating peace and liquidating 'the cold war', and towards Soviet-US rapprochement."[11]

The second book, according to *Hung Chi,* is equally emphatic in stressing the condominium idea:

> The book emphasizes that "the Communist Party of the Soviet Union and the Soviet Government have always attached primary significance to the normalization of the relations between the USSR and the USA and still do so." It cites one argument contained in the resolution on Khrushchov's report at the 21st Congress of the CPSU: "The normalization of the international situation could be helped to a decisive degree by an improvement in relations between the Soviet Union and the United States of America, as the two great powers which shoulder special responsibility for the fate of general peace."[12]

Khrushchev's détente policy was thus based upon the following assumptions:

1) The Administration of John F. Kennedy represented the "sober" forces in the American "ruling class." These forces perceived a détente with Moscow to be in their self-interest and thus could be "trusted."

2) The United States could speak for the entire West, and thus the détente

---

[10] *Ibid.,* p. 3.
[11] *Ibid.,* p. 2.
[12] *Ibid.,* p. 5.

would assume the configuration of an international condominium or dyarchy between the two major powers.

From these two assumptions were to flow the following agreements:

1) further multilateral agreements on the control, prohibition, and destruction of nuclear weapons and conventional armaments, such as a nuclear nonproliferation treaty, a freeze on the production of nuclear weapons, the establishment of regional nuclear-free zones, and various other agreements of a similar character;

2) additional multilateral and bilateral agreements, such as a general non-aggression treaty between North Atlantic Treaty Organization (NATO) and Warsaw Treaty Organization (WTO) countries and a treaty outlawing the use of force in settling territorial disputes and agreements on outer space; and

3) the expansion of consular relations, cultural exchanges, and the granting of generous lines of credit from the United States, the Federal Republic of Germany (West Germany), the United Kingdom, and Japan.

The following expectations and consequences were to materialize on the basis of these assumptions and agreements:

1) The Soviet Union and the United States together would retain their overwhelming nuclear superiority and thus be able to jointly enforce the peace (preserve the status quo?).

2) Japan and Germany would be prohibited from acquiring nuclear weapons and their revisionist ambitions could be contained and blocked by joint Soviet-American action.

3) The nuclear development of France and China would be arrested, or at least considerably inhibited and retarded.

4) China's revisionist and expansionist aspirations would be contained and blocked by the United States with the tacit support of the Soviet Union.

5) The so-called "madmen" or "hawks" in the United States would be isolated and kept out of power and hence away from the nuclear button.

6) A general relaxation of international tensions would ensue which would undercut the attractiveness of the appeals in the United States for more aggressive action, dispel the anti-Communist hysteria, and thus relieve the pressures upon the Administration demanding the "export of counterrevolution" to put down "popular uprisings" and "wars of national liberation" which could then continue unimpeded along their natural course. Without a "Soviet threat," Khrushchev reasoned, internal social revolutions in various parts of the world would no longer be perceived as a threat to the United States.

7) A rapid rise would occur in Soviet economic development with a corresponding rise in the standard of living.

VII. THE FAILURE OF CONDOMINIUM

Undoubtedly the condominium conception of a détente still holds some attraction for individual members of the current Politburo, and it remained, by default, the basis of the Brezhnev-Kosygin foreign policy for the first two years or so although with significant modifications.

The entire structure of Khrushchev's détente policy, however, rested upon the assumption that the Kennedy Administration represented the "sober" forces in the United States and that these forces would continue to determine United States policy. Furthermore, it presupposed that Moscow and Washington shared an interest in containing German, Japanese, and Chinese revisionism. Khrushchev's policy posed a serious threat to the social position, status role, and general interests of powerful, but numerically small, sociofunctional and socioinstitutional groups like the Party apparatus, heavy industry managers, and the traditional military. Instead of conceiving and executing his détente policy so that the interests and needs of these groups might be painlessly accommodated, Khrushchev brusquely attempted an "end run" by appealing to those broad social constituencies whose interests would be enhanced by his détente policy in a bold effort to envelop and isolate his detractors in a sea of "democracy."

Aside from the serious internal dislocations among social priorities implied by his policies Khrushchev's strategy and behavior were also exposing the Soviet Union to new diplomatic and security vulnerabilities, and this too contributed to the tactical area of agreement between Khrushchev's faction and his opposition. Khrushchev's policies threatened the interests of his factional opposition while his behavior alienated his own faction and his détente strategy made the Soviet Union diplomatically and militarily vulnerable.

Both Kosygin and Brezhnev were closely associated with Khrushchev's détente policy; they subscribed to the Khrushchevite division of the American "ruling class" into "sober" and "mad" elements. Although they too were predisposed to recognize President Johnson as a representative of the former, they probably showed more concern about a possible shift in the American political equilibrium to the right. Khrushchev's ouster in October 1964 thus came hard on the heels of a number of events which ominously pointed toward the crystallization of simultaneous crises in Sino-Soviet and Soviet-American relations. The nomination of Senator Barry Goldwater as a Presidential candidate in 1964, President Johnson's Tonkin Bay retaliatory strikes, Mao Tse-tung's open bid for some 500,000 square miles of Soviet territory, and China's imminent explosion of an atomic bomb all likely played a catalytic role in Khrushchev's ouster since they all took place in the months just prior to Khrushchev's denouement.

A new flexibility, combined with a more soundly conceived, better integrated, and more systematic strategy and bolstered by a revitalized consensus, was needed in order for Soviet leaders to be better prepared for whatever unforeseen contingencies might evolve out of the new and confused American political situation as well as out of the ominous uncertainties of China's new capabilities.

The displacement of Khrushchev probably did not dispel the doubts of the factional groupings that were unenthusiastic about the entire détente policy although the new Brezhnev-Kosygin regime was probably more likely to assuage the wounds and grievances of the factional opposition, particularly the traditional military, and to show greater sensitivity to their interests and hence may have been initially armed with a new consensual mandate charged with reviewing and revising existing policy if necessary. Thus, unlike Khrushchev, the new team was poised and prepared for any contingency which might develop out of the American election, ready to plug the gaps in Khrushchev's détente strategy if the détente policy continued, and also amenable to trying a new approach to Peking.

After five years of the Johnson Administration the Soviet leadership, on balance, probably feels that international stability works to the advantage of the United States in particular and the status quo in general. Since international stability is inherently antirevolutionary, it surrenders the political and diplomatic initiative to the United States as the paramount power in the world and as the chief guardian of the status quo. The Soviet position in world affairs, instead of being enhanced, was diminished to that of a tired, worn-out revolutionary power content with permanent status as "Number 2" while the United States was left free to flex its diplomatic and military muscles all over the world and subtly to undermine the Soviet position in Eastern Europe with seductive policies of "bridge building" and "peaceful engagement." While the Johnson Administration faithfully refrained from aggressive and overtly hostile moves against the Soviet position in Eastern Europe, its selective enticement of individual Communist states proved to be a device against which the unimaginative Soviet leaders had no defense except military intervention to arrest the growing forces of autonomy. Furthermore, China had been progressively transformed from an alienated ally into a hostile and threatening neighbor while the world Communist movement was fractured and demoralized and the national liberation movement was deprived of its protective umbrella.

Confident of its superior power and relying on the Soviet Union to refrain from any action that might endanger Soviet-American collaboration, the United States massively escalated the war in Vietnam, systematically bombed

Moscow's ally, and landed Marines in the Dominican Republic to prevent the establishment of a revolutionary-oriented regime. Furthermore, not only in Moscow but also in Belgrade, Cairo, and elsewhere, particularly after the Arab-Israeli war of 1967, the impression that the Johnson Administration had been using the détente not to preserve international stability but to devise a cleverly conceived political offensive against Soviet and radical nationalist positions all over the world achieved widespread acceptance. The Dominican affair, the ouster of President Sukarno in Indonesia and of João Goulart in Brazil, the fall of Kwame Nkrumah in Ghana, the overthrow of Mohammed Ben Bella in Algeria, the Greek military takeover, and finally the Israeli attack upon Egypt appeared to many in Moscow as part of an overall United States design. Abdul Nasser openly complained in Cairo that the chief danger to peace and progress was the absence of any force that could deter or contain the United States while the Italian Communist paper, *Rinascita,* flatly claimed that the Johnson Administration was pursuing a cleverly concealed "roll-back" policy:

> For the policy of the *status quo* and the attempts to divide the world into zones of influence between the two super-powers, U.S. imperialism is gradually substituting a revised and corrected re-edition of the old policy of *roll back,* giving birth, within the framework of nuclear coexistence with the U.S.S.R. (caused by reasons of *force majeure*), to a series of local interventions (economical, political, military) designed to modify the world equilibrium by means of setting up reactionary régimes, or by support given to them, and liquidation of the progressive forces and movements in individual countries.[13]

VIII. The Temptations of Strategic Superiority

One of the constants of the world situation during the past six years has been the American superiority in missile and thermonuclear capability. Instead of contributing to international stability it has been accompanied by instability, but an instability which the Soviet leaders may have perceived as favoring American interests. This has raised in the Soviet mind the entire question of whether the United States is deceptively palming off disequilibrium working in its favor as international stability. The degree to which the Soviet leaders perceive this asymmetric relationship in strategic power as contributing to the Johnson Administration's audacity and boldness in assuming the role of "international gendarme" is crucial to any realistic assessment of meaningful arms control agreements with the Soviet Union.

Since the Brezhnev-Kosygin regime soon after taking office embarked upon an accelerated program of narrowing or eliminating the American lead in strategic striking power not only by stepping up the production of inter-

[13] *Rinascita,* August 4, 1967, as cited in Zbigniew Brzezinski, "Peace and Power," *Encounter,* November 1968 (Vol. 31, No. 5), p. 5.

continental ballistic missiles (ICBM's), improving and refining existing weapons, hardening its launching sites, and expanding its nuclear naval capability but also by deploying a modest antiballistic missile (ABM) system around Moscow, it is obvious that the Soviet leaders are convinced that the narrowing or elimination of the strategic gap is a necessary prerequisite to an effective policy of deterring the United States from acting out its role as "world policeman." On the other hand, it has been the dominant view of the Johnson Administration since about 1965 that the United States possesses an invulnerable and "assured" capability whose effectiveness will not be eroded by the achievement of Soviet strategic and nuclear parity. While this view is not without its detractors, there is an equally forceful view that the achievement of parity will contribute to a more stable mutual deterrence and improve the chances for arms control and other agreements because it will eliminate the essentially psychological and symbolic sense of inferiority in Moscow without at the same time affecting the actual power equilibrium.

This view, of course, assumes that psychological and symbolic inferiority exerts only a peripheral influence on the behavior of nuclear powers. But we really do not know to what extent the strategic superiority of the United States was the decisive incremental factor impelling it to behave with relative impunity in peripheral areas of the world while simultaneously deterring vigorous Soviet action against its own recalcitrant client states in Eastern Europe, to say nothing of deterring more aggressive Soviet activity in other areas, i.e., deterring a possible Soviet intervention in the Arab-Israeli war to prevent the ignominious defeat of its Arab client states. To what extent, for example, were the Soviet move against Czechoslovakia and its threatening gestures against Rumania and Yugoslavia the reflection of a greater confidence inspired by the relative growth of its missile and nuclear power? Does this mean that as the Soviet Union approaches parity with the United States it will manifest less self-restraint in its behavior?

The assumption that the Soviet leaders seek parity as a terminal goal in order to establish symbolic equality with the United States and as a necessary prerequisite to negotiations on other issues on equal terms bears careful scrutiny. Undoubtedly, some Soviet leaders subscribe to this view, but others probably do not. The crucial unknown is the degree to which a significant element in the Soviet leadership believes that Soviet strategic superiority is a feasible goal and that its achievement will transfer the initiative to Moscow and bring about a reversal of roles between the two global powers. It is an unpalatable but ineluctable fact that once the Soviet Union achieves parity, it will be in a better position to strive for superiority.

Although the Soviet proponents of parity might warn the advocates of superiority that given the resources and capabilities of the United States, the Soviet Union cannot hope to win a renewed arms race without straining its

economy, provoking internal discontent as a consequence, and forever for-
feiting an opportunity to reach substantial agreements on the basis of equality,
the advocates of superiority might well rebut as follows: The United States is
now psychologically, militarily, and politically on the defensive, bruised and
humiliated by the Vietnamese war, alienated from its allies in Western Europe
as a consequence, wracked by internal racial disorders, youthful rebellion, and
conflict between rich and poor, and afflicted by political malaise and war
weariness. No administration could confidently hope to mobilize the necessary social support and political unity to engage in another arms race without
aggravating even more these "internal contradictions." Furthermore, the argument might run, the United States position in the third world has been dis-
credited by its counterrevolutionary interventionism, and a strategically superior Soviet Union could not but revive the morale of revolutionary forces,
regimes, and movements in underdeveloped countries, frighten America's
NATO allies into opting for neutrality, isolate West Germany, solidify the
Soviet position in Eastern Europe, reunify the world Communist movement,
force Israel into a dictated settlement with the Arab states, and place China
on notice that Moscow is not to be trifled with. While such a policy might
run the risk of encouraging a mutually defensive Sino-American rapprochement—which they might argue is even more likely otherwise—this view
might hold that it is even more likely that China, confronted with a powerful
Russia, might alter its attitude toward the Soviet Union, particularly if Mao
Tse-tung passes from the scene in the meantime.

Will the Soviet leaders opt for such a policy? Probably not, but it cannot
be excluded as a tempting possibility. If it has any viability as an alternative,
considerable responsibility must be placed upon the Johnson Administration
for demonstrating that strategic superiority does make a difference in spite of
the fact that the Soviet Union possessed an "invulnerable" second strike with
"assured" destructive capabilities. But the "assured" destructive capability of
a strategically inferior Russia was of a limited character as compared with the
nearly *absolute* level of "assured" destructive capability possessed by the United
States, and it was this condition of asymmetry that made the difference.

The diplomatic utility of strategic superiority defined in terms of a unilateral first-strike capability should not be obscured by the miasma of controversy generated over the rationality or irrationality of nuclear war. As an
instrument of diplomatic blackmail strategic superiority apparently retains its
effectiveness, for such a capability can be a powerful factor in the deterrence
and paralysis of responses to military and diplomatic initiatives in areas marginal to the interests of the global powers. The Soviet leaders may opt for a
first-strike capability not for the purpose of initiating and winning a nuclear
war with the United States but in order to escalate the risks of American coun-
teraction to Soviet initiatives. Strategic superiority thus could provide a kind

of protective umbrella for Soviet diplomatic maneuvers and would enable Moscow to maximize its options in foreign policy. Whereas parity enables a power to opt for stalemate or various levels of de-escalation in its diplomacy, strategic superiority allows not only stalemate or de-escalation but also a limited range of escalation in foreign policy behavior.

If it is a main current objective of the Soviet Union to contain and deter American power rather than to erode or roll it back, then the achievement of strategic parity might be sufficient to achieve this goal. Since it appears that the Administration of Richard Nixon is seriously contemplating a reduction in American international obligations—surely neither withdrawal nor isolationism, neo or otherwise—agreements on arms control which would stabilize the existing distribution of power might well offer a welcome respite to both parties. Unfortunately, however, parity as a concept and as a reality virtually defies the precise, calibrated measurement which is demanded to make it a mutually acceptable formula, whereas superiority is much easier to measure and define, particularly when the margin of superiority is substantial. The inability to arrive at a mutually satisfactory definition of "parity" may constitute an insuperable roadblock to agreement in spite of the willingness of both parties to accept it in principle, and the temptation for either Washington or Moscow—or both—to strive for a measurable degree of superiority as a consequence may be unavoidable.

Even if the Soviet leaders opt for parity and if an acceptable formula is devised, it is not likely that the Soviet Union will abandon its role as a global power. This means that although Moscow may accept a freeze on missile or atomic capability and even a limited cutback in strategic force levels, the Soviet leaders will continue to develop conventional military capabilities sufficient to enable them to compete with the United States on a global scale. This means that the Soviet leaders will perceive a need for expanded naval capabilities—aircraft carriers, helicopter carriers, naval infantry (marines)—and long-range air troop carriers to enable them to provide sufficient forces either to deter the United States from intervening or to permit their own intervention. This also suggests that the Soviet Union will seek to acquire the use of foreign ports and bases in friendly countries in the Mediterranean, the Indian Ocean, and Southeast Asia. Latin America, except for Cuba, will probably remain off limits for the time being, but this does not exclude a little Soviet reverse "bridge building" and "peaceful engagement" with Latin American regimes of various hues, the current flirtation with Peru being a good example of future Soviet behavior. While such a policy might infuriate Castro and Latin American revolutionaries, it will nevertheless be a useful device to weaken the United States position in Latin America in the interests of Moscow as a global power if not a revolutionary one.

On the other hand, the Soviet Union will probably erect new barriers and obstacles to "peaceful engagement," "bridge building," and *"Ostpolitik"* in Eastern Europe. Moscow is determined to preserve its empire in Eastern Europe—the "Socialist commonwealth" doctrine is sufficient indication of this —and it may even take additional measures to domesticate Rumania and intimidate Yugoslavia, but its fear of an increasingly bellicose China may be the decisive factor exercising a restraining influence on Soviet behavior in Europe. Moscow's quick and prudent withdrawal of its Berlin threat in March 1969 was probably encouraged by the armed incursion of the Communist Chinese in the Ussuri Valley region of the Soviet Far East.

IX. THE CHINESE PUZZLE: THE TRIANGULATION OF GLOBAL POWER

Any realistic assessment of the prospects for international stability will increasingly depend to a large extent upon the growing capability of China and the intensity and scope of its ambitions as a world power. For the moment Chinese aspirations and behavior pose a greater threat to the Soviet position than to the American, and Peking may actually be in a position to cripple the Soviet ambition to be an effective global competitor with the United States just as it has effectively crippled the Soviet leadership of the world Communist movement. Soviet-American relations are thus an integral part of a complex and intricate triangular relationship between Moscow, Peking, and Washington in which cause and effect have become inextricably merged and incapable of being disentangled. The behavior and conduct of each actor in this curious *ménage à trois* has a multiplier impact upon the reactions and responses of the other parties in the triangle which in turn set in motion feedback effects upon the actors themselves and then radiate out to affect their relations with other states in the international community. This strange triangular relationship was apparently set in motion back during the days of the "spirit of Geneva" in 1955, although the United States was unaware of its intimate involvement as a third party in a fragile Sino-Soviet partnership until after the Cuban missile crisis when it became unambiguously clear that the single greatest factor affecting Sino-Soviet relations was United States conduct, behavior, and intentions. Unwittingly, American responses and reactions were registering their impact upon Sino-Soviet relations in an active and fundamental way which in turn reshaped Chinese and Soviet attitudes toward the United States although it has been recognized since the Camp David era that the United States was always at least a peripheral and passive influence on Sino-Soviet relations.

While it cannot be documented with absolute certainty, the root cause of Sino-Soviet differences appears to be the United States and the divergent images of its intentions and behavior which are perceived in Moscow and Peking. If it is the root cause, Khrushchev's détente policy and its implications for the world Communist movement emerge, in retrospect, not as simply the reflections of his personal idiosyncrasies (which certainly dominated his style and mood) but as a realistic policy corresponding to the vital interests of the Soviet Union as a global power and hence virtually unavoidable in its essentials if survival is accorded top priority in Soviet foreign policy calculations. The policy could accord different priorities to internal interests (heavy industry over light, armaments over butter, etc.), could be carried out with greater or lesser flexibility, enthusiasm, finesse or style, cynicism, and wisdom, and could be compressed within the shell of a "harder" or "softer" line, but any Soviet group which placed survival at the top of its priority list would have to seek some form of rapprochement with the United States to maximize its chances for survival rather than depend indefinitely upon the vagaries of spontaneous deterrence, chance, accident, miscalculation, or error. Khrushchev in his own clumsy and bungling way had intuitively grasped the vital essentials of a realistic foreign policy. The challenge of Communist China made it impossible for Moscow to maintain its half-century oscillation between being a state and the center of a world revolutionary movement, and Soviet leaders were finally confronted with the moment of elemental contradictory truth: Pursuing world revolution could only maximize the prospects of total physical annihilation as both a state and the center of a messianic movement, and Moscow had to choose between survival and doctrinal virtue.

Ironically enough, continued Sino-Soviet hostility would encourage Soviet tractability elsewhere. Because of its geographical position the Soviet Union is peculiarly vulnerable to an encirclement strategy. As long as China sustains its hostility, Moscow cannot afford to antagonize its neighbors in the West for fear of some nightmarish Sino-German coordination of pressure, if not actual collaboration, against the Soviet Union. The inopportune Chinese military incursion in the Soviet Far East just as Moscow was reapplying pressure on West Berlin may have been an esoteric Chinese bid to Bonn for informal cooperation. Moscow, a capital not unversed in the nuances and subtleties of esoteric communication, lost no time in sounding out both Kurt Georg Kiesinger and Willy Brandt about the state of Sino-German relations, noting in particular that West Germany is China's most active trading partner in the West. The quick relaxation of Soviet pressure on Berlin, however, was certainly not unnoticed by Bonn, whose leaders soothingly assured Ambassador Semyon Tsarapkin that West Germany would not seek to exploit Soviet difficulties with the Chinese—which of course can be interpreted as a threat as well as a promise.

The Chinese danger thus serves to encourage the Soviet leaders to seek some sort of accommodation with the United States, but at the same time they probably realize that their open paranoia concerning China exposes them to some serious vulnerabilities. For example, the United States may thus find

a vested interest in sustaining and aggravating Sino-Soviet relations in order
to dampen Soviet appetites for adventures elsewhere.

As long as China is hostile to the Soviet Union, Moscow retains a vested
stake in the perpetuation of Sino-American hostility, for a rapprochement
between Peking and Washington would enable the Chinese to concentrate
their full fury against the Russians. A Chinese-American reconciliation is by
no means considered an impossibility by Moscow. Significantly, the Soviet press
has charged on more than one occasion that the Chinese leaders are plotting
a rapprochement with the United States and Soviet writers condemn with
unusual vigor any intimation by Western writers or spokesmen that a Sino-
American rapprochement might be a distinct possibility. On February 21,
1967, *Krasnaya Zvezda,* for example, charged that both Washington and
Peking were maneuvering toward a possible reconciliation. The Russian Army
newspaper complained that the "Taiwan lobby" was curiously inactive and
had been replaced with a "Red China lobby." It condemned the alleged secret
understanding between China and the United States about the Vietnam war
designed to prevent a Sino-American confrontation and accused the "ruling
circles" of Washington of favoring Mao Tse-tung's retention of power because
of his anti-Soviet policies:

> About the middle of 1964, something strange began to happen with the Tai-
> wan Lobby. The press which earlier carried a hard line against Peking and
> had stood like a mountain behind Chiang Kai-shek, began to soften its tone.
> The same metamorphosis occurred with leading businessmen, senators and
> government leaders. . . . In Washington, there is open talk that the ruling
> circles of the United States are interested in the retention of power by Mao
> Tse-tung.[14]

One of the genuine fears of some Soviet leaders is that a Sino-American rapprochement might enable China to devote greater attention to its unredeemed
territories in the north.

The peculiar fluidity of Sino-Soviet-American relations has seriously complicated the impact of the Vietnamese war on future international stability.
Khrushchev had virtually abandoned Vietnam; his successors reasserted Moscow's presence for a complex of reasons, some of them contradictory: It was
expected to give Moscow a measure of control over the situation and an opportunity to claim credit in the event of its successful resolution and was designed to be part of a plan to reduce or eliminate the sources and causes of

---

[14] *Krasnaya Zvezda,* February 21, 1967, *Cf.* also *The New York Times,* July 21, 1966. On the other
hand, Taipei has expressed concern that the turmoil on the Chinese mainland might precipitate a joint
Soviet-American intervention resulting in "another Yalta, a Russo-American deal at China's expense."
(*The New York Times,* February 19, 1967.) And in March 1969 Peking made the strange charge that
the visit of Soviet journalist Victor Louis to Taiwan was part of a scheme to collude with Chiang Kai-
shek against Peking. The Soviet fear of a Sino-German and a Sino-American rapprochement directed
against Moscow has become a recurrent theme in the Soviet press since March 1969.

Sino-Soviet friction. While Khrushchev's successors wanted to heal the breach with China, they also wanted to pursue the détente with the United States, although in different form. Since the Chinese felt that a Soviet-American détente was incompatible with a Sino-Soviet reconciliation, they spurned the Soviet olive branch. In the meantime the war in Vietnam escalated, Moscow became the chief supplier of arms to the North Vietnamese, and Soviet-American détente was thus made more difficult.

On the whole, the Soviet leaders have exerted their influence in favor of a negotiated resolution of the war, which the proponents of expanded Soviet-American détente viewed as an obstacle to improved relations. As the war was intensified and prolonged, the balance of sentiment in the Politburo shifted as suspicions of the Johnson Administration's intent increased. Relations with both Peking and Washington seemed to have deteriorated and the Soviet perspective on Vietnam became ambiguous and ambivalent. To some Soviet leaders the war remained an insuperable barrier to expanded cooperation while to others the inconclusive character of an intensified conflict which strained American economic and military capabilities, aroused domestic agitation, and diverted the United States' attention away from other areas appeared to pay off greater dividends than would a settlement itself. Thus, while Moscow continued to work on behalf of a settlement, it simultaneously exploited the war by exacting informal and implicit concessions from the United States concerning Eastern Europe in return for Soviet efforts on behalf of ending the war.

Since the advent of the Paris negotiations the Vietnamese war has become essentially a peripheral factor in Soviet-American relations although the Nixon Administration is still relying on Moscow to influence Hanoi toward an acceptable conclusion of the conflict.

X. The Soviet Union and the United Nations

How will all this affect Soviet behavior in the United Nations? Probably not very much. It is not necessary to recapitulate at this point the Soviet view of the UN as essentially an expedient instrument of policy. Increasingly, the Soviet leaders resort to UN bodies when it is clearly in the Soviet interest to utilize its facilities and forums to block whatever action it may take that adversely affects Soviet interests. Moscow stepped up its interest in the UN after Stalin's death, particularly after 1955, not because its basic image of the UN had been altered but rather because Khrushchev reasoned that Stalin was too dogmatic and rigid to exploit fully the possibilities offered by the UN and had too quickly dismissed it as no more than an instrumentality of United States foreign policy.

Generally speaking, Soviet behavior in the United Nations is usually an extension or reflection of Soviet behavior elsewhere. Soviet interest shifts from one organ to another depending upon their relative usefulness, always primed, however, to insist upon the right of a Soviet veto, whether formal or informal. Thus, when the Soviet Union was making its principal thrust in the third world, Soviet utilization of the General Assembly as a vehicle for its policies was at its zenith. Since Moscow was wooing the excolonial states of Africa and Asia, Soviet policy was essentially supportive of Afro-Asian positions. Soviet disenchantment with the General Assembly took form when Moscow realized that Soviet support of anticolonial positions could not be converted into effective Afro-Asian support for Soviet causes and coincided with the disappointing results of Khrushchev's efforts to gain influence in the third world in return for an expensive outlay of resources invested in an ambitious economic assistance program. Moscow retrenched from its overextended position to a few key countries ruled by radical nationalist regimes and moved toward an accommodation and détente with Washington. As a consequence Moscow betrayed a renewed interest in the Security Council where the two global powers could arrive at mutually acceptable positions with minimum intrusion by the smaller powers.

One might conclude that as a general rule if the Soviet Union resorts to the General Assembly as its chief UN vehicle, then Moscow is in a state of intense rivalry with the United States, while if it employs the Security Council as the principal forum in the UN, Soviet policy is oriented toward accommodation and détente with the United States. One might even go further and suggest that a certain functional division of labor has been devised for the Security Council and the General Assembly. On matters of shared interest and concern with the United States the Soviet Union will turn to the Council; on matters reserved for competition and rivalry Moscow will employ the General Assembly. The Security Council thus becomes a forum of accommodation and the General Assembly an arena of conflict. Issues which the Soviet leaders prefer to handle outside the UN represent residual areas of condominium, i.e., the duo-monopolistic preserve of the two global powers.

The area of possible Soviet-American agreement remains fairly large, but perhaps it has contracted somewhat from earlier possibilities and is under constant scrutiny by more skeptical members of the Politburo. Even during the grimmest period of American escalation in Vietnam the Soviet leadership entered into a number of agreements with the United States, the most important of which was the 1968 Treaty on the Nonproliferation of Nuclear Weapons. Various bilateral cultural exchange programs, treaties on outer space, the consular agreement of 1964, the Moscow–New York air agreement of 1968, and the important agreement adopted as Security Council Resolution 255 (1968) of June 19, 1968, whereby the United States and the Soviet Union jointly agreed to come to the assistance of nonnuclear powers threatened or attacked with nuclear weapons,[15] were all signed during this period.

Both the United States and Russia will probably reaffirm the sanctity of their respective spheres of influence, the latest manifestation of this tacit agreement being the mild American reaction to the events in Czechoslovakia. The questions of "bridge building" and "peaceful engagement" remain moot at the moment while Yugoslavia's relationship to the "Socialist community" remains an undefined area. Although the European status quo has been somewhat disturbed, both parties seem to have a greater interest in preserving it than upsetting it.

In the Middle East Russia and the United States appear to be moving in the direction of an imposed settlement whose outlines remain obscure. Moscow will continue to expand its involvement in the Arab world, seek naval bases on Arab territories, and provide more credible and effective guarantees against another Israeli attack. What the Soviet leaders will do if the Arab states take the initiative or if a conflict inadvertently breaks out remains an enigma. Apparently this is one of the most controversial issues in the Politburo, with some members apparently encouraging the Arabs and others counseling caution.

In the Far East Moscow still appears to have more of an interest in ending the Vietnamese war than in seeing it continue despite its obvious usefulness in maintaining a large American military force on the Asian mainland to the south of China. Moscow's relative indifference to the destruction of the Indonesian Communist Party and its support to Pakistan and India are reaffirmations of its Chinese encirclement policy. The key to Soviet success here largely depends upon the United States, and Sino-American relations may turn out to be the most important conditioner of Soviet behavior elsewhere.

Since the Soviet Union is too powerful not to challenge the United States, we can expect a continuing rivalry between the two global powers during the next decade, but increasingly it will assume traditional patterns. Not only will the leadership crisis in the Soviet Union be temporarily resolved, but given the advanced average age of the Soviet gerontocracy,[16] the world can expect a sudden and massive generational shift in Soviet leadership during the next decade. This new leadership, unlike the existing one, will be largely a product of the post-Stalinist era. It will not be psychologically crippled or morally corrupted by the cruel Stalinist legacy; it will be neither ideologically committed to the residuary rotting corpus of Stalinist mythology nor obligated by self-interest to preserve and perpetuate residual Stalinist institutions and processes. This new leadership, furthermore, will not be conditioned by the fears and anxieties of the Stalinist years which have been such a crucial factor

[15] This resolution was adopted in connection with the 1968 Nonproliferation Treaty.
[16] The average age of the Politburo is 59. The youngest member is 51, the oldest is 70.

in shaping the outlook of the current leadership. How this next generation of
Soviet leadership will repudiate or reaffirm the Soviet past remains an enigma,
but it is extremely likely that all of our assumptions concerning Soviet behavior and purpose will once again be subject to critical reexamination and
reassessment.

The United Nations, the United States, and the Maintenance of Peace

Inis L. Claude, Jr.

THIS essay is addressed to the issue of the extent to which and the ways in which the United Nations may serve the interest of the United States in the maintenance of world peace during the decade that lies ahead. It rests upon two assumptions, both of which require careful qualification: first, the assumption that the United States has, and recognizes that it has, a fundamental interest in international peace; second, the assumption that the United Nations is in principle an organization dedicated to the promotion of international peace.

The first assumption must be qualified by the acknowledgment that the United States does not regard every outbreak of violence in the international realm as equally threatening to its interests; it does not take the doctrine of the indivisibility of peace as literal and absolute truth. Moreover, the enthusiasm of the United States for the condemnation and repression of international violence is limited by the conviction that resort to force in some circumstances may be necessary and salutary. The United States has in recent years encountered situations which it has interpreted as justifying and requiring military action, and it must contemplate the possibility that similar situations may arise in the future. "Peace at any price" is not the American theme, nor is total renunciation of the national right to decide upon and undertake acts of coercion a feature of American foreign policy.

These two positions—that some disruptions of the peace may be tolerated and that some circumstances may demand even unilateral resort to violence—may be regarded by some as evidence of American cynicism, of commitment to the goal of world domination by the United States, achieved by force if necessary, rather than to the ideal of world peace. In the more orthodox American view of the matter, which I share, these positions reflect sophistica-

INIS L. CLAUDE, JR., a member of the Board of Editors of *International Organization*, is Professor of Government and Foreign Affairs at the University of Virginia, Charlottesville, Virginia.

tion rather than cynicism. Far from indicating callous disregard for global order, they reflect an awareness of the cruel complexities of the international system and a rejection of the view that a simple "Thou shalt not fight" formula can cut through all the difficulties. Indeed, a strong case can be made for the proposition that these qualifications of the commitment to nonviolence do not qualify but rather serve to define and to implement the basic American commitment to world peace. The commitment is to the *general* stability of the international order, and it may be argued that the maintenance of this stability permits and even requires a hands-off attitude toward certain conflicts that appear to be not only isolated but isolable. In other situations national willingness or determination to fight may, while possibly producing some bloodshed, prove indispensable to the avoidance of general international conflict. In short, commitments to world peace and to nonviolence are not necessarily identical. This is not to argue that the United States has mastered the art of maintaining world peace, nor is it to deny that the actual behavior of the United States may on occasion contradict rather than serve the objective of world peace. It is simply to insist that the qualifications imposed by the United States upon its commitment to nonviolence do not invalidate its proclaimed devotion to the ideal of world peace; it is to defend the assumption that the United States has, and recognizes that it has, a fundamental interest in international peace.

The second assumption, pertaining to the dedication of the United Nations to global pacification, is subject to the observation that the stated purposes of an organization are not necessarily its operative purposes. Constitutional dedication is less decisive than political determination; examination of the politics of the United Nations is superior to perusal of its Charter as a means of identifying the Organization's actual objectives. The Charter's affirmation of the aim of promoting and maintaining peace is not irrelevant. It provides a standard against which the propriety of various purposes that the Organization may be made to serve can be judged, and it establishes the orthodoxy into which all heresies must be squeezed by whatever ingenious methods their proponents can devise. It cannot, however, provide a guarantee that the uses to which the United Nations is put will invariably be conducive to or even compatible with world peace. Given the facts that the primary participants in the shaping of United Nations policy are the Member States, that these include virtually all the states of the world, and that their membership carries with it no automatic transformation of their attitudes and objectives, it would be surprising indeed if United Nations policy were characterized by single-minded and undeviating devotion to the cause of international peace and order.

If we approach the record of the United Nations in the mood of one who seeks to analyze the working of a political institution rather than that of one who is concerned with the advancement of a sacred cause, we find ample evidence of the variety of uses for which the Organization may be available. These range from efforts to develop a durable system of peace, through programs only tenuously related, if at all, to the problem of peace, to activities in support of attacks upon the status quo which, whatever their justification, tend to be disruptive of the peace. While we cannot take it for granted that the United Nations will function consistently as an agency of pacification, we can assert that its constitutional mandate defines the Organization's proper role in these terms and assume the possibility that the Organization may be directed and controlled by those who give priority to its actual and potential capability for contributing to peace.

I return to the original issue: Assuming that the United States has a fundamental commitment to world peace, though it be a commitment qualified by denial that every conflict must be treated as a threat to the general order and by refusal to renounce the possibility of unilateral military action, and assuming that the United Nations is properly conceived as an agency to be used for the maintenance of peace without forgetting that it may be directed toward other and possibly contradictory objectives, to what degree should the United States rely upon the United Nations for the keeping of the peace in the years immediately ahead? What role can the United States reasonably expect the United Nations to play in the furtherance of world order? What potentialities inhere in the Organization which the United States and like-minded states might develop and exploit in the interest of peace? How, in other words, should the United Nations figure in the American approach to the problem of world peace?

The first essential step in the approach to the issue that these questions elaborate is to develop a sensible reaction to the prevailing ideology of multilateralism in international relations. I refer to the point of view according to which collective or multilateral decisions, actions, and programs are regarded as intrinsically preferable to those deriving from the policy processes of a single state.[1] Resting upon the assumption that multilateralism guarantees policy that is uniquely effective, wise, and virtuous, this ideology tends to inspire a mood of doctrinaire antiunilateralism; emanations from Foggy Bottom are automatically to be disparaged and deplored while Turtle Bay is to be regarded as the authentic source of whatever is constructive, decent, and desirable in international relations.

There is evident merit in this emphasis upon the importance of developing and the value of using the collective instrumentalities of the international system. The establishment of international organizations and the systematic de-

[1] I have attempted a critical analysis of this doctrine in "The Vogue of Collectivism in International Relations," *Interstate* (University College of Wales, Aberystwyth), November 1968 (No. 1, 68'69), pp. 14–18.

velopment of multilateral processes are among the most promising phenomena of international relations in the twentieth century, and states, particularly powers great enough to consider thoroughgoing independence of operation an alternative plausibly open to them, may profit from the reminder that they have a stake in the ordering of the global system which can be promoted only by flourishing international organizations. Moreover, there *is* strength—moral and political if not military—in numbers, and many national heads *may* be wiser than one; to give earnest consideration to the will and judgment of the community of states, whether expressed by consensus or by majority vote, is an act of prudence and conceivably of virtue.

Nevertheless, it seems that the doctrine of multilateralism should inspire pragmatic consideration rather than dogmatic acceptance. The relative effectiveness of unilateral and multilateral activities is an issue to be examined in the concrete case, not to be settled by reference to an abstract formula. The quality of policy—its wisdom and propriety—is not a function of its unilateral or its multilateral origins. Since international unpopularity may prejudice the results of a national foreign policy, statesmen are well advised to pay careful attention to the multilateral reception of national behavior but not to pay it automatic deference. Sound and necessary policy is no more so for its having emerged from an international organization and no less so for its having been produced and carried out by a single government. Intelligent foreign policy is a sufficiently rare commodity that it should be welcomed wherever it can be found.

One should also deal cautiously with the advice to treat the making of foreign policy as an occasion for conferring authority and prestige upon the United Nations, as if the latter were a muscular organism that requires exercise to grow strong and avoid atrophy. Quite aside from the fact that overburdening is as great a peril to the world Organization as inactivity there is the central consideration that the United Nations is a means and not an end. Strengthening the United Nations is important, but it deserves a lower priority than dealing successfully with the problems that literally involve the destiny of man. The responsible statesman faces a dilemma that entitles him to something better than ritualistic advice—namely, to sensitive and sympathetic understanding of his predicament. He *ought* to be concerned with the long-term development of an effective system of world order; he *must* be concerned with the short-term solution of pressing problems. He is fortunate when there is no difficulty in reconciling these two concerns. He begins to earn his pay when he grapples with situations involving a conflict and requiring a choice between system building for the long run and problem solving for the short run. This, I suggest, is the nature of the dilemma that American policymakers can expect to confront with some frequency as they consider the relevance of the United Nations to the problem of maintaining world peace in the forthcoming decade. In such situations the doctrinaire insistence that their correct course is to turn to and defer to the United Nations is unconvincing, just as the easy assertion that they should follow the national interest is unrevealing; their responsibility cannot be intelligently discharged by the application of a formula.

A fascinating and significant shift is now occurring in the political symbolism of the United Nations as it relates to American foreign policy. Until recently participation in and support of the United Nations by the United States was above all a symbol of America's new internationalism, its abandonment of the isolationist tradition, and its commitment to the steady and dependable performance of an active role in world affairs. It can be argued that this is what the formation of the League of Nations and subsequently the United Nations was primarily aimed at achieving; the organizations were designed to entice the United States into a leading role in international relations. The American decision to abstain from the League amounted to a rejection of that new role, and the decision to join the United Nations reflected the reconsideration that had been stimulated by World War II and symbolized the reversal of the earlier decision. For many of the founders of the United Nations this transformation of the American position provided the basis for whatever optimism they felt concerning the stability of the postwar international order. They rejoiced at the return of the prodigal Great Power, served up a fatted calf in the form of the veto privilege, and contrived to place the United Nations in the United States in the hope that this would make it easier to keep the United States in the United Nations. American internationalists similarly treated ratification of the Charter as the symbol of belatedly triumphant Wilsonianism in the struggle over United States foreign policy, and they have regarded attentiveness to the United Nations as the essential manifestation of the American resolution to continue in the new role, an earnest of the sincerity of the American conversion to internationalism. Passionate warnings about the danger of neglecting or bypassing the United Nations have come largely from nervous internationalists seeking reiterated assurances as to the solidity of the American commitment.

Considering this background there is a certain irony in the fact that American political leaders today are tending to use the United Nations as a symbol of the possibility of the substantial reduction of the international responsibilities of the United States. The bitter controversy over Vietnam has produced massive pressure against the continued performance of the role of "world policeman" by the United States. Protest against the American military action in Vietnam is doubtless strengthened by the fact that this action does not enjoy the official endorsement of the United Nations and has indeed incurred widespread censure within the Organization. If the American action had been launched in conformity with a United Nations mandate or had been granted formal support by the United Nations, it would presumably have engendered less criticism. However, most of the substantive arguments advanced in condemnation of the American engagement in Vietnam would apply even if the United States were acting for, with, or through the United Nations; in that case it would be logical for those who accept these arguments to denounce the United States for having perverted the United Nations, for having twisted arms to secure endorsement or sponsorship of the Organization for what might still appear to them an unjustified and unwise policy. In short, those who have argued most vociferously that Vietnam should have been left to the United Nations have not, in my judgment, been motivated so much by the conviction that the United Nations should have intervened in that unhappy country as by the conviction that the United States should not have intervened there. Nevertheless, the reaction against Vietnam in the United States is increasingly finding expression in assertions of the proposition that international organizations, not the United States, should engage in the messy business of keeping order where chaos threatens. There is a strong and understandable urge—though it may not be a realistic one—to shift to other shoulders, usually identified vaguely as those of the United Nations, the burdens, the costs, the risks, and the blame that this business entails. Political leaders, bowing to the necessity of making concessions to the Vietnam-generated demand for American retrenchment, develop the theme that the United States should abdicate the policeman's role to the United Nations.

In his 1968 presidential campaign speeches Hubert Humphrey accepted the proposition that the United States has burdened itself with excessive commitments in international affairs and promised careful trimming of those commitments with a view toward shifting greater emphasis to domestic problems:

> The lesson [that we have learned from Vietnam] is . . . that we should carefully define our goals and priorities. . . .
>
> . . . I would insist as President that we review other commitments made in other times . . . that we carefully decide what is, and is not, in our national interest.
>
> . . . .
>
> . . . if I am President, I owe it to this nation to bring our men and resources in Vietnam back to America where we need them so badly . . . and to be sure we put first things first in the future.[2]
>
> Our world role in the next ten years will be different from that in the last. There are pressing problems at home, which cause us to place careful priorities on allocation of resources abroad.[3]

[2] The passage is from the text of a television address, published in *The Washington Post*, October 1, 1968, p. A 6.

[3] From a speech delivered in San Francisco on September 26, 1968. *Ibid.*, September 27, 1968, p. A 6.

From this point he moved directly to the position that primary responsibility for the maintenance of peace should be transferred to the United Nations:

> I pledge to you . . . that one of the high priorities of my Presidency will be to strengthen the peacekeeping and peacemaking capacity of the United Nations.
>
> This is our third step toward a new strategy for peace: To make the U. N. the instrument for controlling conflict it has so far failed to be.
>
> The United States cannot play the role of global gendarme. The American people don't want it, and the rest of the world won't accept it. We know better today than yesterday that "the illusion of American omnipotence"—in D. W. Brogan's phrase, "is an illusion."
>
> But the alternative to American peacekeeping cannot be no peacekeeping. It must be peacekeeping by the United Nations or by regional agencies.[4]

Humphrey was not advocating a return to isolationism. In the speeches that I have cited and in others he was explicit and emphatic in his insistence that the United States should not draw back within itself and abandon its active role in world affairs. Moreover, he did not suggest that this country could or should simply delegate its responsibilities to the United Nations, but, recognizing the existing limitations of that Organization, he asserted that the United States should promote and support the development of the capacity of the United Nations to assume the major burden of coping with threats to the peace. He stressed leadership and partnership; the United States should work with other states and through international agencies to maximize the possibility of multilateral action and thereby to minimize the necessity for unilateral American action in keeping the peace.

Nevertheless, it is clear that Humphrey was making an effort to assure the electorate that if he became President he would act in accordance with the widespread demand for reducing the commitments of the United States, and it is significant that he treated the United Nations as a vehicle for realizing this objective, an agency potentially capable of providing an "alternative to American peacekeeping." His references to the limitations of the United States, the need to turn primary attention to domestic problems, and the consequent urgency of reducing our foreign involvements underlay his proposal to place greater reliance upon the United Nations and other multilateral agencies. As he presented the matter, American retrenchment was to be facilitated rather than inhibited by the membership of the United States in these organizations. Despite his reminder that this country would have to exert itself to expand the capacity of the United Nations and other agencies for undertak-

---

[4] *Ibid.* Cf. this comment concerning the mood of the new Administration of Richard Nixon: "There is a disposition . . . to be chary of any more Vietnams—to shy from unilateral entanglements and rely more on international organizations to police the peace and good order of the world." (" 'Let Us . . . Go Forward Together,' " *Newsweek,* January 27, 1969, p. 19.) Whether or not this is an accurate appraisal of the Nixon Administration's attitude it is a striking example of the widespread tendency to regard action by multilateral agencies as an alternative to American involvements.

ing heavier responsibilities the central theme of his remarks was that international organizations might in some measure relieve the United States of its
international burdens.

The significant point of this analysis is that Humphrey's position represents
the reversal of the conventional symbolism according to which the United
Nations is conceived as a means of calling in the United States to redress the
balance of forces in the world. It calls in the United Nations to cover the partial retreat of the United States, to help this country get itself off the international hook. The world Organization is invoked to symbolize and legitimize not the American commitment to internationalism but an American
shift toward a more limited global role.

Humphrey lost the election, but I see no evidence that his defeat should be
construed as a repudiation of the position discussed above. On the contrary,
it may be argued that his electoral failure is at least partly attributable to the
fact that his movement in the indicated direction was too little, too late, and
insufficiently convincing to many of those who have traditionally provided
the major support for American commitment and involvement in world affairs. The dominant mood in the United States is one which favors the deflation of foreign policy, as Walter Lippmann has described it,[5] and which
is no longer so concerned about the danger of bypassing the United Nations
as about the possibility of buck-passing to the United Nations.

As we consider the potentialities of the United Nations for contributing to
the maintenance of peace and order in the next decade, we must confront
the question of the impact upon the Organization of this American mood and
the trend in American foreign policy that it foreshadows. Generally, the
record suggests that American retrenchment will, while creating a need for
the United Nations to expand its role in world politics, reduce rather than
increase the probability that it will and the possibility that it can do so. In
most areas of activity the rule of thumb has been that the less the United
States is willing to do, the less the United Nations can be expected to do—
and vice versa. It is open to question whether that relationship can be reversed,
whether the objective of increasing the activity of the United Nations to permit and compensate for the diminution of the activity of the United States
can be achieved. How capable a buck receiver can we realistically expect the
United Nations to become?

I suggest that the conception of the United Nations as a possible substitute
for the United States in carrying out some of the tasks that may be required
for the maintenance of world peace provides too limited a basis for the consideration of the relationship that should prevail between the global Organization and its most powerful and influential Member. The nature and identity
of the United Nations can be conceived in several ways with varying implica-

[5] See his column in *The Washington Post*, February 9, 1969, p. B 1.

tions for the functional relationship between the Organization and the United States.

The United Nations may be conceived first of all as an entity in itself, a synthetic but separate actor on the international stage, created by states and dependent upon them for its survival but capable of acting in its own right. This conception focuses upon the Secretariat and in particular upon the Secretary-General—those who in a special sense constitute the Organization. This bureaucratic entity is largely controlled and directed by states, but states do not compose it; it is for every state an "other," an agency external to itself.

Second, the United Nations may be regarded by the United States or any other Member as a vehicle for other states, a mechanism for the registration of their judgments, the rendering of their decisions, and the facilitation of their joint action. Looking at it in this way, a particular state sets aside its own membership and involvement and envisages the Organization as a collective "them" distinguished from the national "us." Thus, it becomes possible to speak of the United Nations as assisting in our economic development, improperly meddling in our affairs, or approving our policy.

A third conception of the Organization brings one's own state back into the picture along with the other states and the supporting staff. The United Nations becomes a combination of "them" and "us," a setting within which "we" interact with the massive "them" and its component parts, competing and cooperating, winning and losing, persuading and conceding.

These three versions of the United Nations may be tagged as "it," "they" (or "them"), and "we and they" (or "us and them"). Clearly, these are alternative conceptions that do not require a definitive choice but are available for periodic selection. No one of them expresses the exclusively correct perception of the United Nations, and resort to all of them poses no problem if we keep clearly in mind which of them we are dealing with at any given time.

As "it" or "they" the United Nations is theoretically eligible to substitute for the United States in the performance of tasks that may be regarded as conducive to peace. The United States can conceivably reduce its involvement by standing aside in favor of "it" or "them." We should be very clear that what this means is that the buck is passed to the United Nations Secretariat, to an indeterminate group of other states, or to some combination of the two. The questions of what functions should be handed over in this fashion and of what burdens the United States might wish to dispose of in this way must be considered in relation to a third question: What tasks can "it" and "they" reasonably be expected to be willing and able to undertake?

The "we and they" conception of the United Nations, on the other hand, provides no scheme for American disengagement. It involves action by the United States in combination with other states through, or under the auspices of, or with the sanction of, the United Nations. Unless the record of the past misleads us as to prospects for the future, the contributions of other states will vary directly, not inversely, with the contributions of the United States. In matters ranging from the defense of the Republic of Korea (South Korea) to the funding of multilateral economic aid and technical assistance programs major American commitments have been the key to the involvement of other states; if the United States had done less, it seems unlikely that others would have done more. In the area appropriate to action by "us and them" American retrenchment can be expected to spell United Nations retrenchment; and if the United Nations is to be made a more adequate and vigorous organization, this will mean more, not less, responsibility and involvement for the United States.

The classical notion of the potential and desirable contributions of general international organizations to the maintenance of peace assigns primacy, in importance if not in sequence, to the peace-enforcement function, the mobilization of collective pressure and action—by military means if necessary—to control states breaking or threatening to break the peace. This originally implied the operation of a reliable and generally applicable system of collective security, promising quasi-automatic action by a quasi-universal body of states to squelch any aggression that might occur. While the idea of such a system is no longer taken seriously, the basic objective that the theory of collective security was designed to serve, the development of a systematic means for compelling states to refrain from disruptive international behavior, remains central to contemporary thought and aspiration concerning world order. The question of United Nations peace enforcement figures prominently in the standard agenda of those who ponder the future role of the United Nations in the maintenance of peace.

I submit that if the United Nations has a peace-enforcement system in its future, that system will be a function of "us and them," not of "it" or "them." To discuss the repression by the United Nations of aggression or other disruptive behavior is to talk not about how to reduce the commitments of the United States but about how to maintain and increase them. Considering the United Nations apart from the United States, I see no evidence that it has, and no prospect that it will develop, either the power or the political will requisite for the coercive restraint of peacebreakers. Any conceivable United Nations function in this vein would seem to involve the Organization's serving as a vehicle for action led by and heavily dependent upon the participation of the United States rather than as a replacement for the weary, frustrated, and disillusioned American "world policeman."

To view the matter in this light is to regard the enhancement of the role of the United Nations in peace enforcement as a very unlikely prospect at least for the next few years. At most the Organization can be expected to carry out the function of authorizing and encouraging Member States to undertake joint resistance to breaches of the peace. Such joint actions are improbable except as enterprises under American leadership, and the facts that few states are disposed to follow the United States and that the latter is increasingly indisposed to take the lead in enterprises of this kind of militate against their occurring. If situations develop which the United States regards as sufficiently threatening to the stability of the global order to require an effective military response, this country will have to choose between acting and not acting; the choice of leaving it to the amorphous "them" of the United Nations will not be available. If it decides to act, the United States will and should welcome the legitimizing endorsement of the United Nations, to be sought in the "we and they" forum of that Organization, but in most circumstances it will be unlikely to find that endorsement obtainable. Failing that, the United States will have to decide whether the case justifies or demands that it proceed without United Nations support. Many of the states that are least likely to give their approval to American action in cases such as these can be expected to appeal for coercive measures in situations involving residual colonialism and recalcitrant racialism, cases in which the United States tends to regard coercion as having peacebreaking rather than peace-maintaining consequences. Thus, it may well be that United Nations policy will be supportive of ventures to which the United States will be unwilling to commit its power and that the United States will think it essential to invest its power in ventures to which the United Nations will be unwilling to lend the support of its policy. The combination of United Nations policy and United States power in a mutually supportive relationship may be difficult to achieve in the years that lie ahead; that is to say that the United Nations is unlikely to play a prominent role in the enforcement of peace against determined troublemakers.

Peace enforcement is not, however, the sole or necessarily the most important function in the realm of peace maintenance. Perhaps the most significant development in the thinking of scholars and statesmen about international organization in the postwar period has been their gradual emancipation from the collective security fixation, their breaking out of the intellectual rut in which it was taken for granted that the suppression of aggression was so crucial a function of general international organizations that if this function could not be exercised, the only issue worth thinking about was how to make its exercise possible. Dag Hammarskjöld gave dramatic and forceful expression to the new and less constricted approach to international organization when he put the question of how the United Nations could contribute directly to keeping the peace when it could not enforce the peace and answered the question by formulating the theory of preventive diplomacy, now generally known as peacekeeping.[6]

[6] See his *Introduction to the Annual Report of the Secretary-General on the Work of the Organization, 16 June 1959–15 June 1960* (General Assembly *Official Records* [15th session], Supplement No. 1A).

The provision and the management of peacekeeping operations constitute the primary function which from the American perspective lies essentially within the province of the United Nations understood as "it" and "them." This function, designed to induce and facilitate the standing off of the super-powers at a safe distance from the scene of potentially spreading trouble, is the major exception to the general rule that American inactivity tends to promote the reduction rather than to stimulate the increase of United Nations activity. In this instance the willingness of the major powers to become or to remain disengaged from the situation is a basic requirement for successful action by the United Nations. Moreover, the disposition of the United States and the Union of Soviet Socialist Republics to regard and treat the United Nations in third-person terms enhances the prospect that each of them will consider the Organization sufficiently impartial to be trusted with the carrying out of the peacekeeping function. This is preeminently the functional sector in which United Nations action may be conceived as a substitute for American action, where "leave it to the United Nations" can be regarded as the invocation of a meaningful and preferable alternative rather than as a slogan designed to excuse inaction.

There is a limit, however, to the necessity for and the virtue of the American treatment of the United Nations in its peacekeeping role as a third party rather than a "we and they" grouping. While emphasis upon the "otherness" of the United Nations is conducive to its political eligibility to serve the Great Powers by ministering to their need for avoidance of confrontations, it does nothing to remedy the deficiency of the Organization in the resources required for meeting the practical problems involved in rendering such service. To put the matter bluntly, the United Nations has encountered such formidable difficulties in peacekeeping operations, ranging from the threat of bankruptcy to the development of political discord threatening to disrupt the Organization, that the will of "it and them" to continue this kind of service has been placed in question. There is an unpleasant analogy between the effects of Vietnam upon the United States and the effects of peacekeeping ventures, notably the Congo operation, upon the United Nations; the American "policeman," embroiled in what he regards as peace enforcement, is no more sourly convinced of the truth of the Gilbertian maxim concerning the unhappiness of the policeman's lot than is the United Nations "policeman," recently experienced in the perils of peacekeeping.

A major task for the United States in the next few years is to promote the development of the capacity of the United Nations to conduct peacekeeping operations without thereby jeopardizing its survival. Such enterprises may always present more than routine problems, but it should be possible to remove them from the category of traumatic experiences for the Organization. While the conduct of peacekeeping operations requires that the United States stand aside and defer to "it and them," the creation of adequate United Nations potential for exercise of this function demands a "we and they" approach on the part of the United States. This country cannot perform the task alone. Some of the most critical contributions—the provision of the appropriate personnel for operations in the field, for instance—are dependent upon the will of states far removed from American influence. Nevertheless, American leadership is vital. The truth is quite simply that unless the United States takes the lead in promoting the solution of problems relating to the authorization, management, and financing of peacekeeping, those problems will remain unsolved and will spoil the future of this new and promising function of the United Nations.

In any case, United Nations peacekeeping has a limited range of application. It is not, even in theory, a technique suitable for dealing with the great bulk of the situations and events that may endanger the peace. It is certainly not applicable to situations of the kind that most explicitly and directly threaten the peace: those which involve a belligerent so determined and powerful that forcible resistance on a substantial scale is indispensable. We must be very clear about the point that it is as unrealistic to consider the United Nations a potential substitute for the United States in cases of that type as it is inappropriate to regard the United States as a substitute for the United Nations in cases where the interested parties are willing to accept the interposition of a politically disinterested force to calm an explosive situation. One may legitimately argue that the United States should not have intervened in Vietnam to deal with what it regarded as a case of indirect or covert aggression, but one cannot realistically suggest that the United Nations might have acted in lieu of the United States to carry out the mission that the United States attempted; the alternative was that the task would not be undertaken, not that the United Nations would undertake it. The essential point is that there are basic differences between peace enforcement and peacekeeping that indicate the ineligibility of the United Nations for the former and its eligibility for the latter. Peace enforcement requires power that the United States has and policy that the United Nations is unlikely to engender or even to support. Peacekeeping requires a political stance that is conceivable for an international organization but not for a Great Power and agents whose effectiveness depends not upon the power but upon the presumed impartiality of their states.

To say that the potential scope of peacekeeping is limited and uncertain is not to minimize its potential importance and value. The cases appropriate for its exercise may be few, but their significance may be critical; it takes only one uncontrolled fire to develop into an uncontrollable conflagration. A situation that causes both the United States and the Soviet Union to sense and acknowledge the need for a buffer to forestall their competitive involvement is by definition a dangerous one. If it inspires them also to welcome and support the initiation of a United Nations peacekeeping operation, it becomes a hopeful situation. Working imaginatively and persistently at the task of achieving the solution of the problems that inhibit the continuation and further development of the world Organization's peacekeeping role is the most important way in which the United States can promote the usefulness of the United Nations in the maintenance of peace.

Beyond the realm of peace enforcement and peacekeeping there obviously lies a broad functional terrain upon which the United Nations can operate to promote world peace and order. Major challenges to the wisdom and ingenuity of those who put the mechanisms of the United Nations to use are posed by the problems of promoting peaceful settlement of disputes and peaceful toleration of unsettled disputes, peaceful change and peaceful resistance to change. The United Nations will presumably continue to provide the setting for a considerable portion of the rapidly expanding business of international relations in future years—for much of the debate and the diplomacy, the conduct of negotiations and the registration of consensus, the declamation and the consultation that mark the interaction of states in an increasingly intimate but explosive world. Still farther from the edge of conflict the United Nations will have the opportunity to engage in peace-building activities no less important than operations bearing more directly upon specific areas of friction.

The United States has a stake in the development and use of the United Nations as a contributor to world order in all these respects, but for the short-term problem of dealing with threats to the peace its best hope of obtaining substantial assistance from the United Nations seems to lie in the possibility of strengthening the will and capacity of the Organization—of "it" and "them"—to perform the peacekeeping function.

We live, and will continue for the foreseeable future to live, in an international system plagued by the actuality and the potentiality of conflicts between states, over states, and within states—conflicts which in varying degrees endanger or involve the possibility of endangering the general stability of world order. The variety of potential crises is enormous; the possibilities include direct clashes between the United States and the Soviet Union, between either of them and the People's Republic of China (Communist China), between either of them and a member of its own or of the other's system of alignment, and between states or groups of states outside these blocs. The range of dangerous action that must be anticipated extends from overt and clear-cut aggression to the most subtle and ambiguous forms of intrusion, from direct confrontation of hostile states at territorial boundaries to competitive involvement of external powers within the political life of third states.

How should the United States respond to the procession of crises that seems certain to bedevil the world in future years? I have contended that it can look to the United Nations as an agency of action for the maintenance of peace only in those instances where the parties involved and the potentially intrusive Great Powers value the avoidance of continuing and expanding conflict so highly that they are prepared to welcome or accept the intervention of a United Nations peacekeeping force. The ability of the United Nations to perform even this function will be precarious until and unless solutions are found for the grave problems, fundamentally political in nature, that previous performances have entailed. The United States will be well advised to do all that it can to enhance the general capacity and eligibility of the United Nations to engage in peacekeeping operations, to examine conflicts that arise for evidence of their susceptibility to management by such means, and to encourage and support peacekeeping by the world Organization whenever this seems feasible.

Beyond this we encounter the range of cases where the consensual basis for United Nations peacekeeping is lacking and cannot readily be contrived, where one or more of the parties is more devoted to the conduct of a struggle than to the enlistment of assistance in calling off the struggle; in such instances the issue is not peacekeeping but peace enforcement, the threat or the use of force to counter the action being undertaken. The United States may find itself in any one of several situations: 1) It may be resolved to take action, with or without the collaboration of other states, at the behest of the United Nations or with the latter's approval; 2) it may be unwilling to participate in action endorsed or demanded by the United Nations; 3) it may be opposed to action undertaken by other states with the sanction of the United Nations; 4) it may think it necessary to take action, alone or with others, without the approval or even in the face of the disapproval of the United Nations; 5) it may abstain from involvement and urge other states to do likewise. In cases of this variety the potential function of the world Organization has to do with the legitimization of action by states. The United Nations may endorse or condemn, encourage or discourage, military intervention in situations of conflict; it offers no substitute for the power of states, but its machinery provides facilities for multilateral efforts to influence the policies of states.

I can conceive of no pat formula for determining the proper course of the United States in cases of the kind under consideration. Acting, or refraining from acting, in conformity with the resolutions of United Nations organs is highly desirable—though less because of the presumption that there is virtue in adherence to the "will of the United Nations" than because of the recognition that there is pragmatic advantage in concerting American policy to the fullest possible degree with that of other states. Similarly, Congressional and public opinion and reaction within the United States must be considered and anticipated since the effectiveness of foreign policy is a function even more of domestic than of international acceptance and support. Ultimately, however, the task of statesmanship is to judge whether American involvement in a given situation is more likely to produce consequences that weaken or that strengthen the stability of the general international order. Such judgments can never be certain, but they must be made, with wisdom if possible and courage if necessary. Neither passivity nor active engagement on the part of the United States is in principle the key to the management of international crises. Responsible leaders of the United States can neither evade nor delegate the burden of deciding, case by case, how American policy and power are to be related to the objective of the maintenance of peace.

Arms Control and International Order

LINCOLN P. BLOOMFIELD

I. THE PARADOXES OF THE PRESENT

A VISITOR from another, more advanced, planet would find many extraordinary paradoxes on earth, but surely the most extraordinary would be the fantastic destructive potential of nuclear weapons which contrasts starkly with the primitive and near-impotent institutions of global peacekeeping. He might marvel that a breed capable of producing the wealth for a $185 billion armory of lethal devices, let alone the technology for killing several hundred million humans in a single exchange of nuclear weapons, had not also produced a workable international order capable of regulating such apocalyptic man-made power.

Alas, no such international order exists today, and the prospects are not encouraging that it will exist within the foreseeable future. The nuclear arms race is accelerating. Such stability as has existed between the nuclear capabilities of the Union of Soviet Socialist Republics and the United States may be in process of being undermined by the apparently inexorable rhythm of action and reaction. The newest spiral takes form with two developments. One is MIRV—multiple independently targetable reentry vehicles—which can produce several times more widespread destruction and fallout than today's already huge inventories of deliverable intercontinental nuclear weapons. The other potentially destabilizing development is the antiballistic missile (ABM) which most experts agree can always be overcome by increasing numbers of offensive weapons. Carried to extremes, both could conceivably lure a nation into harboring the one misconception that could be fatal for much of humanity—the mistaken belief that it can strike another nation, using nuclear weapons, without being intolerably damaged in return.

Mankind is not totally impervious to the stark lessons of this process. There

LINCOLN P. BLOOMFIELD, a member of the Board of Editors of *International Organization,* is Professor of Political Science and a senior staff member of the Center for International Studies, Massachusetts Institute of Technology, Cambridge, Mass. The author wishes to acknowledge the major contribution made to this article by Irirangi Coates Bloomfield.

was more progress in the 1960's than before toward limited agreements bearing on the dangers of nuclear warfare. The United Nations played a part in most of these agreements, either in exhorting the nuclear powers to act, in sponsoring the negotiations, or in formally acknowledging and thus in a sense "codifying" an agreement after it was reached. But as an institution capable of altering in any major way the behavior of the nuclear-weapons powers the UN has been powerless apart from such marginal effects as an expression of generalized world opinion may have on nations that are entirely free to disregard it for reasons of state.

The UN cannot disarm the nuclear-weapons nations. It has neither carrots nor sticks with which to bend them to the will of even an overwhelming majority of nations. It can sometimes influence and even coerce states; given Soviet-American collaboration, it is even theoretically possible that the three lesser nuclear-weapons powers—the United Kingdom, France, and the People's Republic of China—could be deterred and even crushed. But if either of the two giants decides to launch its fearful strategic might, the international community as presently constituted has no way to alter their decision, however fateful that decision for much of the planet.

There is irony in the fact that in many other ways the world *has* in fact been changing and moving in the direction of international cooperation. The planet Earth is diverse, pluralistic, and, increasingly interdependent. This reality of widely distributed political and economic power is reflected in a whole gamut of institutional forms ranging from the European Economic Community (EEC) to the Organization of African Unity (OAU), to the Council for Mutual Economic Assistance (CMEA), to the International Communications Satellite Consortium (Intelsat), to the UN itself. Restraints on unilateral action, and to a degree on the use of force, do in fact abound, all bespeaking functional, politically useful, and otherwise serviceable means of pooling power for the attainment of common goals.

All of this ought to gladden the hearts of nineteenth-century liberals and twentieth-century idealists whose logic led them to predict just such a development. For even the utopian visionaries who expected the nation-state to give way to a global brotherhood never quite foresaw the irrelevance of national boundaries to radio waves, satellite orbits, and the phenomenally growing transnational business corporations. As the late astronaut Edward White said about his earth-girdling flight, "I never did see any national boundaries."

This, then, is the supreme paradox the extraterrestrial visitor would encounter: the stark reality of a bipolar strategic world existing within the equally real multipolar world of diplomacy, interdependence, regional groupings, economic networks, international organizations—indeed, multipolar in every sense but that of the *ultima ratio* of raw power to destroy.

But there's the rub. For when it comes to the root of national sovereignty—

unilateral decisionmaking about war and peace—there is neither world instrument nor agency of genuine control, regulation, or even deterrence. Apart from the North Atlantic Treaty Organization (NATO) and the Warsaw Treaty Organization (WTO)—both at base military alliances—the UN and other agencies represent only feebly the reality of multipolar political power that coexists with bipolar military strength.

Many believe that UN agencies are most useful not for collective security but for advancing the process of modernization in the developing countries. The first UN Development Decade (UNDD) failed to come near the goal of 5 percent annual growth rate in gross national product for the developing countries or one percent of GNP contributions by the developed nations. Yet at the same time global military expenditures now take more than 7 percent of the world's gross product. In money terms they are equivalent to the total annual income produced by the one billion people living in Latin America, Southeast Asia, and the Middle East. They are greater by 40 percent than worldwide expenditures on education by all levels of government and more than three times worldwide expenditures on public health.[1]

Given these various realities, what connection can, and should, exist in this age between the arms problem and the international order? What in fact has the connection been? What is the potential in the short- and middle-term future? And what should be the posture of the United States toward the role of international organization in moderating the arms race?

II. THE CHECKERED HISTORY

Given the dreary record of failure of efforts to achieve significant disarmament prior to World War II, it was an act of realism for the planners of 1943–1945 to accept as a fact of life the retention of national military forces. The UN Charter envisaged such forces being used to carry out the will of the Security Council in the event of breaches of the peace or acts of aggression. At the same time it made only the most cursory references to the need for regulating armaments and formulating principles that might govern such a program. Nevertheless, the new dimension of weaponry revealed at Hiroshima and Nagasaki little more than a month after the Charter was signed prompted an immediate about-face, at least on the part of the Western powers.

The United States' monopoly on the new destructive magic gave it an unparalleled strategic advantage. But it also carried with it a deep sense of unease, even guilt, set against a historical backdrop of unwillingness to conduct a policy of *Machtpolitik*. Beyond this it gave a focus to national idealism. The United States thus sought, through the Acheson-Lilienthal-Baruch Plan,

[1] *World Military Expenditures and Related Data: Calendar Year 1966 and Summary Trends, 1962–1967* (Research Report 68–52) (Washington: Economics Bureau, United States Arms Control and Disarmament Agency, December 1968), pp. 1–2.

to place atomic energy under international control with adequate safeguards. This in turn set a pattern for negotiating within the UN rubric that persisted for a decade. The failure of this unprecedented act of national renunciation can be seen in retrospect to have been due to several factors, each one of which remains pertinent to the search for a safer world.

First, the Baruch Plan was undoubtedly seen by the Soviet Union as preventing it from attaining the sophisticated military, and perhaps other, technology already achieved by the United States through its development of atomic power. Soviet determination to achieve parity with the United States was progressively revealed in the years after 1945. Despite an inferior industrial base, much of it ravaged by war, the Soviet Union matched the American atomic explosions after four years (1949), duplicated the American hydrogen explosion after only one year (1953), became the first power in space (1957), and was subsequently thought to be leader in number of nuclear delivery vehicles—an erroneous judgment which nevertheless became an issue in the 1960 Presidential elections and is now probably true at least for land-based intercontinental ballistic missiles (ICBM's).

Each side has invariably framed its arms control proposals in ways that would confer on it strategic or political advantages. The Baruch proposal could be interpreted as doing so for the United States by vesting control in an international agency whose political complexion would be overwhelmingly non-Communist. The Soviet Union sought to improve its position by calling for banning the nuclear bomb without controls, by promoting the so-called Gromyko Plan for the control of atomic weapons which would have nullified the United States advantage, and by pushing for reductions in conventional weapons by ratios that would preserve Soviet superiority.

Throughout this early period the wartime coalition was rapidly collapsing, and the two parties found themselves at loggerheads over Greece, Berlin, and Korea—indeed, the whole agenda of powder keg confrontations between the Western and the Communist worlds that came to be known as the Cold War. In this setting the disarmament negotiations themselves were from the start adversary proceedings and worse. As such, conducting them in open UN forums yielded maximum propaganda advantage to the side whose rhetoric had the most popular appeal.

A second factor involved in the failure to reach agreement to prevent national exploitation of atomic energy had to do with the kinds of safeguards demanded by the West. The problem of how to determine who might be cheating on an arms control agreement arose with the Baruch Plan, and the question of inspection and verification has bedeviled every serious effort at disarmament since that time. Western insistence that international controls be agreed to and spelled out before any actual disarmament was a measure of the profound distrust between the two superpowers. It has since come to be acknowledged that the Soviet government feels an overriding domestic political necessity to maintain rigid internal control, as well as a fear of penetration verging on the neurotic. Given this, Western insistence on control measures that threatened to penetrate and open up Soviet society (and which in some Western minds explicitly aimed at transforming the Soviet system) was unfeasible and thus no contribution to arms-controlling ends.

For their part the Soviets insisted on prohibitions ahead of the institution of controls. Moscow's mobilization of captive "peace forces" for ban-the-bomb propaganda indicated little serious intention to negotiate. If the Soviets *were* serious they could assume that their high degree of internal secrecy would protect them while in turn they would be able to detect cheating by open societies on any arms limitations that might be agreed to. Each side's position was to a degree self-serving and advantage-seeking and in all events self-defeating to the degree that either genuinely favored substantial arms control. Only as the search began for nonintrusive measures of control, substituting for nosy humans such technological surrogates as observation satellites, array seismographs, and other remote control sensors, has it been possible to make progress. The 1963 Treaty Banning Nuclear Weapons Tests in Atmosphere, in Outer Space, and Under Water and the 1967 Treaty on the Principles of the Activity of States in the Exploration and Use of Outer Space, including the Moon and Other Celestial Bodies are the most notable examples to date.

A third disqualification of the Baruch Plan was that its proposed international control organ would not have been subject in its operations to the great-power veto that was already paralyzing the UN Security Council. Soviet unwillingness to yield any part of its central sovereign powers to a numerical majority of nations which were, by Marxist-Leninist definition, hostile remains a fact of political life today no less than in retrospect it was in 1946. With the tremendous increase in number of nonaligned states in the UN and the general weakening of great-power alliance systems the comparable reluctance of the United States to subject itself to majority will was greatly reinforced.

To recapitulate, the main factors that torpedoed the early arms negotiations were: Soviet determination to achieve parity; the attempt by each side to seek strategic advantages; blatant Soviet propaganda on the issue; Soviet sensitivity to outside intrusion; and the unwillingness of the Soviet Union to forego its veto. The fact that the parties did not cease talking altogether is a tribute to the power of public opinion which refused to accept as permanent the notion of an uninhibited atomic arms race. It is also a tribute to the existence of a neutral forum during the worst days of the Cold War even if the forum was used primarily to seek support for a position rather than to arrive at a meeting of minds.

By the early 1950's events were occurring that eventually modified the positions of the principal parties and the pattern of their relationship. The American and Soviet hydrogen bomb tests in the years 1952–1954 raised still further the level of concern about the consequences of a race for weapons deadly enough to destroy whole societies. Soviet bombers gave to Moscow at least a one-way capability to threaten the continental United States, long considered invulnerable. Just over the horizon were new delivery systems that would revolutionize strategy and open outer space and the seabeds to potential militarization.

These technical-military developments coincided with significant barometric changes in the political climate. Stalin's death in 1953 brought a less paranoid regime to power in Moscow. In Washington a sense of increasing peril to the human race prompted President Dwight D. Eisenhower to call for an international program to develop peaceful uses for the atom. Three years later the idea was successfully institutionalized with the establishment of the International Atomic Energy Agency (IAEA). Incidentally, this negotiation was conducted outside the UN Disarmament Commission because the United States did not consider the idea a disarmament proposal. In recent years the safeguards developed by IAEA and the vast expansion of its program currently envisaged under the 1968 Treaty on the Nonproliferation of Nuclear Weapons have come to have much significance for arms control and disarmament.

In 1953 in a new disarmament subcommittee of the UN Disarmament Commission—the first negotiating forum limited to those states "principally involved" and by far the most harmonious to date—there was for the first time a considerable narrowing of differences. The West abandoned its long-held dysfunctional insistence on international ownership of fissionable materials and operation of nuclear facilities and accepted the notion of ultimate control through the Security Council. The Soviet Union in turn accepted the principle of retention of nuclear weapons until a second phase of disarmament, the setting of specific force levels (rather than ratios), and even the notion of permanent control posts. In 1955 in a basic reversal of position the Soviets acknowledged that no conceivable control measure could any longer uncover all the fissionable material already produced. Finally, concern was increasing about the health consequences of nuclear atmospheric fallout. However, the implications of the technological advances were still insufficient to overcome fundamental political hostility and mistrust. In late 1955 the United States announced that it was placing a "reservation" on all its previous disarmament proposals on the grounds that the American position required reexamination; we will never know what might have flowed then from acceptance, at least in principle, of the apparent new Soviet flexibility and reasonableness.[2]

[2] For a detailed analysis of the disarmament diplomacy of the period see Lincoln P. Bloomfield, Walter C. Clemens, Jr., and Franklyn Griffiths, *Khrushchev and the Arms Race: Soviet Interests in Arms Control and Disarmament 1954–1964* (Cambridge, Mass: M.I.T. Press, 1966).

By the mid-1950's the strategic situation began to be generally acknowledged to be dramatically different from ten years before. In the years of United States nuclear-weapons monopoly American security had been based on the doctrine of deterrence through the threat of massive retaliation. With enormous destructiveness available to both powers it became increasingly clear that the implication of massive retaliation was mutual annihilation. This mutual balance of terror was reinforced when each side attained a relatively invulnerable capacity to retaliate with a devastating nuclear riposte even after being struck with a surprise blow. But even as intercontinental missiles of megaton yield began to enter superpower inventories by the scores and then hundreds, the search began for a more flexible range of military capabilities that would make possible an initial response to local aggression on a less apocalyptic scale than launching Soviet or American intercontinental missiles. These "flexible" or "graduated response" doctrines had the aim of gradually raising the threshold between conventional and nuclear weapons.

A new Ten-Nation Committee on Disarmament was formed in 1959 which reflected for the first time parity between the Western and the Communist worlds. But after a brief embroilment over rival blueprints for general and complete disarmament the Committee was abandoned by the Soviets in 1960. Such agreement as was reached in that period was on the principles to govern general and complete disarmament, the so-called McCloy-Zorin Agreement negotiated privately in New York the following year between the United States and the Soviet Union. Similarly, the effective negotiating that led to the Partial Test Ban Treaty of 1963 and the establishment of the "hot line," plus the informal agreement in 1964 to reduce the production of fissionable materials, took place bilaterally and offstage and was spurred by the world's closest brush so far with nuclear disaster—the Cuban missile crisis of 1962. This extraordinary period of agreement also featured some tacit measures, including a mutual reduction in defense budgets, a general policy of unprovocative troop deployments and the avoidance of overflights, and the pointed failure of either side to develop a "doomsday" weapon.

The mid-1950's had seemed to culminate a period of maximum danger; by the mid-1960's the world looked relatively stable, and people began to discount the all-out war that had earlier dominated their fears. The capacity each side now possessed for a second strike after absorbing an initial attack— thanks to the evolving technology represented by hardened missile sites and by the mobile underseas *Polaris* system—was now operative and enabled both sides to think in terms of protracted coexistence instead of conflict. When the two superpowers wished to talk they had little difficulty in arranging private negotiations.

In this context the role of the United Nations even in disarmament diplomacy became distinctly secondary by comparison with the period when it had been the sole forum and source of organized pressure. Its role was to suggest, urge, and approve—a role neither of the major parties appears to regard as important. The growing sense of human helplessness in the face of mounting destructive power was never thenceforth left in doubt by the speeches and resolutions of a United Nations that after 1955 approached universal representation, apart from Communist China and the divided countries. But this moral and political pressure never seemed to be enough in itself to move the nuclear-weapons countries to decisive action (and, it must be said, the smaller countries showed little disposition to disarm themselves). Then, as now, it was only the mutual recognition of the dangers by the parties themselves that finally brought them together. Whereas the first ten years of arms discussions took place in the UN setting—and were barren—the second decade increasingly saw private negotiations between the parties most concerned, negotiations that more and more bore fruit.

But if the history was not actually cyclical, it was not linear either. The whole apparatus of mutual strategic deterrence was a fragile one, depending wholly on statesmen being rational, making similar calculations, and accurately reading each other's often cryptic signals. The fear of preemptive war remained and with it the fear of war by accident or miscalculation. Still unresolved was the prospect that the atmosphere and the environment would be increasingly polluted by malignant fallout from nuclear testing. And in the 1960's two events further skewed the pattern that seemed to be developing: the emergence of Communist China after 1964 as the fifth nuclear power and the Americanization of the war in Vietnam culminating in the 1965 United States decision to bomb the Democratic Republic of Vietnam (North Vietnam).

The significance of a Chinese nuclear capacity cannot yet be fully evaluated with any confidence. But its bearing on the strategic arms control equation was undeniable. We have learned that communication, in the full sense of correct mutual perceptions and reliable contact, is all-important in maintaining a tolerable equilibrium in the presence of indescribably destructive weapons. But good communication with the Chinese Communist government is at a minimum in both Western and Soviet worlds. The dangers Chinese isolation holds for the future are evident when one considers that the stability provided by the balance of terror has come to depend on the clearest possible understanding of intentions. Indeed, uncertainty about Chinese intentions provoked increasingly widespread disquiet as China opposed one after another of the partial measures of arms control overwhelmingly approved by others (although not by General Charles de Gaulle). Apart from proposals for nuclear-free zones in the Pacific and elsewhere China opposes any form of nuclear control short, it says, of a total ban. The general concern on the part of a UN majority about China was reflected in a General Assembly resolution late in 1965 calling for a world disarmament conference, outside the United Nations—which could thus include China.[3] (China declined the gambit.)

The American decision in 1965 to bomb North Vietnam, a close ally of the Soviet Union, placed a new public chill on relationships between Washington and Moscow. In competition with the Chinese for the leadership of the Communist world, the Soviet Union could not afford to appear intimate with the United States; but neither could it afford to ignore the dangers of the arms race or appear indifferent to others' aspirations to limit it.

This ambivalence characterized Soviet approaches to two major arms control measures that a strong common interest continued to commend to both superpowers despite the growing distraction and embarrassment of Vietnam. The common interest sprang from the inexorable rush of technology that put squarely before the powers the problem of outer space and the threat of further spread of nuclear weapons.

Outer space represented for both the major powers a challenging area for one-upmanship in scientific know-how and exploration. Given the primarily military cast of the Soviet space program, as well as the pressures on the part of some American military figures, it was also a disturbing extension of the area of possible conflict. The comparative ease with which agreement had been reached in 1959 on the demilitarization of Antarctica, contrasted with the complexities that had beset the fruitless negotiations on disengagement in Europe, set an important precedent for foreclosing outer space from national exploitation and a probable arms race. It was nevertheless an act of statesmanship for the two major powers to agree, as one of their historic understandings reached in 1963, that they would not place in orbit weapons of mass destruction. The role of the UN was to provide an Assembly resolution recording that agreement.[4]

After many further crises and unremitting efforts on the part of the UN Committee on the Peaceful Uses of Outer Space (which operated entirely by consensus and never by majority vote) the Treaty on Principles Governing the Activities of States in the Exploration and Use of Outer Space, including the Moon and Other Celestial Bodies, was concluded in 1966. It established the principles of international cooperation in space and applied to space the principles of international law and the UN Charter. It provided that all installations on the moon or other celestial bodies would be open to other states on a reciprocal basis provided reasonable notice was given. This compromise fell far short of effective prelaunch inspection which the United States had sought. But while payloads cannot be identified short of "screwdriver" examination, significant unexplained space activity can be detected by remote

[3] See General Assembly Resolution 2030 (XX), November 29, 1965.
[4] See General Assembly Resolution 1962 (XVIII), December 13, 1963.

electronic monitoring devices. More to the point, aggression from space is equally discouraged by existing nuclear deterrence on earth. The UN General Assembly approved the Treaty in 1966, and it came into effect in 1967.

Of the two historic agreements the Nonproliferation Treaty had by far the higher political content. There is a certain logic in the proposition that all the Great Powers named in the Charter might possess a nuclear-weapons capacity without seriously distorting the pattern of world order the Charter sought to develop. By 1965 the five countries named in Article 23, paragraph 1, of the Charter as permanent members of the Security Council had such a capacity.[5] But there is nothing self-limiting about the technology. Twenty or more countries have the industrial base, the wealth, and the trained manpower to join the nuclear club in the next few years if they develop the will to do so. The problem of understanding intentions under such circumstances appears insurmountable and the opportunities for nuclear blackmail are thus virtually limitless. Moreover, the countries most likely to go for nuclear weapons are parties to local conflicts that have come to be the most numerous cause of potential entangling confrontations between the two big powers.

This was obviously not a problem the Great Powers could solve between themselves. An effective nonproliferation agreement requires the cooperation of all the other states in the world. On the other hand, in the actual negotiation of the Nonproliferation Treaty issues such as inspection, safeguards, and the relationship of the European Atomic Energy Community (Euratom) to IAEA could only be solved by bilateral talks, a process made infinitely more difficult by the intensifying American involvement in Vietnam.

In those circumstances, with the superpowers needing both the active cooperation of the nonnuclear weapons powers *and* a multilateral cloak for bilateral negotiations, the United Nations once again became very useful to them. In 1965 the long-dormant Disarmament Commission, which comprises the entire UN membership, was reactivated and in turn called on the Eighteen-Nation Committee on Disarmament (ENDC), established in 1962, to negotiate a pact to halt the spread of nuclear weapons.

The pair of landmark international arms control agreements was achieved in 1966–1968 despite both the Vietnam war and the 1967 June war in the Middle East fought by client states of both sides. They were negotiated by a combination of bilateral and multilateral negotiating techniques. The comprehensive Outer Space Treaty was negotiated almost exclusively within the UN Committee on Peaceful Uses of Outer Space; the Nonproliferation Treaty followed a seesaw pattern between the two major powers, the ENDC, and the General Assembly.[6] The role of the multilateral bodies was, first, to call

---

[5] It is, of course, the government of Communist China which possesses a nuclear-weapons capacity, rather than that of the Republic of China (Nationalist China) which represents China in the Council.

[6] A third arms control agreement, the Treaty for the Prohibition of Nuclear Weapons in Latin America, which did not primarily concern the superpowers initially, was debated and endorsed in principle in the Assembly in 1963, negotiated outside the United Nations, and then given UN endorsement.

for such a treaty, second, to provide forums for widespread participation in the process, and, third, to legitimize the results by substantial votes of approval and the registration of the treaty when ratified.

But particularly in negotiating the Nonproliferation Treaty something more was involved. For the first time in the armaments field smaller powers have some real leverage over the superpowers; the potentially nuclear among them show decreasing willingness to renounce their own nuclear options in the absence of evidence that the superpowers are also prepared to do some renouncing. Those asked to take the pledge have made it clear that much of the world is no longer satisfied just with the absence of great-power conflict and is increasingly concerned to recapture for the needs of a newly articulate humanity the vast resources diverted to the strategic arms race.

It was pressure from the nuclear have-nots that forced the superpowers to insert Article VI into the Nonproliferation Treaty committing them to pursue negotiations in good faith on effective measures toward the cessation of the arms race at an early date (which became in turn a debating point in the hands of opponents of the United States decision in 1969 to go ahead with the *Safeguard* antiballistic missile system).

It was pressures of the same sort that forced the two superpowers to agree in 1967 to the holding of a conference of nonnuclear weapons states—a step that institutionalized still further the already portentious split of UN members into Great Powers and others—a split comparable to the lineup in the UN Conference on Trade and Development (UNCTAD) of the "group of 77" developing states versus all the others.

One might go beyond this and generalize that the constant pressures on the nuclear powers to negotiate, to control, to disarm, and to make available to poorer countries the economic resources thus freed had an additional, cumulative effect that is difficult to measure but is nonetheless real. It would be an imprudent historian who would write off as utterly meaningless for arms control the aggregated whole of international conference diplomacy, its machinery, and its politics.

But, historic as these various agreements were, the sum of arms control achievements to date is modest. Nuclear-weapons tests are banned in the atmosphere, outer space, and underwater but not underground (and two of the five present nuclear-weapons powers, France and Communist China, have continued to poison the atmosphere with testing). A few areas are to be spared the curse of nuclear weapons—Antarctica, outer space, possibly Latin America if the Tlatelolco Treaty on the Prohibition of Nuclear Weapons in Latin America is ratified. There is some prospect, but no assurance, that the states of the world will have the wit to add the ocean floor to that brief list.

Even one of the modest list of agreed measures is subject to uncertainty. The Nonproliferation Treaty may never be ratified by enough of the near-nuclear states to make it truly effective. There remains profound dissatisfaction with the Treaty's built-in notion of first- and second-class nations as a permanent classification. If the nuclear-weapons nations cannot show progress toward self-renunciation of some of their freedom of action, it will reinforce the already disturbing likelihood that other key nations will not consent to remaining nuclear have-nots.

Several aspects of the experience to date are worth summing up: the concentration in the years 1963–1969 of such formal arms control progress as there has been since the nuclear age began; the fact that all of the achievements inside the UN were preceded by bilateral negotiations outside the UN; the continuation in that six-year period of recurrent superpower political crises and unilateral acts (e.g., the 1962 Cuban missile crisis, the Vietnam war, Czechoslovakia) all strongly implying that arms control negotiations are not precluded but rather necessitated in a world subject to such fierce perturbations; and the rise of Communist China at the Soviet's rear.

The historical record demonstrates clearly that in this same period there has on occasion been something that could be called pre-détente, at least enough to generate modest arms control agreements. Nevertheless the underlying political confrontation between the Western and Soviet worlds continues, a fact underlined by the odious Soviet-bloc occupation of Czechoslovakia in August of 1968. So far there is little evidence that those with super power assign more than nuisance weight to "the opinion of mankind" as manifest in exhortations, injunctions, or even "commands" by numerical majorities of nations. In part this is because absolute power bestows the right to be indifferent. In part it is because of the obvious irrelevance of many lesser states to the strategic issues under discussion. In part it is because the superpowers do not really know how to go about substantially disarming. And in part it is because things have not gotten really bad enough for them either to disarm significantly or to pay serious attention to the opinion or the machinery of the majority.

III. Prospects for the Future

The great disparity between national destructive power and international order was not much bridged in the 1955–1969 period of modest arms control agreements. For the future the link between armaments and the international order will continue to be a function of two things: the faltering, but not completely unhopeful, progress of the United Nations; and yet another spiral in the "action-reaction" cycle of strategic nuclear weapons, this one possibly accelerating the race between offense and defense in ways that could upset the present equilibrium, such as it is. As of the end of the 1960's and the opening of the decade of the 1970's it was difficult to be confident of basic improvement. Numbers of elements in the picture contribute to pessimism although, as I shall attempt to show, there is nothing inevitable about them.

In this picture is, first, the growing potential of a China still profoundly hostile to the United States, the Soviet Union, and the United Nations; second, the continued, if diminishing, fundamental divergence of American and Soviet political goals and values; third, the continuing relative ineffectiveness in the political and security field of the UN as presently constituted; and, fourth, the prospect of a new round in the strategic weapons race that may be destabilizing to the precarious equilibrium under which the world has in recent times sheltered.

An element in that strategic equilibrium has been the certain superiority of offensive weapons over any realistically conceivable active defensive system. So assured was the capacity of each power to inflict devastating retaliation, even after absorbing a first strike, that attention could be focused on damage limitation. Intercontinental ballistic missiles that were acquired beyond the minimum required to deliver the number of warheads that would inflict "unacceptable damage," suggested by former Secretary of Defense Robert McNamara to be 400 or so,[7] could in combination with the *Polaris*-launching submarines be aimed at remaining enemy missiles to limit the additional damage such forces could inflict. But there was an upper limit even to this damage-limiting capability (particularly if no substantial enemy missiles were left unfired) and the key calculation was still of massive mutual deterrence through "assured destruction."

There it might have rested indefinitely had it not been for a Soviet decision to deploy an antiballistic missile system in the mid-1960's around Moscow. After considerable private and public soul-searching the United States government decided in September 1967 to deploy *Sentinel*—a so-called "light" ABM system directed specifically at the potential threat from a Communist China become irrational (or a stray incoming warhead fired by accident or by another small power) but employable also against the Soviet Union.

Expert opinions differ considerably about the degree of effectiveness an ABM system can achieve. There are even respectable arguments that all-out ballistic missile defense should be encouraged as a stabilizing step. But the logic of action and response is invariably to match an improvement in the defense by stepping up the offensive capability another notch or two. The weapon that makes this feasible—and adds a major new stage to the arms spiral—is the multiple independently targetable reentry vehicle. When fully perfected, MIRV will supply in the *Poseidon* and *Minuteman III* systems the capacity to deliver several warheads from a single rocket, each against a separate target and each with considerably more accuracy than is presently

[7] See the McNamara posture statement, *The Fiscal Year 1969–73 Defense Program and the 1969 Defense Budget* (Washington, 1968), p. 57.

possible. Hence the possibility that with an even smaller number of missile launchers than the enemy one side could acquire the power to destroy all the other's silo-emplaced missiles and other targets as well. The Subsonic Cruise Armed Decoy (SCAD) system will add to this offensive capability by multiplying the capacity of individual bombers. This quantum jump in the offensive could in turn prompt the other side to go for an all-out ballistic missile defense or an increased strike capacity.

In response to the Soviet ABM deployment, which seems so far to be limited to the Moscow area, the United States made the decision to go ahead with the testing of MIRV's. There is no reason to believe Moscow is not already responding to both American "prudential" developments with a "prudential" MIRV program of its own, perhaps reconfiguring its SS-9 missiles. The United States decision in the spring of 1969 to modify its *Sentinel* system showed that deployment decisions were not necessarily inexorable. But the process taken as a whole is hard indeed to turn around or even slow down.

In the face of this prospect what routes are open to the United States in seeking genuine security? How is the American national interest to be best served? Must it rely entirely on its *own* resources and capacity to muster superior strength? Is the nuclear race so central to the security equation that United States policy must focus on *bilateral* deals with its superadversary and negotiating partner? Is genuine security in the ICBM age still available through *alliance* arrangements with like-minded countries? Is the problem of arms control so interwoven with the interests of the world as a whole that remedies should be looked for mainly on a *global* basis through a multilateral framework?

It seems obvious that the preferred path to safety through the minefields of the arms race is through negotiations or at least tacit agreement between the nuclear giants. Only there can decisions be made that are essential in stemming the course of escalation in weaponry and strategic doctrine. Agreement between the Big Two is an absolute precondition to security over the years ahead. More than ever before national security does not and can not lie in going it alone.

The reasons for this are found in two great dangers that inhere in the latest reciprocal example of what former Secretary of Defense McNamara called the "mad momentum" of the arms race.[8] First, it could raise defense costs to the point of further imperiling domestic American life in the face of acute social disorders. Even more perilous to the peace of the world, it could lead one side or the other to the condition that is above all to be feared: the belief that it can with relative impunity launch a successful first strike against the other. Thus, unless the superpowers set limits to the offensive and defensive

---

[8] In the same speech in which he announced the deployment of the *Sentinel* system, September 18, 1967. For the text see *The New York Times*, September 19, 1967.

capabilities that each has the technical competence to possess, the world is in for a time that could be infinitely more dangerous, and certainly more expensive, than ten years before. The strategic arms limitation talks (SALT) between Moscow and Washington could be among the most important ever held.

But the prospects for success in thus moderating the newest arms spiral are only modest; too much suspicion and hostility underlie the *marriage de convenance* between the United States and the Soviet Union to allow great hope for its genuine consummation even when right reason demands it. Deterrence against miscalculation must be maintained resting both on the American capacity for assured destruction and the visible will to resist on the part of the non-Communist states lying in the path of expanding centers of Communist power.

The UN by itself can contribute little to this particular problem. If the cycle of reaction and counterreaction is to be broken, it can only be done on the basis of a hardheaded recognition by the two parties themselves that their vital interest lies in avoiding such a new escalation. As with other forms of arms control, the role of the UN and associated disarmament and diplomatic forums is secondary but not inconsequential. It lies, as before, in imposing continuing pressure, however marginal, for agreement and in providing sites for negotiation, expert assistance, and parliamentary leadership. If an agreement can be reached, there is certainly a role for the international community to bring pressure on the two miscreant nuclear powers, France and Communist China, to join in the agreed international arms control regime.

This brings us to the other half of the equation: the role and the capacity of the UN and related international organizations both to affect the arms race and to discharge tasks of international order that may be demanded by arms control and disarmament agreements.

In the current historical period the willingness of the two key nuclear powers to let the UN influence their actions has not much increased. American interest in bestowing new authority on the UN seemed to diminish as the "swirling majorities" of the Assembly demanded action on their racial and economic concerns and as the promise of UN peacekeeping seemed to dwindle in the face of the insistence on the part of several Great Powers to have their own way or not play. Soviet interest in the UN may or may not have increased in terms of the latter's more congenial political climate. And both Moscow and Washington, correctly in the author's opinion, reject the open forums of the UN as a place to do the serious business of regulating the power relationships between the giants.

But two positive trends could also be discovered. First, on a more general level, the United States and the Soviet Union were increasingly utilizing UN machinery to conduct private negotiations and to register such agreements as they were able to reach privately. It was even possible that they would try to reactivate the Security Council for peacekeeping and other limited security purposes.

More specifically, much has been said and written about the UN's role as inspector of arms control and disarmament. This author earlier thought that perhaps the greatest potential value of the UN in disarmament and arms control lay in impartial organizations for inspection and verification.[9] With non-intrusive "national" inspection being emphasized for strategic weapons controls the prime use of the UN may be rather to bring Soviet-American pressure on others, and to actually make the Nonproliferation Treaty effective will require just that.

At the same time under the Nonproliferation Treaty international machinery must grow to meet the requirement of inspection of the nuclear reactors of nonnuclear-weapons powers, plus those peaceful-use reactors placed under voluntary control by the United States (and hopefully the Soviet Union). Already in this connection as of 1969 the International Atomic Energy Agency had 40 inspectors drawn from 25 countries, with 200 to 250 estimated to be needed by 1973. (Three hundred sixty research reactors were already in operation with 80 more in commercial use.) The IAEA teams in 1969 were making periodic unannounced inspections of 70 nonmilitary reactors in 30 countries.

A further call for international organization involvement in arms control inspection was the United States proposal in April 1969 that IAEA take over sole responsibility for verifying compliance with a cutoff in the production of nuclear materials for weapons purposes. (The United States had previously specified "adversary inspection" by each superpower of the other's compliance.)[10]

Other new potential areas of cooperative and possibly multilateral activity were being signaled by such straws in the wind as then Arms Control and Disarmament Agency Director William C. Foster's proposal to the First (Political and Security) Committee of the UN General Assembly on December 5, 1968. As a step toward a comprehensive nuclear test ban the United States formally proposed a program of underground nuclear explosions with the collateral objective of serving as means of worldwide seismic investigation.[11]

Yet another possible expansion of UN "disarmament activity" could be the international arrangements called for by Article V of the Nonproliferation Treaty to make nuclear explosion for peaceful uses available to the nonnuclear countries.

[9] See Lincoln P. Bloomfield, *The United Nations and U.S. Foreign Policy: A New Look at the National Interest* (rev. ed.; Boston: Little, Brown, 1967), Chapter 8, "Disarmament and Arms Control."

[10] See statement by United States representative Adrian S. Fisher to the ENDC, April 8, 1969. (*The New York Times*, April 9, 1969.)

[11] Department of State *Bulletin*, January 20, 1969 (Vol. 50, No. 1643), pp. 59–60.

Conventional arms are by no means unimportant. Other desirable tasks for the international community in conjunction with the Great Powers lie in making general any agreements that can be reached on regional arms controls, notably on regulating arms transfers to the Middle East and the underdeveloped world,[12] and in publicizing the international arms traffic as the League of Nations sought to do.

But I have emphasized the problem of nuclear weapons because of their obvious capacity to shatter civilizations. Put differently, the world could endure another conventional war, however terrible, and still survive as a going concern. But the societies based in the temperate zones of the planet could not survive an all-out thermonuclear exchange between the two giants. In this connection the UN can be crucially important in extending the concept of nuclear-free zones to the seabed, to Africa, and if possible to areas where nuclear weapons may already be stationed, notably Central Europe, as part of a more general settlement of the division of Europe.

Great problems often turn out to be interrelated. I referred at the outset to the UN Development Decade. Even if we avoid all-out war, other responsibilities face mankind as it struggles to master its economic and social problems. According to a recent survey total armed forces and military-related employment comes to over 50 million—larger than the total population of France. It is about 4 percent, or one in 25, of the economically active population of the world. Although in absolute numbers this employment may be larger in the developed than in the less developed countries, it is in the latter, where trained and educated manpower are relatively limited, that the diversion of skills from the civilian economy may represent the more serious factor affecting economic progress.[13] This serves to reinforce all the other reasons why, utopian as it seems, a generalized agreement to limit conventional arms as well as nuclear weapons and armed forces represents a long-term interest of all mankind—and therefore of the United States. It scarcely needs saying that if such an arms-limiting agreement was in fact reached and implemented, a whole new environment would have been created in which international law and order would flourish precisely because they would be more essential to the peace than they are in a world of limitless "self-help."

Like so many other contemporary problems this one demands a time scale that compresses the more natural evolution of man and his institutions. In historic terms we might in another century or so foresee agreement on an effective world order sufficient to guarantee and enforce general disarmament among the nations. Correctly rejecting the wait as undesirable, some believe that *nuclear* disarmament could take place without accompanying institutions

---

[12] See Lincoln P. Bloomfield and Amelia C. Leiss, "Arms Control and the Developing Countries," *World Politics*, October 1965 (Vol. 18, No. 1), pp. 1–19.

[13] *World Military Expenditures and Related Data*, p. 6.

of enforcement and the like and that this might happen if the superpowers became sufficiently frightened at the implications of their own strength or worried enough about soaring costs. But the lack of disarmament action as a result of the Cuban missile crisis of 1962 casts doubt on the "sufficiently frightened" scenario; mounting defense budgets, despite exigent social needs in both countries, seem so far to invalidate the motivation of economic burden.

The superpowers remain physically capable of acting unilaterally, of deterring unilaterally, of being isolationist or interventionist in conflict situations, and of wreaking worldwide havoc unilaterally. It is, on the record, far from easy to think of persuasive incentives for the United States or the Soviet Union to forego freedom of action in the name of a more workable and reliable world order. Existing international organization machinery seems to offer few incentives or disincentives that are convincing to either superpower. Those who believe that a real strengthening of international institutions to the point of rendering them capable of enforcing world law is in the common interest have yet to demonstrate the values and utilities in a way that is persuasively cost-effective to the national-security-minded political or military leader of a Great Power. If no other argument were available, a case can still be made that decisionmaking time available for last-minute deterrent actions (not for retaliation, as this seems increasingly irrelevant) precludes full-scale UN debates.

But the security equation is getting less rather than more reassuring. The costs and embarrassments of submission to the "democratic" procedures of multilateral organizations may come to be worthwhile if the benefit is to be saved from one's own ultimate folly. Moreover, the world is changing and with it the Soviet Union, the staunchest defender of untrammeled national sovereignty against multilateralized authority. Both superpowers will demonstrably benefit from an improved set of international rules and action agencies to cope with local peacekeeping situations that, numerically at least, are among the most likely potential triggers for superpower confrontation. Both will continue to benefit from the availability of a mix of multilateral instrumentalities, diplomatic fig leaves, and even persistent pressures on the part of the great majority of nations of the world.

Utopia is not to be looked for, and it may be enough if the superpowers develop the wit between them to control the "mad momentum" that weapons technology generates. But one can at least speculate on the possibility that they will begin to have to take the collective security aspects of the UN more seriously if they are to complete the Nonproliferation Treaty structure which specifically includes great-power guarantees to countries without nuclear weapons. Perhaps genuine collective defense of those threatened by aggression will become more of a reality if the superpowers are sufficiently motivated to keep the nuclear monopoly. At a minimum perhaps that same incentive to react responsively to threatening situations will enhance the more limited, but most needed, peacekeeping capabilities of the Organization. Here again, as with anything else in the realm of peace and security, American-Soviet agreement remains an indispensable condition for progress and eventual success.

As though to underscore the infernal complexity of man's greatest problems, the place of Communist China may be seen both as a reason for quickening the pace of American-Soviet cooperation and at the same time as an element of any future UN and thus a potential hazard to that cooperation.

Nothing about the problem is easy, simplistic nostrums to the contrary. But as President John F. Kennedy said in his last year:

> There are no permanent enemies.
>
> Hostility today is a fact, but it is not the ruling law. The supreme reality of our time is our indivisibility as children of God, and our common vulnerability on this planet. [14]

---

[14] From a speech to a joint session of the Irish Parliament, June 28, 1963.

International Organization and the Rule of Law

Louis Henkin

"International-Law-and-Organization" has become a hyphenated conception but the implied interrelations are assumed rather than explored. All international organization, of course, may be seen as an aspect of law partaking of its forms and sharing its purposes. Law and organization have in common that, in both, nations eschew laissez-faire and "going it alone" and identify and prefer common interests. Often, on the other hand, one thinks of international organization in contradistinction to law as making different promises, suffering different limitations, evoking different loyalties.

I shall not explore these relations here, nor, despite the title of this article, do I propose to weary further that tired phrase "the rule of law" or to add to the rhetoric it has profused. My concerns in these pages can be stated in specific questions: How has international organization reshaped the compass and modified the content of international law? How has it influenced the attitudes of nations toward law, in particular the disposition to govern their behavior by their legal obligations and to resort to legal processes for the settlement of differences? To what extent do the achievements—and failures—of international organization reflect the influence, and accord with the interests, of the United States? And what are the implications for the United States in the years ahead?

The questions are specific and clear; the answers can only be suggestive. One cannot readily isolate international organization from other forces to determine its proper responsibility for change in law or national behavior. One cannot measure or weigh international law or the "rule of law," how they were before the day of international organization, how much international organization has added to or subtracted from them, how they might have been had there been no international organization. One cannot measure

Louis Henkin is Hamilton Fish Professor of International Law and Diplomacy, Columbia University, New York.

or weigh the significance of law in a nation's foreign policy and the extent to which international organization has modified that significance. Nor can one readily determine the interests of any one nation, even the United States, and identify, disentangle, and appraise its influence in complicated activities of complex international organizations. A look to the near future of law and organization, moreover, implies impossible predictions about all of international life: about relations between nations, war and peace, order and disorder, continuity and change. A look at implications for the United States must predict also the future of American society and of political forces within it. Yet there are judgments that can be made and portents that can be discerned, and they support impressions about the condition of the "rule of law" and of the causes which law serves.[1]

INTERNATIONAL ORGANIZATION AND THE MAKING OF LAW

International organizations contribute to the ends which law pursues, building order and promoting the common interest. They also contribute to the law itself. They reflect, and create, an attitude that sees law as the fulfillment of their activities and the principal means of assuring their purposes. They promote, facilitate, expedite, and improve the making of law by bringing nations together and emphasizing their common interests; by identifying problems that might lend themselves to law and developing possible legal "solutions" for them; by providing personnel, machinery, and processes for the various stages of international legislation from conception to enactment.

International organizations have helped make—and unmake and remake—international law.[2] To begin, every international organization represents new law at its birth, for it is itself a child of law. The charters of the United Nations and the specialized agencies, the treaties creating the North Atlantic Treaty Organization (NATO) and the Organization of American States (OAS) down, say, to the arrangement for operating the Cape Spartel Lighthouse[3] are formal international agreements; the least of them prescribes law

---

[1] There is relevant background and broader consideration of some matters dealt with here in my book *How Nations Behave: Law and Foreign Policy* (New York: Frederick A. Praeger [for the Council on Foreign Relations], 1968).

[2] I consider principally universal organizations and others in which the United States participates; other organizations, notably the European Communities and broader European institutions, have made major contributions to law and the rule of law that impinge also on the rest of the world, not least on the United States.

[3] This most "meager" multilateral "organization" that comes to mind was established in 1865 to direct, administer, and financially support the lighthouse which had been built by the Moroccan government at Cape Spartel. See Convention concerning the Cape Spartel Lighthouse, May 31, 1865, in George P. Sanger (ed.), *United States Statutes at Large* (hereinafter cited as *Stat.*), Vol. 14 (Boston: Little, Brown and Company, 1868), pp. 679–681; *United States Treaty Series* (hereinafter cited as *TS*) 245 (Washington: U.S. Government Printing Office). The Convention was terminated by protocol on March 31, 1958. See *United States Treaties and Other International Agreements* (hereinafter cited as *UST*), Vol. 9 (1958) (Washington: U.S. Government Printing Office, 1959), pp. 527–530; *Treaties and Other*

for participation in and governance of the organization and for the execution of some functions and contains some undertakings by members, if only the obligation to contribute to the budget. Some organizations are appendages to agreements prescribing substantive law, and the implementation of that law is their raison d'être—e.g., those established by the commodity agreements (coffee, cotton),[4] old and new arrangements regulating fisheries (whaling, salmon, halibut, tuna),[5] the General Agreement on Tariffs and Trade (GATT). Some organizations brought new relationships requiring new law: The United Nations has general law in its Convention on Privileges and Immunities and bilateral law in the Headquarters Agreement with the United States; NATO produced its Status of Forces Agreement and other arrangements supplementing the obligations of the North Atlantic Treaty. Some organizational charters include independent undertakings by the members—for a notable instance, the provision in the UN Charter prohibiting the use of force.

Several international organizations have developed international law by

International Acts Series (hereinafter cited as TIAS) 4029 (Washington: U.S. Government Printing Office, 1958); United Nations Treaty Series (hereinafter cited as UNTS), Vol. 320 (1959), No. 4639 (New York: United Nations), pp. 103–109. Control was returned to the government of Morocco.

[4] See "Multilateral International Coffee Agreement," September 28, 1962, in UST, Vol. 14 (1963), Part 2 (Washington: U.S. Government Printing Office, 1964), pp. 1911–2202; TIAS, 5505 (Washington: U.S. Government Printing Office, 1964); UNTS, Vol. 469 (1963), No. 6791 (New York: United Nations), pp. 169–413. See also "Multilateral Articles of Agreement of the International Cotton Institute," January 24, 1966, in UST, Vol. 17 (1966), Part 1 (Washington: U.S. Government Printing Office, 1967), pp. 83–105; TIAS, 5964 (Washington: U.S. Government Printing Office, 1967). See also "Multilateral International Sugar Agreement," December 1, 1958, in UST, Vol. 10 (1959), Part 3 (Washington: U.S. Government Printing Office, 1960), pp. 2189–2422; TIAS, 4389 (Washington: U.S. Government Printing Office, 1960); UNTS, Vol. 385 (1961), No. 5534 (New York: United Nations), pp. 137–357. See also the amended constitution of the International Rice Commission, November 23, 1961, in UST, Vol. 13 (1962), Part 2 (Washington: U.S. Government Printing Office, 1963), pp. 2403–2417; TIAS, No. 5204 (Washington: U.S. Government Printing Office, 1962); UNTS, Vol. 418 (1962), No. 1613 (New York: United Nations), pp. 334–347.

[5] E.g., International Convention for the Regulation of Whaling, December 2, 1946 (Stat., Vol. 62 [1948], Part 2 [Washington: U.S. Government Printing Office, 1949], pp. 1716–1729; TIAS, No. 1849 [Department of State Publication 3383] [Washington: U.S. Government Printing Office, 1949]), implemented by the Whaling Convention Act of 1950 (Stat., Vol. 64 [1950–1951], Part I [Washington: U.S. Government Printing Office, 1952], pp. 421–425; United States Code, Title 16: Conservation [1952 ed.; Washington: U.S. Government Printing Office, 1953], 916–16L); Convention for the Establishment of an Inter-American Tropical Tuna Commission, May 31, 1949 (UST, Vol. 1 [1950] [Washington: U.S. Government Printing Office, 1952], pp. 230–246; TIAS, No. 2044 [Department of State Publication 3851] [Washington: U.S. Government Printing Office, 1950]; UNTS, Vol. 80 [1951], No. 1041 [New York: United Nations], pp. 3–25); Convention between the United States of America and Canada Concerning the Sockeye Salmon Fisheries, May 26, 1930 (Stat., Vol. 50 [1937], Part 2 [Washington: U.S. Government Printing Office, 1955], pp. 1355–1361; TS, No. 918 [Washington: U.S. Government Printing Office, 1937]); Convention for the Preservation of the Halibut Fishery of the Northern Pacific Ocean and Bering Sea (UST, Vol. 5 [1954], Part 1 [Washington: U.S. Government Printing Office, 1955], pp. 5–11; TIAS, No. 2900 [Department of State Publication 5372] [Washington: U.S. Government Printing Office, 1954]); Convention with Canada and Japan on High Seas Fisheries of the North Pacific Ocean, May 9, 1952 (UST, Vol. 4 [1953], Part 1 [Washington: U.S. Government Printing Office, 1955], pp. 380–420; TIAS, No. 2786 [Department of State Publication 5202] [Washington: U.S. Government Printing Office, 1954]); Interim Convention on North Pacific Fur Seals (United States, Canada, Japan, Soviet Union), February 9, 1957 (TIAS, No. 3948 [Washington: U.S. Government Printing Office, 1958]).

promoting multilateral conventions. From its birth after the First World War, for example, the International Labor Organization (ILO) has prepared and sponsored more than 100 conventions establishing common minimum standards in regard to conditions of labor and other aspects of individual welfare.[6] Since the Second World War other international organizations have also sired law in their areas of interest—e.g., the conventions of the International Civil Aviation Organization (ICAO) on international aviation.[7] Some organizations have "spun off" international law and agreements out of general political and social preoccupations. The UN itself has been midwife (or godmother) to multilateral conventions on subjects ranging from arms control to human rights to standardized road traffic signs.[8] For their members the inter-American organizations have developed conventions relating to war and peace as well as the status of aliens, automotive traffic, and cultural relations.[9] Unheralded, undramatic but important contributions to daily law have been made by other institutions falling within the spectrum of international organization: Since League of Nations days the International Institute for the

[6] As of the end of 1966 there had been 126 such conventions. See *Yearbook of the United Nations: 1966* (New York: United Nations, 1968), p. 978.

[7] The 1944 Convention on International Civil Aviation (Chicago Convention) which is the constitution of ICAO was accompanied by the International Air Services Transit Agreement and the International Air Transport Agreement. Since then there have been other agreements including modifications of earlier agreements e.g., of the 1929 Convention for the Unification of Certain Rules relating to International Transportation by Air (Warsaw Convention) which established rules relating to air transportation, including limitations on the liability of carriers.

[8] As of December 31, 1967, 131 treaties had been developed under the auspices of the UN and the specialized agencies for which the UN Secretary-General was the depositary. See *Multilateral Treaties in respect of Which the Secretary-General Performs Depositary Functions: List of Signatures, Ratifications, Accessions, etc. as at 31 December 1967* (United Nations Publication Sales No: E.68.V.3 [UN Document St/Leg/Ser.D/1]) (New York: United Nations, 1968). Special mention is due also to the International Law Commission (ILC) which with devotion and competence has proposed conventions containing new developments in the law, as well as the new law that is inherent in clarification and codification of old law.

[9] Some of these antedate the hemisphere's involvement in the Second World War, e.g., the convention between the American republics regarding the status of aliens in their respective territories, February 20, 1928 (*Stat.*, Vol. 46 [1929–1931], Part 2 [Washington: U.S. Government Printing Office 1931], pp. 2753–2756; *TS*, No. 815 [Washington: U.S. Government Printing Office, 1930]; *League of Nations Treaty Series* [hereinafter cited as *LNTS*], Vol. 132 [1932–1933], No. 3045 [Geneva: League of Nations, 1932], pp. 301–311); convention concerning artistic exhibitions, December 23, 1936 (*Stat.*, Vol. 51 [1937] [Washington: U.S. Government Printing Office, 1938], pp. 206–229; *TS*, No. 929 [Washington: U.S. Government Printing Office, 1937]; *LNTS*, Vol. 138 [1938], No. 4356 [Geneva: League of Nations, 1938], pp. 151–171); convention providing for creation of the Inter-American Indian Institute, November 1, 1940 (*Stat.*, Vol. 56 [1942] [Washington: U.S. Government Printing Office, 1949], pp. 1681–1715; *TS*, No. 978 [Washington: U.S. Government Printing Office, 1942]). More recent ones include the 1947 Inter-American Treaty of Reciprocal Assistance (Rio Treaty) (*Stat.*, Vol. 62 [1948] [Washington: U.S. Government Printing Office], pp. 1681–1715; *TIAS*, No. 1838 [Department of State Publication 3380] [Washington: U.S. Government Printing Office, 1949]; *UNTS*, Vol. 21 [1948], No. 324 [New York: United Nations], pp. 77–185); convention on the regulation of inter-American automotive traffic, September 19, 1949 (*UST*, Vol. 3 [1952], Part 3 [Washington: U.S. Government Printing Office, 1955], pp. 3008–3061; *TIAS*, No. 2487 [Department of State Publication 4606] [Washington: U.S. Government Printing Office, 1952]); and convention for the promotion of inter-American cultural relations, March 28, 1954 (*UST*, Vol. 8 [1957], Part 2 [Washington: U.S. Government Printing Office, 1958], pp. 1903–1935; *TIAS*, No. 3936 [Washington: U.S. Government Printing Office, 1957]).

Unification of Private Law has been promoting common law, particularly in matters which spill over national frontiers, for example, its recent draft law for international sales; the Economic Commission for Europe (ECE), the International Chamber of Commerce (an international organization at least by some definitions), and the new UN Commission for International Trade Law (UNCITRAL) are also raising law and increasing order in international trade. The Hague Conference for Private International Law, striving for uniformity in the rules determining which nation's law shall apply in a multinational transaction, has been sufficiently successful to attract participation by the United States.

International organizations contribute to the sum of international law by other kinds of lawmaking. Some organizations promulgate regulations or make decisions of quasi-legislative character:[10] In the International Monetary Fund (IMF) the Executive Board can limit national modifications of the rate of exchange of their currencies; the International Whaling Commission can modify regulations limiting the kinds of whales that may be caught and in what season.

International organizations also make law in less formal ways. In the UN every organ interprets the Charter to determine its own prerogatives and sometimes those of other organs. The General Assembly, in particular, has repeatedly overridden claims that it was exceeding its Charter authority: It has successfully claimed the power to discuss and make recommendations on issues of war and peace (Korea), on self-determination (French Algeria), on human rights (South Africa); it has purported to make binding assessments for contributions to various UN programs, e.g., the United Nations Emergency Force (UNEF).

The General Assembly has also "legislated" substantive international law. It did so by interpreting the Charter—as when it held that the Charter barred "indirect aggression."[11] It adopted a regime for outer space giving it substantial legal quality even before it was formalized by multilateral treaty. It affirmed "the principles of international law recognized by the Charter of the Nürnberg Tribunal and the judgment of the Tribunal." It "declared" principles of international law, or recommended policy based on particular interpretations of law, e.g., that the use of nuclear weapons is unlawful. Its various resolutions on national sovereignty over natural resources inevitably helped modify the law relating to expropriation of alien properties. There have also been ten

[10] Usually these require unanimous consent or are only recommendations, for especially since the early postwar days (in the UN Charter and the Bretton Woods agreements) nations have been generally unwilling to submit to decisions to which they do not consent. But submission to regulation is in some cases the condition of some advantage: for example, accepting inspection is the price of receiving fissionable materials through the International Atomic Energy Agency (IAEA). Within smaller groupings or in regard to specific subjects all the participants sometimes subject themselves to "supranational" regulation, but vetoes or various forms of weighted voting protect the more important states.

[11] E.g., General Assembly Resolution 380 (V), November 17, 1950 ("Peace Through Deeds").

formal "declarations," beginning with the Universal Declaration of Human Rights, which while not purporting to have the quality of law, have in differing degrees entered the stream of international law and influenced national behavior.

The special climate of the UN has achieved some status as law for political "principles" and has given unusual growth to other law with political overtones. Even now "self-determination" may not be strictly a legal principle, and surely there is no agreement on its definition and reach, but it has effectively "outlawed" traditional Western colonialism on the colored continents. The stigma that has attached to colonialism, and the political influence of the erstwhile colonies, concentrated in the United Nations, have tended to modify law as it relates to their former status, e.g., the law governing succession by states to the rights and obligations of their predecessors. (There is also talk of new applications of *rebus sic stantibus* and of a doctrine that gross "inequality" in bargaining power is a basis for invalidating or escaping treaty undertakings.) Discrimination on the basis of race may already be a violation; witness various near-unanimous General Assembly resolutions and the opinions of several judges of the International Court of Justice (ICJ) in the South West Africa case. In the mysterious ways in which customary international law is born many elements contributed by international organizations (including the Universal Declaration, the finally completed UN covenants, debates in the Assembly, the work of the Human Rights Commission, regional agreements and institutions) may also be helping to create—eventually, slowly—some universal customary law on human rights generally.

THE SIGNIFICANCE OF THE CONTRIBUTION TO LAW

In sum, it is easy to show that international organization has helped add to the body of international law; it is less easy to measure the size and weight of this contribution, and I do not know how to begin to assess its significance for international order or justice or general welfare. Some law might well have come without the intermediation of any international organization; some would probably not have been made, or been made as well or as expeditiously, but for the efforts of some international organization; some is uniquely the child of organization. Some of the law which international organization has fathered or brought to maturity is universal in design and reach; some applies only to a few countries. Some "universal" agreements have been widely adhered to or generally accepted as law even by nations that have not bothered to accede formally; some will remain at best a special regime for a few adherents. Some law promotes common or reciprocal interests in a traditional international activity; other law is concerned to regulate subjects not previously of international concern. Some law seeks to struggle with fundamental disorders; some would improve a small facet of human activity of some small international consequence. Much of the new law which comes with or from international organization aims directly not at order but at distributive justice and general welfare.

Significance, of course, is often in the eye of the beholder. It is commonly accepted that the most important development in international law in our times, born together with the most important development in international organization, is the prohibition on the use of force in the UN Charter (although there is debate as to the scope of the prohibition and particularly of the "self-defense" exception to it; debate continues also as to whether that law is viable, perhaps even whether it is desirable). Despite abiding weakness in what was done high place would have to go, too, to the law designed to bring order into international money and banking and international trade;[12] to the charters of the International Bank for Reconstruction and Development (IBRD) and of other specialized agencies and the functional agreements they promoted; to the law of the European Communities, radiating influence far beyond Western Europe. The "principle" of self-determination has helped remake the map of the world; it is the banner leading the struggle against embattled remnants of white colonialism and racism in Africa; it continues to influence the international relations of former colonies—most of the states of the world—and to affect all relations in a divided, changing world.

The conventional law promoted by international organization includes some that seems trivial (but may be widely accepted) and some that is important by any standards (and, partly for that reason, might remain an ideal). Nations, of course, have been more willing to accept law that is not onerous, that will not subject them to intrusive enforcement or other sharp international scrutiny. In special contexts they have responded to humanitarian appeal and the pressures which it generates, particularly if the obligations seem limited and temporary—as in the Convention Relating to the Status of Refugees and its implementations by the UN High Commissioner. On the other hand, universal human rights covenants, for example, are a major promise, but it remains to be seen how many nations will adhere to them and how many will accept the protocol providing for a modicum of "enforcement."

It is relevant to note also law which international organization has not made. Much failure-to-do is implied in what it did, which in many instances indicates that it could go that far and no further. International organization has not altered the processes of lawmaking: The principle of unanimity remains largely intact in regard to general lawmaking; where law can in fact be made by majorities, some nations at least have vetoes or special voting rights. The General Assembly has arrogated much legislative authority in regard to white colonialism and racism where proliferating new nations have

12 Principally the Articles of Agreement of the International Monetary Fund.

been joined by old nations that are sympathetic, feel guilty, or are striving to please. But eager majorities have not been able to impose law on the rich and powerful, nor have majorities been willing to attempt to make law of general applicability binding on themselves as well.[13]

In content, despite the efforts of international organization international law remains primitive, leaving many relations between nations unregulated and disorderly. New undertakings directly to strengthen the fabric of peace may not be necessary, for many think the UN Charter has done all that law can do to that end and that further undertakings—including, for example, definitions of aggression—would add little, could not be negotiated, and might dilute what has been done. But there has been no success, for instance, in reinvigorating the provision in the Charter outlawing *threats* of force, widely disregarded, as by the Arab states against Israel. And neither the Charter nor older international law unambiguously and effectively deals with a major contemporary disorder: "Intervention" in the affairs of other nations cries for refined definitions and revised regulations, depending on circumstances, purposes, means. There has been only little law controlling armaments: We do not even have yet some important, practicable, "preventive" agreements, for example, to extend the ban on nuclear testing, to avoid the development or deployment of antiballistic missiles, to limit the military uses of the sea and its bed, to add controls in outer space; it is not yet clear how successful will be the attempt to prevent the spread of nuclear weapons. Although there is some law and some order in commercial affairs, international organization has not yet succeeded in establishing stable, effective regulation of money or trade. It is just beginning to think about new problems raised by new technology—outer space, the deep sea, weather control. It has not helped resolve particular critical issues in old law, e.g., as to the requirement of compensation for expropriations of alien property—or old differences as to the width of the territorial sea and new ones about the continental shelf.[14] There could be much more law establishing rights and obligations between nations generally, including the basic obligation to accept each other's existence even if there is no desire to maintain relations. Surely, international organization has not established a welfare society in which the society and its members have an obligation to promote the general welfare and the minimum welfare of each— as by financial assistance and beneficial discriminations in trade. It has not yet established a minimal unitary society in which what states do in their own territories vis-à-vis their own inhabitants is of concern to all and must meet minimum standards, e.g., the right to an education, to liberty, to due process of law.

[13] I discuss the legal status of General Assembly resolutions in *How Nations Behave*, pp. 163–173.
[14] See, e.g., Louis Henkin, *Law for the Sea's Mineral Resources* (New York: Columbia University Institute for the Study of Science in Human Affairs, 1968), pp. 14–24.

INTERNATIONAL ORGANIZATION AND RESPECT FOR LAW

Any judgment on the contribution of international organization to the rule of law must weigh not only the law it has helped make or has not succeeded in making but also its influence on national behavior in respect of law. International organization, indeed, can contribute to order without making law, as when it helps persuade nations to live by tacit agreements or to avoid anti-social conduct that is not unlawful. The rule of law, on the other hand, is not built with paper laws, not even when they are made by international organization. The question is whether law works. Our question is whether international organization has helped see to it that law is observed or has otherwise shaped how nations behave under law.

Contrary to common misconceptions, nations generally observe their international undertakings because observance is generally in the national interest, whether egoistic or enlightened. It is rare that a violation brings advantages that outweigh the direct cost in the probable response of the victim and the indirect costs to a nation's friendly relations, its credit, dependability, respectability, to its general interest in keeping the system going, in some instances also to aspirations to leadership and to special influence in international relations.

International organization has generally enhanced the forces that make for law observance. In the round the forces that support international organization also create respect for law: Both law and organization reflect the need for cooperation and emphasize the common or reciprocal interests of nations. International organization also increases points of contact and interdependence and creates additional "constituencies" for cooperation both in international bodies and within nations and their governments; the same institutions and constituencies tend to promote the law's success, and some international organizations themselves have grown a kind of "executive" function corresponding to the legislative achievements I have described.

That international organizations make law gives them also the interest and influence to see that the law is effective. In some cases, we have seen, an international organization exists to assure that a particular law is faithfully executed—as in GATT or the IMF. The principal purpose of the UN (and. locally, the OAS) is to maintain international peace and security, especially the observance of the law outlawing the use of force. Even in a highly "political" context relating directly to peace and security the North Atlantic Treaty Organization, for example, involves nations in detailed implementation of the North Atlantic Treaty, fosters expectations and habits of compliance, creates a bureaucracy and a constituency with an active interest in keeping the obligation intact, subjects would-be violators to pressures to observe and the threat of unpleasant consequences if they do not. International organizations that promote multilateral conventions also have an interest and an influence in promoting their observance.[15] When international organization contributes to the law of daily intercourse, say, the rules and forms of trade, the law created is virtually "self-executing," there being every reason for nations to accept and respect it.

The UN in particular, I believe, has added an important increment to the forces that support observance of international law. While the victims of most violations of international law do not wish to "internationalize" them and other UN Members resist involvement, violations of the law of the Charter surely, and some other important violations probably, come before the Organization, become the business of all UN Members, and inevitably engage them in the controversy. Neither the powerful few nor the mass of the Members can easily refrain from putting their influence behind the observance of law—as in Korea, at Suez, in Kashmir in 1965. Even in the so-far-incurable Middle East the UN is continuously and inextricably involved, hearing and resolving, condemning and exhorting, trying to prevent, deter, or terminate fighting. Of course, the UN still cannot itself "maintain international peace and security," for the original conception and the original hopes which died early in the Cold War have not revived despite occasional détente and burgeoning new foci of political power in groupings of new nations. The UN, indeed, has been virtually irrelevant in a few cases, particularly where a major power has seen a major interest to be vindicated regardless of political cost—Tibet, Hungary, and Czechoslovakia, some might add Guatemala, the Dominican Republic, and Vietnam.

But in the sum, contrary to common misimpressions, there have been few instances since 1945 in which nations—including the most powerful nations—have engaged in "war," in full and sustained hostilities, even in circumstances in which in the past such use of force might have been expected. (I speak of international war as distinguished from intervention in internal wars, as to which the law is less certain, the facts often unclear, and the role of the UN inevitably circumscribed.) For this major development in international order, I am satisfied, substantial credit is due to the law of the UN Charter reflecting new international attitudes and to the deterrent influence and occasional intervention by the UN Organization. Every nation that considers using force or committing any other violation likely to come within the UN's ken knows that it will have to face charges, probable condemnation, perhaps even some sanctions; no nation is indifferent to adverse UN votes and actions, and it will have to see strong advantages in the violation to offset that additional

---

[15] Notably, the Constitution of ILO requires governments to report what measures they have taken to give effect to their obligations under conventions they have ratified. The reports are scrutinized by a committee of experts and governments may be called on to reply to the committee's criticism. ILO has also developed special procedures for the handling of complaints and the settlement of disputes.

cost. The existence of the UN also, I believe, affords general protection to the weak against pressures from the strong that were common in an earlier day.

The influence of the UN, however, is not simple, uniform, or in one direction. The UN is a political body reflecting the distribution of power and other forms of influence in the world refracted through the particular medium of the UN Organization; its judgments on legal issues are also political. The temptation of majorities to adopt law that applies particularly to the few has its counterpart in an unequal enforcement of law. Law observance is not encouraged if an international organization applies a double standard or if its approval or condemnation is not based on "neutral" legal principles. Perhaps the UN had no choice but to discontinue discussion of the invasion of Czechoslovakia by the Union of Soviet Socialist Republics in 1968 after the victim's representatives indicated that its cause would not be helped thereby. But the UN does not help the rule of law when it condones India's conquest of Goa, when it tolerates perennial Arab threats to destroy Israel, or if it permits the growth of the impression that it will acquiesce in a special "rule" permitting the use of force by the Soviet Union against members of its bloc or by African nations against the remnants of white colonialism or racism. It is not the rule of law when the UN takes action against violation of human rights in some countries but not in others or when a principle of universal membership is invoked to support a seat for Communist China but is abandoned to support exclusion of the Republic of South Africa. There is a disturbing tendency within international organizations to disregard constitutional limitations and to disdain established procedures and due process. There is an abiding danger that majorities will loosen the restraints of law generally, converting legal questions back into political ones to be decided by *fiat* of majorities. And who can say how much such politicization might cost the rule of law as compared with what international organization contributes to it?

INTERNATIONAL ORGANIZATION AND INTERNATIONAL ADJUDICATION

Those who were nurtured on the spirit of The Hague at the turn of the century and its realizations between the wars must be particularly disappointed at the stagnation and decline of international adjudication and arbitration in our day. International organization has not produced a judicial achievement comparable even to its modest legislative and executive contributions although there was much more to build on. The great hope, the International Court of Justice, has had few cases, and its advisory function has not made a major contribution to the development of international organization or international law or to the settlement of disputes between nations.[16] International

16 Between 1922 and 1939 the Permanent Court of International Justice (PCIJ) considered 66 adversary proceedings and handed down 27 advisory opinions. Since 1945, although it might have been ex-

arbitration too has languished. The Permanent Court of Arbitration has had little business; *ad hoc* arbitration is at best sporadic and has not been a common recourse for the resolution of important issues. The decline of third-party decision, I emphasize, does not necessarily reflect a decline in respect for law. Nations with good records for law observance have still been reluctant to submit to adjudication in principle or actually to go to court.

Principally, perhaps, hopes for third-party decision fell victim to the early postwar polarization. Even for the nations of the West—the ICJ's "natural" constituency—sharpening political differences with aggressive Communism brought an atmosphere not conducive to law: Legal issues were "politicized" leaving few which countries were willing to entrust to law and on which they felt they could afford to lose in a judicial tribunal. (Within the blocs, too, tightened alliances made it easier to resolve disputes without cumbersome, slow, expensive judicial process.) On the other side, Soviet ideology, even after the death of Josef Stalin, rejected the conceptions of "neutrality" of principles and impartiality of persons which are crucial to third-party decision.

Proliferating new nations, too, have not become clients for judicial or arbitral tribunals. The new nations have been cautious in regard to the law of the society into which they were born as well as the institutions which implemented it. That the judges of the ICJ have been old in years, traditional in spirit, largely Western in their origins and training may also have deterred erstwhile Western colonies from resorting to the Court; perhaps, too, a passion for nonalignment made them reluctant to commit themselves to institutions which the Soviet Union basically rejected. Adjudication, also, is expensive and slow and most new nations would have to depend on Western lawyers to represent them. Like the Communist countries, moreover, though for different reasons, new nations have not been prepared to risk adverse decision. When Thailand lost a case to Cambodia, it turned on the Court while Cambodia did not necessarily turn to it.[17] The South West Africa debacle in the ICJ gave the former colonies reason—or pretext—for looking askance at that institution.[18] In the result most nations have not accepted the Court's compulsory jurisdiction and few nations have actually brought proceedings before

pected that the ICJ would be a more important and effective body, the ICJ has considered 50 adversary proceedings and handed down thirteen advisory opinions. Numbers apart, the ICJ has not had the impact which many had hoped for.

[17] *Case concerning the Temple of Preah Vihear (Cambodia v. Thailand), Merits, Judgment of 15 June 1962: I.C.J. Reports 1962.* Thailand, to show its displeasure at having lost the case, refused to attend meetings of the Southeast Asia Treaty Organization (SEATO) and the Geneva conference on Laos. (*The New York Times*, June 20, 1962.) Thailand also recalled its ambassador to France, presumably because two French lawyers represented Cambodia in the case, and cut off trade with Poland, apparently because the President of the Court at the time was a Polish national. (*The New York Times*, June 23, 1962.)

[18] In 1966 a bare majority in effect reversed an earlier decision and held that under the League of Nations mandate Ethiopia and Liberia did not have a justiciable claim to challenge apartheid in South West Africa.

it. There has even developed a resistance to accepting the principle that the Court should be the ultimate arbiter of disputes arising under particular treaties. It is given no role in the implementation of the human rights covenants; the 1967 Protocol to the 1951 Convention relating to the Status of Refugees was designed so as to permit new parties to enter a reservation to the provision in the original Convention for settlement of disputes by the ICJ.[19] Arbitration, too, has suffered because there has not been acceptance by disputing parties of common principles and values and shared confidence that there are arbitrators who will apply them evenhandedly. Again, for various reasons nations have preferred to rely on diplomacy or self-help or to leave disputes unsettled.

Perhaps third-party decision has suffered in some measure from the growth of political and economic organization. To an extent organization has served the same function, ordering relationships in accordance with law: Matters producing issues that in an earlier day might have gone to a tribunal are now within the jurisdiction of an international organization, and in successful organizations some issues do not arise while those that arise are "worked out" or are decided by administrative bodies within the organization. (In the European Communities there is a court, too, although its business is also limited.) In some instances international organization has discouraged third-party decision because it has subordinated legal principle and impartial determination. Those in command of political processes prefer to use them to legislate what they desire instead of "abdicating" that power to a court or even an arbitral body. In the UN and its specialized agencies requests for advisory opinions are infrequent, for majorities prefer to extend their authority by their lights rather than risk having the Court limit it by interpretation of constitutional documents. In the settlement of disputes, too, majorities, and often one or both parties, prefer the diplomatic arena where they dominate or participate in the process to putting important issues out of their own control into the distant hands of Fifteen Old Men or even three "experts" *ad hoc*.[20]

I do not suggest that one should write off international adjudication and arbitration. Only recently the pressures of common interest have produced wide acceptance of a convention, prepared by the World Bank, for arbitration of disputes between nations and foreign investors; it remains to be seen how much arbitration there will in fact be, but the Convention may be even more successful if it serves to encourage governments and investors to avoid disputes or to settle them "out of court." As regards the ICJ even today, between some nations, the Court is used to resolve important, difficult, "technical" dis-

---

[19] Under the original Convention the ICJ clause was not open to reservation. Compare Articles 38 and 52. The 1967 Protocol permits new adherents to reserve that clause. It was to encourage adherence by those who might refuse to adhere to the 1951 Convention because of the ICJ clause that the Protocol was drafted in an unusual, almost grotesque form.

[20] See footnote 16 above.

putes, e.g., how the bed of the North Sea shall be divided under the 1958 Geneva Convention on the Continental Shelf.[21] Between some countries the threat of a suit in the ICJ might still deter a violation, as it did when the United Kingdom reconsidered breaking its agreement with France to join in building the *Concorde* airplane. In the future even new nations may yet begin to turn to the Court as experience and participation in the process of lawmaking and in the membership of the Court render the institution less alien and distant. Surely in their relations *inter se* new nations will have to consider adjudication or arbitration—perhaps by judges of local origin or by regional tribunals.

THE ATTITUDES OF THE UNITED STATES

An inquiry into the implications for the United States of the impact of international organization on international law might begin by recognizing that —in regard to law at least as much as elsewhere—what international organization has done and not done is in substantial measure due to the United States, to its policies and diplomacy, to its preeminent contribution in money, personnel, ideas, and initiatives, as well as to its restraints. The policies of the United States, however, have not been uniform or of one piece; nor, of course, have they always and completely prevailed.

The Making of Law

The attitudes of the United States toward the legal activities of international organization reflect attitudes toward international law generally. Law is in this country's history and traditions, its constitutions and institutions, its values, its "style," its "national character." It was conceived in a "decent respect to the opinions of mankind," born in the heyday of the "law or nature," fathered and raised by men who respected law. A written constitution and a Supreme Court enjoining the complex divisions of federalism and separated branches and the limitations of the Bill of Rights have molded many national problems in legal cast.

Law has always been prominent in American foreign policy. (Indeed, American policy is often criticized for an excess of "legalism.")[22] From the beginning lawyers have been major actors in the conduct of American foreign relations, and lawyers in and out of government have exerted due—some will say undue—influence upon it. The organization of government today includes

---

[21] The issue was recently before the Court in two cases, one between Denmark and the Federal Republic of Germany (West Germany), the other between the Federal Republic and the Netherlands. A judgment generally favoring Germany's position was handed down in February 1969.

[22] See in particular George F. Kennan, *American Diplomacy: 1900–1950* (Chicago: Chicago University Press, 1951), pp. 95ff. I deal with this and other criticism in *How Nations Behave*, Chapter XVIII, particularly pp. 254–261.

important roles for the Attorney General and particularly for the Legal Adviser of the Department of State who has a substantial staff of lawyers integrated into the process of making policy.

In its foreign relations the United States has long recognized its particular interests in law. The first modern "new nation," it early sought protection for its independence in the law of nations. Later, geographic isolation, natural wealth, and the desire to be let alone enhanced its support for the conservative influence of law to promote order in relations between nations. Its rise to wealth and power and a major role on the world scene revealed additional interests in the uses of law.

Of course, like other nations the United States has sought its own blend of freedom from the law's restraints and pursuit of law's advantages. At different times it has had different answers to how much confidence it had in law as a means to peace, security, order, justice, and welfare; how much interest it saw in freedom from law and in the flexibility of diplomacy; how much freedom it was prepared to sacrifice for some particular advantage or common enterprise. In our day, in the beginning—in the glow following victory in the Second World War—the United States seemed committed to new reaches and new horizons for law. It contributed handsomely to the faith, hope, and enlightenment that helped produce the UN Charter, the Statute of the ICJ, the charters of the International Bank and the Monetary Fund and other specialized agencies. The law and the organization implied in the Acheson-Lilienthal plan for the international control of atomic energy were revolutionary, and its authors, surely, did not share the later cynicism that suggested that the United States relied on the Senate to save it from its own proposal. Even the notorious Connally Amendment to the American acceptance of the compulsory jurisdiction of the ICJ (reserving for the United States final say that a case against it would not lie because it involved a matter essentially within the domestic jurisdiction of the United States) appeared originally as an excess of caution by a few senators, not as a lapse from idealism reflecting resistance to adjudication.[23]

One can debate whether this early enthusiasm for law was the victim of Soviet aggressiveness and the Cold War or whether it would in any event have dissipated in the morning after the glory of war's end. The fact is that for two decades now American policy, while not devoid of generosity and enlightenment, has been marked by "realism," caution, reliance on its own power and its own diplomacy, reluctance to submit even secondary interests to the judgment of others. Yet there has been an important place for international law, as for international organization, even in "realist" policies. "Realist" American officials, too, have come to recognize international organization as a new, different, but integral component in international diplomacy;

[23] See footnote 33 below.

they have been known to appreciate law as a basic instrument of diplomacy as well as its fulfillment. Although like other powerful nations the United States has often resisted assuming the restraints of law and has chafed under some it had assumed, in principle and in general it has recognized its particular interests in promoting and living by law. It has seen its interest in international stability and has recognized the uses of law to promote it. It has appreciated law as the ripe fruit of diplomacy building reliable expectations and confident relations. It has known the convenience of common standards and common forms. It has enjoyed the legitimacy which law can give to its own actions and the limitations which law imposes on the behavior of others. It has recognized that even the rich and the mighty cannot commonly obtain what they want by force and dictation but must pay the price of reciprocal or compensatory obligations. In some respects, indeed, its wealth and power gave the United States a special interest in law: It is deeply dependent on stability in trade and finance; it has particular concern for strategic stability and for limitations on its powerful rival, the Soviet Union, say, by agreement to limit the development of new weaponry. It has learned that power and wealth hardly assure against—even invite—harassment and that law affords some protection also to the strong against the weak. The United States, moreover, has seen national interest not only in law to provide order but also in law to distribute justice for its own sake and for its influence on eliminating forces that breed disorder.

American appreciation of the uses of law has been wide and continual. The United States has acted and cooperated to codify, clarify, and modernize international law. State Department lawyers, and scholars working outside but close to official bodies, have struggled to reduce the chaos in international fields like the scope of sovereign immunity and the width of the territorial sea. The United States developed its network of bilateral treaties on traditional subjects and added new subjects: relief from double taxation, protection for investments against confiscatory expropriations. Even when the United States sought freedom from restraints on national egoism, as when it claimed the right to exploit the resources of its continental shelf, it did so in the framework of law and legal process, almost singlehandedly launching the doctrine of the continental shelf which later found formal confirmation in the 1958 Convention and wide acceptance even by nations that have not formally adhered to the Convention.[24]

But the attitudes of the United States toward international law must be seen also in what it has not done. Except perhaps during its honeymoon with "internationalism" after the Second World War its uses of law have been limited by traditional attitudes and traditional perceptions of its interests. It

[24] See the Truman proclamation, No. 2667, of September 28, 1945, in *Federal Register*, Vol. 10 (October 1945), No. 191 (Washington: U.S. Government Printing Office, 1945).

has welcomed and sought to modernize law of traditional kinds on traditional
subjects such as responsibility to foreign nationals and the regulation of international transportation and trade; it has not been prepared to join law about
matters on which it has traditionally had freedom of action, e.g., the human
rights of local inhabitants. Even in its modern treaties of friendship, commerce, and navigation it has not been eager to extend law to new areas, especially those traditionally the domain of the states, say by agreeing that aliens
may practice law or medicine.[25] Indeed its changed place in world affairs has
made it less receptive to provisions which it welcomed in an earlier day, like
those providing reciprocal exemptions from military service for resident aliens.
The conflict with Communism has also caused it to retreat from the attitude
that nations generally are friendly and deserve similar most-favored-nation
treatment.

The same attitudes are reflected, of course, in what the United States has
been prepared to do or to have done about law through international organization. At bottom, it has been somewhat uncomfortable about lawmaking
by international organization which, as compared with traditional diplomacy,
engenders special pressures affecting the substance of the law it makes, sometimes seeks for its law some superior status, and often promotes additional
organization which further threatens national autonomy. American hesita-
tions have been reflected in many ways. The United States has adhered to
the law contained in the charters of many international organizations, but as
much as any other nation it has insisted on a veto, the principle of unanimity,
or a voting system in which it has great weight and has resisted involvements
which might subject it to the binding authority of "supranational" bodies in
matters of substantial import. (Even at the height of its internationalism, when
the United States accepted the law of the UN Charter outlawing war and
establishing means to maintain peace, it was not prepared to accept binding
judgment and action not subject to its veto.) It has joined organizations that
could promote order in particular international activities or further the welfare of less fortunate states through financial or other assistance; it has not
been prepared to accept binding regulation by international bodies. It has
accepted substantive law contained in international charters or multilateral

---

[25] In one instance the Executive branch was prepared to accept such provisions but the Senate insisted
that the states remain free to limit the practice of the professions to aliens. See Treaty of Friendship,
Commerce and Navigation between the United States of America and Israel, August 23, 1951, Article
VIII (2), in *UST*, Vol. 5 (1954), Part 1 (Washington: U.S. Government Printing Office, 1955), pp.
550–604; *TIAS*, No. 2948 (Department of State Publication 5490) (Washington: U.S. Government Printing Office, 1954); see also the Senate's reservations in *Congressional Record*, Vol. 99 (July 13, 1953–
July 25, 1953), Part 7 (83rd Congress, 1st Session) (Washington: U.S. Government Printing Office,
1953), pp. 9313, 9314 (remarks of Senator Bourke Hickenlooper). Compare Treaty of Friendship, Commerce and Navigation between the United States of America and Greece, August 3, 1951, Article XII
(1), in *UST*, Vol. 5 (1954), Part 2 (Washington: U.S. Government Printing Office, 1956), pp. 1829–
1921; *TIAS*, No. 3057 (Department of State Publication 5677) (Washington: U.S. Government Printing
Office, 1955).

conventions on traditional subjects—the regulation of international intercourse, cooperation for common "police-power" purposes (suppression of slavery, crime, "vice"); in other areas while it has voted for most of the UN declarations it has adhered to few "UN treaties" and has particularly eschewed the new conventions on subjects which the United States had always considered its own affair. Even in the early days, in the UN Charter it agreed—or thought it had agreed—only to exhortation, not obligation, in regard to self-determination, the control of armaments, human rights, and cooperation for economic and social welfare, and it welcomed the limitations implied in the provision that the UN shall not intervene in matters essentially within the domestic jurisdiction of states. Later, in developing the law of the Charter the United States offered some resistance to the sweep of self-determination and more to assertions by new nations in revolution of national "sovereignty" over natural resources unlimited by law. In the endless negotiations to control armaments, although Americans tend to consider that the record of the United States is far better than that of the Soviet Union, caution—including insistence on verification affording a high level of confidence of detection and deterrence—has led it to agree to very little. Even in relations to its allies, even in NATO, the United States has sought to retain substantial control; it has reserved decision as to the means and timing of American assistance; it has been reluctant to submit American troops to the law and the courts of its allies.[26]

Consider, for a striking example, proposed conventional law for the protection of human rights. The United States is probably second to no other nation in the rights accorded by law to its own citizens. It has insisted on the relevance of human rights to international peace and security. It helped write provisions to promote human rights into the UN Charter and normative protections into the peace treaties with nations vanquished in the Second World War. It joined in developing not only the UN declarations—on human rights, on the rights of the child, on the elimination of all forms of racial discrimination, on the elimination of discrimination against women—but also the draft treaties—the 1949 Convention on the Prevention and Punishment of the Crime of Genocide, the Convention Relating to the Status of Refugees, and the major human rights covenants now finally completed, giving these documents, too, an image out of its own laws. It would be pleased to have other nations adhere to and live by these conventions.

But the United States has not ratified them. American officials consider them largely unnecessary for the United States since our Constitution and laws generally match or exceed the proposed international standards. More important, when Presidents have wished to adhere to them in a spirit of com-

---

[26] At least it has insisted on a clause in the Status of Forces Agreement designed to require the host nation to give sympathetic consideration to requests that it waive criminal jurisdiction over American soldiers and has sought waivers as a matter of course in almost every case.

mon enterprise and in order to establish a common standard, powerful voices in the country have objected. In some cases, it was argued, the conventions go beyond American law, but whether or not they do opponents have maintained that these matters are our own business and have rejected international scrutiny of our doings. (Once they sought to amend the United States Constitution to prevent adherence to such conventions by treaty; recently they have concocted arguments that the United States is barred from joining these efforts by the Constitution as it is.) As a result the United States has refrained from joining even law that for it would be merely an affirmation of old pieties. The executive branch submitted the Genocide Convention for Senate consent in 1949 and it has lain on the Senate table ever since. The United States did not even sign the 1951 Convention Relating to the Status of Refugees which it helped draft.[27] In 1953 Secretary of State John Foster Dulles announced that the United States would not adhere to the human rights covenants then in negotiation. When President John F. Kennedy, perhaps as a first step in reversing the Dulles policy, sent up three small agreements dealing with slavery, forced labor, and the political rights of women, the Senate consented only to the one on slavery, the others being indefinitely tabled.[28]

Respect for Law

While the United States is often reluctant to assume new obligations it is careful to honor those it has accepted; indeed, the care with which it selects and shapes its undertakings is evidence that what it undertakes it intends to keep and generally keeps.

Again, for the United States the lessons of history, the habits of generations, the impulsions of institutions, the attitudes of its people, the influence of lawyers—all promote observance of law. Respect for individuals, enjoined by domestic law, makes it unlikely that the United States will commit certain violations, e.g., infringement of basic rights of aliens. Free institutions deter other violations because they make it less likely that violations will escape detection and censure; the United States is incapable of keeping a secret or denying a true accusation. (Compare the 1960 U-2 incident in the Soviet Union.) The people do not like their government to violate the law or to be caught at it.

[27] In 1968 after seventeen years—perhaps because refugees are not being admitted to the United States in large numbers, perhaps by oversight, perhaps in guilty reaction to its failure to adhere to other covenants—the United States adhered to the 1951 Convention through the back door by accepting the 1967 Protocol which virtually incorporated the 1951 Convention by reference. Entered into force for the United States on November 1, 1968 (TIAS, No. 6577 [Washington: U.S. Government Printing Office], 1968).

[28] See Senate Executive Report No. 17 (90th Congress, 1st Session) (Washington: U.S. Government Printing Office, 1967) and Congressional Record Vol. 113 (November 1, 1967–November 9, 1967), Part 23 (90th Congress, 1st Session) (Washington: U.S. Government Printing Office, 1967), pp. 30902–30909, remarks of Senator William Proxmire and others.

For the United States respect for law is supported by strong reasons of foreign policy. I am not suggesting that the United States commonly sacrifices "national interest" to international law. That is a false issue.[29] Often the law coincides with the interests of the United States as of other countries: If it did not, it would not become or remain law. (Sometimes the influence of the United States can achieve a change in the law, as in the Truman proclamation on the continental shelf.) But even where the United States might act otherwise were there no law or obligation, the United States usually sees its national interest in acting consistently with the law. There are the immediate reasons to keep intact law that it had seemed desirable to make: If the United States thought it desirable to agree to a test ban it would not lightly give up the advantages it saw in the agreement by destroying it. There are also other national interests in observing law, no less real because intangible and difficult to prove or measure. The United States shares the common concern to keep the international system running and orderly. It wishes its relations with other nations to be friendly. It is concerned for its honor, prestige, leadership, influence, and reputation. Since international law was born in the West, Western powers, including the United States, are disposed to be content with their creation. Since law is generally a conservative force, it is more likely to be observed by those content with their lot, and few nations have as much reason to be content as the United States. In our day the United States has a special stake in world order, and its own compliance establishes a comfortable position from which to insist that others do the same. Claiming leadership, it seeks a reputation for international propriety, respectability, and especially dependability. The foreign policy of the United States has depended in particular on its credit and creditability for living up to particular undertakings —to come to the aid of allies[30] or not to intervene in the interal affairs of Latin American countries.

In general, I believe, the record of the United States has been as good as, probably better than, that of most nations comparable in capacity and temptation to disregard the law.[31] It is in relation to the struggle against Communism that the conduct of the United States can be seriously faulted.[32] The believed demands of the ideological struggle and the domestic pressures which that

---

[29] See Henkin, *How Nations Behave*, Chapter XVIII, particularly pp. 261–266.

[30] As in NATO. It has also claimed this as a principal justification for its action in Vietnam.

[31] It is difficult to fault the United States even in regard to the "law" which the UN General Assembly has sought to make, for while the United States has questioned some of that "law," it has not lightly flouted it. Although it rejected the declaration by the General Assembly in Resolution 1653 (XVI), of November 24, 1961, that the use of nuclear weapons (even in self-defense) is illegal, happily, it has not yet had to decide whether to act contrary to that view of the law. It has differed from some extreme positions as to the meaning of the "law" of self-determination but it has not in fact acted contrary to them. It has complied with recommendations of UN organs about which it had misgivings, as in regard to Southern Rhodesia and South Africa.

[32] Caution about adhering to new law, e.g., disarmament agreements or human rights covenants, or to accept compulsory jurisdiction of the ICJ, p. 112 above, is also rooted in part in fear that Communist enemies might abuse such new law or such consent to adjudication.

struggle enhanced have led to occasional breach of treaty (e.g., termination of most-favored-nation treatment for Communist countries), to the U-2 incident, perhaps even to violations of the UN Charter. There was clearly a violation of law at the Bay of Pigs in 1961 (and some have argued, also in the 1962 Cuban missile crisis). Especially—it is commonly accepted—the United States has violated the vague, complex, but real norms against "intervention" in Guatemala, in the Dominican Republic, many think also in Vietnam. The few instances in which the United States has been charged with violating its obligations as host to the United Nations also reflect American concern for "security" in relation to the dangers of Communism, as in failure to grant visas to "subversives" coming to United Nations Headquarters. But even when the United States engaged in illegal or questionable activity, concern for law was not wholly absent. At the Bay of Pigs, for example, ambivalence and restraint, induced in substantial measure by concern for law and obligation, limited the American involvement and left a residue of guilt and penitence that made another such action unlikely. In the Dominican Republic the United States eagerly strove to extricate itself and sought legitimization by the OAS—and, again, repetition appears less likely as a result.

The policies of the United States, then, have largely coincided with the efforts of international organization to improve national behavior in respect of law. As concerns its own behavior, since the United States is generally law-abiding, it has not suffered from the deterrent influence and the "execution" of law by international organization in the past and is not likely to regret them in future. When it fell from legal grace, it did not suffer at the hands of international organization, if only because it had the votes to prevent it. The uses of law by international organization in quest of justice and welfare commonly raise issues not of law observance but of contribution and cooperation. The United States has paid its budget obligations handsomely, and in other respects too it has for the most part been generous and cooperative although there will be debate as to whether it has been generous and cooperative enough.

In reaction to the conduct of other nations, too, the influence of international organization on the side of law and order has had the support of the United States. The failure of the League of Nations is commonly laid to the unwillingness of the powerful to enforce the law, and the United States sought to avoid that failure for the UN. It put its influence particularly behind the law against the use of force: It led resistance to aggression in Korea; it joined against its principal allies at Suez; in the Middle East it has sought to maintain and restore peace and to allocate blame with substantial objectivity. In Hungary and Czechoslovakia, I believe, it was not only a desire to score the Soviet Union but also concern for the law of the Charter that prompted American condemnation of aggression.

The United States has accommodated itself even to the unhappy tendency of international organizations to politicize law in their own operations, particularly to disregard constitutional limitations and established procedures. Violations of constitutions and procedures do not usually damage American interests immediately, directly, or obviously, and it comes easier for American officials to "run with the pack" than to risk a confrontation over principle reflecting intangible longer-term interests. It surely seems easier to give in to the majority wish in these "technical" respects than to have to give them something "real," like more money or some other substantive concession.

The bad times suffered by adjudication and arbitration also do no obvious violence to American policy, and the United States must even bear substantial blame for them. No doubt the United States would like others to resort to the Court to settle disputes but it has not set them an example although adjudication is in its tradition and its spirit and it could easily afford the costs and the risks; instead, this country's lead has been toward diminishing the importance of the ICJ and of adjudication and arbitration generally. The "acceptance" by the United States of the compulsory jurisdiction of the ICJ has been rendered specious by the sturdy survival of the Connally Amendment and its extravagant application belying the narrow conception orginally intended for the American reservation.[33] While resort to the ICJ for the settlement of disputes is provided in a number of treaties, the United States has brought no such disputes to the Court. Nor has the United States sought to use the Court in other disputes with the consent of the other party. It has been party to only one adversary proceeding, brought in 1950 by France in regard to American capitulation rights in Morocco, an anachronism which the United States was already preparing to give up.

Implications for the United States

For the largest part, then, what international organizations have done to make and enforce law reflects what the United States has wished them to do or, at least, has been content to have them do. Much of it the United States is content to have them continue doing. But things have been done and others are threatened that will trouble American policy.

Some of the problems created for the United States are minor. As long as the Connally Reservation persists, for example, it will be a small embarrass-ment giving a small lie to our protestations about the rule of law. (Unhap-

[33] There has been a disposition to treat the Reservation as an absolute "veto" on the Court's jurisdiction rather than as a right to make a bona fide determination in a close case that there is no question of international law or treaty. See "Pending Repeal of the Connally Amendment," *Record of the New York City Bar Association* (Vol. 19, No. 3). Compare the objection of the United States in the *Interhandel* case, where the United States invoked its reservation when Switzerland challenged the right of the United States to sequester property which the United States claimed belonged to an alien enemy corporation while Switzerland insisted it was a neutral Swiss corporation. See *I.C.J. Pleadings, Interhandel Case (Switzerland v. United States of America)*.

pily, we have not yet been embarrassed enough to repeal the Reservation.)
And, in general, failure to promote adjudication and arbitration tends to work
against American interests since the United States often stands to gain from
such impartial decision.

The lawmaking function of international organization also brings its embarrassments. Even formal legislation by multilateral convention, which does
not bind the United States without its consent, imposes political pressures to
which the United States cannot be impervious. The United States is not entirely comfortable when it continues to withhold adherence to convention after
convention on human rights produced by international effort. A Republican
Administration, I venture to guess, is not likely to seek to move the Senate
on the treaties pending before it or to ask its consent to the more comprehensive covenants recently negotiated, surely not to the protocol providing for
their "enforcement" upon complaint of other parties. Abstention by the United
States will encourage others to abstain, reduce the effect of these conventions,
and expose the United States to some criticism at home and abroad, even by
nations with records on human rights far less good than ours and which, if
they adhere to the covenants, might not in fact live up to them. There will be
particular pressures on the United States—concentrated in international organization, e.g., the UN Conference on Trade and Development (UNCTAD)
or the General Assembly—to accept new regimes for international finance and
international trade or to create new organizations with power, say, to regulate
exploitation of the resources of the sea.

More troublesome to the United States than the substance of any law which
international organizations have helped make are the processes by which
they sometimes purport to make it, notably the increasing disposition of the
UN General Assembly to make law by majority vote. The United States has
itself contributed to the "legislative power" of the Assembly during the years
when it commanded overwhelming majorities there. As the United States
has learned, an Assembly that can decide its own authority to "recommend"
action and to assess contributions can, under different influences, accelerate
the processes of decolonization faster than the United States might think desirable, call for sanctions—even military force—against South Africa and
Rhodesia, declare against the use of nuclear weapons even in self-defense. In
the future, although the United States will still often be able to prevent action to which it strongly objects, it will have to reckon with the strong temptation of majorities to assert legislative authority, a temptation that will increase
with continuing frustration and the importance of the interests involved.
While the legal quality and legal effect of General Assembly resolutions and
declarations can be denied, the United States cannot easily and always act
as though the Assembly had not spoken. It might be compelled to go along
with more or less modest extensions of law by Assembly action, whether on

trade, aid, arms control, regulation of the seas' resources, or other "welfare" legislation.

Different difficulties for the United States are promised by the insistence of majorities on pursuing relentlessly a political goal in the guise of enforcing international law. For the United States the principle of self-determination does not prove that all dependencies were ready for immediate independence; certainly it does not warrant the use of external force to bring about decolonization, as in Goa or against Angola or Southern Rhodesia. American policy is opposed to apartheid both in "Namibia" (the dependent area of South West Africa) and in the Republic of South Africa itself, but the United States has been less than enthusiastic about sanctions against the Republic and has resisted some stringent ones. In the future, too, no doubt, the United States will be pushed farther than it wishes to go in these embattled areas.

Of course, the United States must continue to face old questions as to how to "mix" national and international effort. It must decide again and again what it will do unilaterally or bilaterally, what through regional or universal bodies—as for instance in the distribution of financial and technical aid. It must decide where it will seek continued laissez-faire, where regulation by traditional treaties, bilateral or multilateral, where there should be organization, regional or universal. And it must continue to face also the consequences of the inadequacies of international organization for maintaining a legal order. International organization, I am satisfied, has had substantial deterrent influence to make nations observe law, even the law against use of force, but that influence is not enough; witness, for a recent sad example, the fate of Czechoslovakia. Continued insufficiencies will compel the United States to face the perennial problems: whether and how the UN can be strengthened, what supplementary or alternative institutions are called for, how much of the UN's job the United States is prepared to assume, where it will fight or assist others who will, where it will content itself with helpless condemnations.

CONCLUSION

International organization, I conclude, has served the cause of law. It has contributed to the ends which law pursues and to the law itself; it has helped to create an atmosphere of lawfulness, to make law, promote its observance, deter violation. It has, I believe, helped maintain the basic requirement of a legal order: the prohibition of force between nations. But political international organizations—and functional organizations that permit themselves to be "politicized"—have also detracted from the cause of law: They have sought to cloak political principles as law and to impose them on minorities; they have sometimes sacrificed legal principle to the *ad hoc* judgment of majorities; they have sometimes failed to apply law evenhandedly; they have been short-sightedly unprincipled about constitutions and procedures.

International organization, no doubt, will be a source of more law in the years ahead. I do not anticipate a major "breakthrough" to subject to law large anarchic areas in international relations but only "more of the same," more small steps, occasionally one less small in response to crisis. I see hope for law that will achieve some new regime for aid and trade, improve the government of international money and finance, impose some further "preventive" controls on new armaments, set preliminary guidelines for new order in new environments (outer space, the sea), anticipate other new problems to come with new technology (e.g., the awesome implications of weather control). In the future, too, international organizations will promote basic order and respect for law because they are in the common interest. I do not foresee dramatic rededication by nations to law observance, and in some areas some international organizations—the UN—may again encourage violations by those who are confident that majorities will condone or approve them. There is no reason to expect major submissions to supranational authority or renascence of third-party determination as a principal means of enforcing law or developing new law. I am hopeful that international organization will help keep alive the law against force, indispensable foundation for any meaningful order. I am hopeful—though I do not yet see how—that remnants of Western colonialism and racism in Africa, perpetuating a sense of injustice and breeding disorder, might yet be ended or modified without major rents in international society.

There is, and will be, a major contribution to legal order in the busyness of a multitude of organizations engaged in patching or building small additions onto the structure of international society. There is, and will be, a contribution to law when international organizations actively promote a sense of order, enforce law, and deter its violation. Even the most convinced "functionalist" will not claim that today's and the future's organization and law will bring lasting peace, perfect order, impeccable justice, universal well-being. No one would deny that they do and will govern important relations between nations, remove areas of contention, and add a significant increment to order, to justice, to welfare, to "the rule of law."

The contribution of international organization to the rule of law has largely coincided with American interests to date and will probably continue to do so in future. But there are tensions between the law desired by the United States and the law of majorities. The United States is more concerned with the law of order; majorities care more about law that will promote their conceptions of justice and their well-being. International organizations have begun to promote law in areas which the United States has long considered its own business and not a matter for international concern and scrutiny. They—the UN in particular—have sought to create law (without the concurrence of the United States) which the United States rejects. They—the UN in particular—have sought to enforce law against selected recalcitrants in circumstances and by means in which the United States was reluctant to concur. The United States has been more-or-less disturbed when international organization—the UN in particular—has sometimes converted legal questions into political ones, judging conduct not by principle but by the sum of private political judgments of a majority of governments.

Most important, the interests of the United States and of other nations within international organizations may diverge sharply in critical areas. Many nations seem bent on using law to solve "insoluble" political problems—the remnants of colonialism and racism in Africa—and to surmount "insurmountable" economic problems—the widening chasm between the rich few and the many poor. There may be new efforts to consummate the demise of white colonialism and racism by means which the United States will resist. There will be pressures for law on aid and trade going beyond what the United States is prepared to do. One cannot even be confident that there will be no major "radicalization" of international organizations, no attempts to revolutionize the processes of making law, no effort to impose revolutionary law. The disappointments and frustrations resulting from such confrontations may tear at international organization and have other unhappy consequences for American foreign relations, particularly with Black Africa, perhaps even in Latin America.

The United States will be caught between foreign pressures for greater cooperation in international organization and increasing resistance at home bearing the faces of economy and autonomy. If the United States turns inward to its awesome domestic problems of race and city, international cooperation will inevitably appear to involve sacrifice of domestic interests and domestic priorities, and generosity will begin at home and may end there. More conservative administrations and more resistant Congresses may not be easily moved, making life less comfortable for the United States in various international organizations and in its relations with many of their members. Economy drives and decreasing sympathy for some kinds of international organization activities will limit even the kind of cooperation that is easiest for the United States—giving money—although it seems unlikely that Congress would rebel against assessments of the present order of magnitude for the same kinds of purposes; there might be less generosity—for an important example—in concessions in trade policy at the direct expense of segments of the private sector of the American economy.

There will be other tensions. In their national elections in 1968, many believe, the American people voted for "law and order," and the Administration that will be governing in Washington when the next decade begins might claim that as its mandate. That slogan, of course, was strictly domestic in focus, and one cannot assume that a people and a government dedicated to law and order at home will value those goals as highly and pursue them as earnestly in the larger world. Indeed, one can support the view that while—as for our Constitutional fathers—concern for domestic tranquility goes with concern for the common defense, it tends rather to discourage active concern with international disorder. In the wake of Vietnam, and under diverse domestic pressures, the forces for internationalism are weakened and the constituency for cooperation through international organization and international law is in disarray. Traditional supporters may fall away and prospective recruits might turn in other directions. While, after Czechoslovakia, this country might strengthen its defenses, including the international organization and law of NATO, otherwise American internationalism might increasingly give way to some conjunction of isolationism and unilateral interventionism which would not be new to American policy. Internationalists will have no cause to be happier even if such policies are covered over with that specious internationalism which casts upon international organization tasks it cannot do or refuses to give it the means to do them.

And, in general, although a new President and his Secretary and Undersecretary of State are all lawyers, they may strike a note for a kind of law that is not the principal preoccupation of international organization and will hardly interest many other nations—the law of "law and order" that keeps things going along much as they are (albeit more smoothly) rather than the law that helps achieve change; the law of free enterprise and laissez-faire rather than the law of cooperation for the general welfare as conceived by the opinion of contemporary mankind. The United States might indeed tend to see the immediate advantages of autonomy more clearly than the longer ones of organization, of freedom from law more clearly than of order and of justice. If so, it will not lead—or follow—new marches to law, adhere to many new conventions, or accept third-party judgment for issues of substantial importance. In fact, revised conceptions of American interest might even begin to heed old voices that depreciate, deprecate, or dismiss law, erode some of the law that is, make this country less concerned about how others behave in regard to law and less troubled by how American behavior looks to others.

These are not predictions, only fears. Those of us who see the interests of the United States as lying in international cooperation rather than in unilateralism or solipsism, in more law rather than less, in the law that promotes welfare and justice even more than in the law that directly promotes order, must fear these fears and by taking heed strive to end them. Other nations, I believe, also have these fears about the United States, and their fears translate into loss of confidence in us, the weakening of alliances, responsive isolationism or political realignments in various corners of the world. A new Administration should be concerned quickly to prove these fears idle. What we say will be important but, in language dear to the previous Republican Administration, it will take deeds, not words.

The Dimension of Poverty

Patricia W. Blair

Toward the end of the Administration of Lyndon Johnson it became briefly popular to talk about programs for eliminating poverty at home *versus* programs for mitigating poverty abroad. But it can also be argued that the two are sides of the proverbial coin and that the experience of the one has meaning for the other. The present troubles of the domestic "war on poverty" do not diminish the value of the comparison. If anything, they enhance the need to consider the programs together.

The rationale for attacking poverty is much the same at home and abroad though better recognized domestically. The simple moral argument that the rich have an obligation to help the poor ("*God* says so," says a senior development scholar of my acquaintance not entirely facetiously) is perhaps more compelling than it is fashionable to admit. And the connection between poverty and insecurity for the rich has been made frequently. While the urgency of attacking domestic poverty is easier for Americans to see—after all, *our* cities are burning—the argument on the international plane is still obvious enough. Basically, we must simply recognize that we are in the business of building a community, a sense of shared purpose and shared destiny, both at home and abroad. The central values of our own civilization permit no less. "Anti-commitment," as Harlan Cleveland says, is "irrelevant."[1]

At home we have long accepted the proposition that a community must take responsibility for the welfare of all its members and that this will require some form of concerted action in favor of the weak and the poor. If nothing else so dictates, the familiar shrinkage of our planet requires that we apply the same reasoning to the world at large. It would be foolish to convince ourselves that the problem is simply one of economics. "This is the decade of the Negro's claim to full equality in *all* aspects of American life," James Tobin

Patricia W. Blair was formerly editor of the *Development Digest*, a journal prepared by the National Planning Association for the United States Agency for International Development (AID).

[1] Harlan Cleveland, "The Irrelevance of Anti-Commitment," paper presented to the American Political Science Association, September 1968.

has written.[2] Equally, it is the era of the have-not nations' claim to full membership in the world community.

Modern communities do not try to equalize incomes, but they do try to curb gross disparities and to structure policy to facilitate upward mobility for the underprivileged. The width of the still-growing gap between rich nations and poor and the depths of poverty at the lower end surely imply the need for some effort at closing the gap. John Pincus points out the issue:

> The quest for a valid rationale for aid or concessions [to the poor of the world] is ultimately insoluble when we limit our analysis to "objective" considerations, and forgo any resort to questions of values. . . . Once the analysis is done, stubborn issues of equity remain . . . . the case for aid must ultimately rest in part on grounds of income redistribution.[3]

Income redistribution does not seem to be an important international goal, however. The most ambitious official target, as endorsed by the first United Nations Conference on Trade and Development (UNCTAD), is to transfer in all forms only one percent of a rich country's gross national product annually to the developing world, less than half of the proportion of GNP that the United States devoted to European recovery at the height of the Marshall Plan. Even that goal is still far from being met. At best the idea seems to be to bring the poor over some "poverty line" to a point of self-sustaining growth which is presumably reached when concessional aid is no longer considered necessary.[4] This much more modest goal should indeed be feasible. Just as there has been considerable statistical success in bringing American families over the poverty line, there has already been some success in bringing nations over it.[5]

Nevertheless, to continue Tobin's line of argument, "the poverty that remains has become a greater threat to the social order."[6] The reasons are obvious. Now that the grime of hopelessness and inertia has been swept largely away we can see more clearly that racial discrimination, cultural impoverishment, and political inequity are also part of the explanation for the domestic and world poverty gaps; and they account for much of the explosive quality of the drive of the poor to achieve social justice. The abrasive demands of the

---

[2] James Tobin, "Raising the Incomes of the Poor," in Kermit Gordon (ed.), *Agenda for the Nation* (Washington: Brookings Institution, 1962), p. 114.

[3] John Pincus, *Trade, Aid, and Development: The Rich and Poor Nations* (Atlantic Policy Studies) (New York: McGraw-Hill [for the Council on Foreign Relations], 1967), pp. 13–14.

[4] Definition of this "line" is still unclear. Countries with less than $250 per capita income are considered to qualify for "soft" loans from the International Development Association (IDA). The Republic of China (Nationalist China) was "graduated" from aid-recipient status at $190 per capita by AID. Chile, with a per capita income of $691 (1968), is still a major recipient of United States aid.

[5] Although the world poverty gap is still growing, thanks mainly to still-high birth rates in the poor countries, the success stories are numerous enough to prove that the poverty line can be breached internationally. See, for example, the growth experiences of Greece, Turkey, Israel, Mexico, Venezuela, Nationalist China, the Republic of Korea (South Korea), soon Iran, maybe the Ivory Coast, as well as specific sectors like education or industry in country after country.

[6] Tobin, p. 114.

Stokely Carmichaels and the Sukarnos pour out of the same well of bitterness. Building a community, it seems, will require a much more searching look at *all* the needs of the poor and a much greater willingness to listen to the poor themselves. Senator William Fulbright has rightly indicated that we will need to change, if not reverse, the way we have traditionally looked at the world's have-nots:

> As with most important adjustments in human affairs, the first and most important requirement . . . is a change in our *thinking*. . . . We must develop a new idea of generosity, one which purports to help people without humiliating them, one which accepts the general advancement of the community rather than cloying expressions of gratitude as its just and proper reward.[7]

In the past we have tended to assume that "natural" economic growth would gradually eliminate domestic poverty or at least keep it within bounds as a political issue. Similarly, the rich nations once seemed to assume that, with expansion in international trade, development would naturally trickle down to the poor of the world with perhaps a small assist in the way of aid. Some of the new states once seemed to think that independence would "automatically" bring the fruits of modernization. We have all learned that these things will not happen. In international affairs, as in domestic, there is no substitute for policy.

In what follows I will try to show that our policy response to international poverty has been heavily influenced by nineteenth-century images. At best we have moved toward the "Big Government" attitudes of the New Deal: a series of centrally administered welfare programs characterized by minimal provision of material goods and maximum bureaucratic oversight into the life of the recipient. At home, however, our new perceptions are leading to new policy prescriptions. I will try to suggest some of the thinking stimulated by looking at the question of international aid through the lens of these new insights into domestic poverty.

I do not mean in this analysis to deny the very real accomplishments of the existing international programs or to imply that they have nothing to teach domestic ones. Indeed, one can argue that domestic programs have benefited considerably from the international ones and have been able to seek new directions in part because experience has taught us how necessary they are. Nor do I mean to imply that domestic programs do not have their own peculiar debilities or that differences between individual poor do not require different policies. My interest is merely to mine a different vein for whatever ore it may uncover.

[7] J. William Fulbright, *The Arrogance of Power* (New York: Random House, 1966), pp. 240–241.

The Aid Relationship—Outdated Images

The image of Lady Bountiful salving her conscience with a basket of food and castoffs has been outdated in the United States for some time. It is not so outdated when we consider the "aid" programs of the "donor" countries. The very terms evoke the dowager giving away the fruits of her (husband's) labor. In fact, of course, very little has actually been given away to the developing countries of Latin America, Africa, and Asia.[8] Annual transfers from all sources reached $11 to $12 billion in the mid-1960's. In the shorthand generally used all this has come to be counted as "aid." Indeed, real benefits accrue to developing countries from many international transfers of funds or people whatever their terms or auspices. But the transfers have not been charitable donations, nor have they been defended as such. They have included private investment, on which profits are expected, and export credits, whose purpose is to enable the poor to buy the goods produced by the rich. A healthy chunk of the $6–7 billion now being transferred annually under the auspices of donor governments[9] is given for the overt political purposes of the donor or to subsidize elements of its domestic economy. For example, out of the total United States official aid of $4.7 billion in fiscal year 1968 about $500,-000,000 (exclusive of military aid) went to the Republic of Vietnam (South Vietnam), a similar sum was allocated by the Export-Import Bank which lends to promote United States exports, and $1.4 billion was for surplus commodities under Public Law 480, at least a part of which subsidizes American farmers. The amount given or loaned specifically to combat world poverty by promoting development is thus much smaller than the annual aid totals would indicate. And even this is heavily hedged with restrictions to protect the rich countries' balance of payments; this "tying" has the effect of reducing the effective amount of aid as much as 20 percent below the totals indicated.

In the United States, taxpayer mythology seems to envision aid as "handing over bags of money"[10] to irresponsible governments. Actually, of course, American aid money is spent by the government to which it is "given" almost exclusively (98 percent at last count) in the United States for purchases of American goods, to employ American nationals, to subsidize American shipowners, and so forth. Furthermore, the major recipient governments now obtain most of their aid in the form of loans repayable in United States dollars at interest rates ranging as high as 6 or 7 percent a year for official loans and more for private credits. Defaults to date have been minimal. Yet the term "giveaway" persists as does the vague sense of self-satisfaction and superiority associated with giving charity.

[8] The giveaway image may persist partly because the massive funds transferred to Europe under the Marshall Plan *were* largely in the form of grants.

[9] Excluding transfers from Communist countries which seem to run a mere $300–400 million a year.

[10] Editorial in the *Times-Union* (Jacksonville, Florida), February 4, 1969.

The more sophisticated, naturally, have long since discarded the Lady Bountiful image of rich-poor relations. As in domestic life, they have welcomed her displacement by the professional—in this case the development economist rather than the social worker. And indeed this change is a step forward, one for which United States academies and administrators deserve much of the credit. The United States Agency for International Development (AID), the United Nations, the International Bank for Reconstruction and Development (IBRD), the Organization for Economic Cooperation and Development (OECD), and the universities are full of people who have devoted their working lives to the question of what makes for growth in poor countries. A great deal more is known today of the causes of economic backwardness and the engines of growth. But professionalism has its limits. Economic model-building can be just as stultifying, just as self-perpetuating, just as irrelevant to the problems of moving a nation of poor as individual case work can be to the problems of a ghetto. Economics—as even the economists are coming to admit—can provide only partial answers to what is only partly an economic problem.

Closely related to Lady Bountiful (her husband, no doubt) is Horatio Alger. How many times have the poor been exhorted to work harder, to be patient, to pull themselves up by their own bootstraps? Self-help and Operation Bootstrap are clichés in the foreign aid business. Given reasonable opportunity and some luck, poor nations would rather develop on their own. In fact, developing countries as a whole are already financing about 80 percent of their total investment themselves. The rub is that some of the most serious problems of poverty cannot be solved by the single individual or even nation working alone.

Group self-help in the form of political pressure on the rich by the organized poor has probably had rather more to do with escape from poverty than any individual effort. Many now "respectable" development institutions, including the Inter-American Development Bank (IDB), the UN Special Fund, the International Development Association (IDA) of the World Bank, even the Bank's International Finance Corporation (IFC) which encourages private enterprise, owe their origin directly to the insistence of the poor on their "right" to development capital on concessional terms. Unfortunately, the limitations of poor-country "trade unionism" quickly become apparent. The "group of 77" developing countries in UNCTAD, for example, must still depend on the willingness of the rich to make substantive economic concessions. This is partly because organized poor countries cannot do what organized poor laborers can often do: meaningfully withhold their labor. At least for the present the rich countries have little economic necessity to maintain a dialogue with the poor.

Our domestic and international welfare programs have had just enough success to raise the animus of the poor without actually giving them much stake in the national or world community. Tobin's words concerning the poor in the United States apply internationally:

> Simply lifting the bottom of the income distribution will not set the situation right so long as Negroes feel that the institutions of society conspire to confine them to the bottom.[11]

If the general health of the community is the accepted goal, certain things seem to follow. First, the welfare dimension will always be with us. It is hard to envision a community in which *someone* is not weaker than the rest for whatever reason. International poverty programs have consistently been billed as temporary though estimated terminal dates seem to get further and further away. If one focuses only on the middle and larger developing countries, it may one day be possible to end concessional transfers of capital. But I can see no prospect of freeing many of the smallest nations, for example, from dependence on some kind of special international favors.

Individual recipients will change, of course, just as they do at home. Some "make it" to the middle class. Others stabilize somewhat closer to the poverty line. Some strike it rich. Some give up. Some never even try. Aid totals will also change. More importantly, the kinds of policies needed will change. In some cases and in some eras programs should concentrate, as they do now, on helping the poor to generate their own capital; in others concentration may appropriately be on "civil rights" for governments or individuals; in some permanent handicaps will seem to call for specialized rehabilitation or a continuing subsidy, or both; in still others community services may be most helpful.

In addition, the political dimension will require more attention. The poor must be given, and must feel they have, a real stake in the continuation of the community. As lower-middle-class support for the 1968 presidential candidacy of George Wallace showed, a certain prosperity is no necessary cure for political disaffection. When important numbers of people or nations feel unable to make themselves and their concerns politically effective, alienation is the all too likely result. If international programs are to cope with these political factors, they will involve some sacrifice of relative wealth and power on the part of the rich. It is best to face this issue squarely. As long as the institutions of world community seem to conspire to confine today's have-not nations to the bottom, the system will not, indeed, be set right.

This is emotional language. Clearly, it is an emotional issue. Precisely for that reason we need to look for mechanisms and institutions that will help to defuse the situation. These will not be found within the existing aid system where both political and technocratic pressures put a premium on intense

---

[11] Tobin, p. 79.

donor involvement in the affairs of the recipient. Rather, we will have to work toward an international system that offers both rich and poor genuine opportunity for mobility and that requires from both a significant measure of responsibility. The more such a system can be made to work through relatively impersonal, even automatic, mechanisms, the better. For example, we will need to look for the international equivalents of social security systems, labor-management contracts, and other devices that have helped to define domestic relations between rich and poor in a way that is tolerable, if not entirely acceptable, to both at the same time as they permit the necessary change. We will need to ensure that market forces permit the ambitious poor to make gains and consolidate them. In this kind of system aid programs would involve only community activities to deal with removing specific disabilities or compensating for those that cannot be removed.

Lessons from Domestic Programs

This has been a difficult year for proponents of international poverty programs. Just about everyone feels the "disenchantment of the rich" that Robert McNamara, President of the World Bank, complained of.[12] International aid programs have clearly lost whatever dynamism they once had. Perhaps what we lack, as Senator Fulbright says, is a way of thinking about poverty and the poor that would help us to strike out in new, more purposeful directions.

Here, although distance doubtless lends enchantment to this observer, aspects of the early days of the war on poverty seem worth investigating. In implementation these programs suffered from the same kinds of disabilities as international ones: administrative confusion and overlapping, insufficient funding, inadequacies of personnel, corruption. Nevertheless, some of them seem to have had a strength and relevance not always present in their international counterparts.

Venturesomeness

Part of the reason for the chaotic administrative state of the domestic poverty programs is that they are, or at least were, experimental. Programs ranged from education for preschool children to model cities, from mobilizing unemployed youth to encouraging black capitalism, from cooperatives for the rural poor to employment of the aged. And each facet was accorded substantially more than pilot-project status. In contrast, international poverty programs have tended to put their most important resources at the service first of one then another presumed cure-all, with never enough time or money for results to show. Theodore Geiger lists some of the different approaches:

12 Robert McNamara, "Address to the Board of Governors," address delivered to the World Bank's Board of Governors, Washington, September 30, 1968, p. 3.

> Beginning in the early 1950's, a succession of simplistic prescriptions . . . were confidently expected to overcome easily and rapidly the obstacles impeding economic growth and social change. Such development panaceas have included capital investment, technical assistance, community development, comprehensive national development planning and . . . educational development. [Today Geiger might have added birth control and private incentives.] All of these . . . are necessary parts of an effort to accelerate . . . growth . . . , but even together —much less individually—they do not encompass the many interrelated . . . factors involved in the social process.[13]

Where experiments were undertaken, they were too often in the form of small pilot projects so well coddled that success could not be repeated on a broader scale.

Furthermore, the war on poverty early and wisely exhibited a willingness to seek new faces, a certain mistrust of the older bureaucracies. In retrospect, the early foreign aid programs made a mistake in relying for technical expertise on secondment from functional agencies—the United States Department of Agriculture and the Bureau of Reclamation, the Food and Agriculture Organization (FAO), the International Labor Organization (ILO), etc. In too many instances these agencies happily unloaded their most mediocre talent and in too many instances these men still embarnacle the aid organizations.

For policy direction the aid programs have developed a cadre of development professionals. Their successes have been in the areas where competent bureaucrats can be expected to succeed: in coordination (about 25 percent of official United States transfers to developing countries are now discussed jointly with other donors in settings variously labeled consortia, consultative groups, etc.); and in ordering of priorities (within countries this is done through devices like country programming and between them through concentration of aid in about a dozen key, usually large, developing nations). Nevertheless, except for the American Peace Corps and related international efforts the *panache,* the esprit, of the early war on poverty and of some early foreign aid efforts has eluded the international programs for too long. It has vanished now from the domestic programs too. But I am not sure we can expect rejuvenated poverty programs either at home or abroad without it.

Civic and Social Awareness

In the United States the range of community action programs and the courses in political effectiveness and Afro-American history are reflections of an emphasis on civic and social awareness. Partly under their impulse the importance of the civic and social aspects of world poverty has come increas-

[13] Theodore Geiger, *The Conflicted Relationship: The West and the Transformation of Asia, Africa and Latin America* (Atlantic Policy Studies) (New York: McGraw-Hill [for the Council on Foreign Relations], 1967), p. 277.

ingly to be recognized.[14] It may be, as some say, that long-run social and political goals can be pursued only at the expense of short-run economic growth.
That case is by no means proven, however. In any event, both appear necessary
to the task of modernization, to say nothing of the principles of equity.

The American Congress has insisted on including this aspect of modernization in international aid programs. Somewhat to the dismay of economically
oriented professionals Title IX of the 1966 AID legislation directs that

> emphasis shall be placed on assuring maximum participation . . . of the people
> of the developing countries through the encouragement of democratic private
> and local governmental institutions.[15]

American aid administrators are still trying to find useful ways to translate
this directive into actual programs.

Although civic and cultural programs are more difficult to fashion, their
results more difficult to measure, and their goals indubitably more controversial, the thrust of Title IX is a positive addition to the development lexicon.
Adapting it to multilateral development institutions may prove particularly
difficult. Politically sensitive and vulnerable by nature, the staffs of these institutions tend to see themselves as "neutral" technocrats concerned only with
what will maximize economic growth. Perhaps more than others they hesitate
to consider problems of *distributing* growth and they fear that emphasis on
popular participation will only exacerbate those problems. Furthermore, the
representatives of the world poor at international organizations often come
from privileged groups with little concern for, if not active fear of, sharing
power or wealth in their own countries. American leadership may thus be
particularly important. Max Millikan suggests that

> the fact that Americans are now aware of problems of bringing about an ade-
> quate level of participation by elements of their own population should make
> discussion of these problems with foreigners easier rather than harder.[16]

Cultural Openmindedness

One element that appears in some domestic poverty programs has yet to
take root in their international counterparts. Aside from some "orientation"
programs there seem to be few equivalents to the "sensitivity" sessions for
social workers, teachers, and other domestic aid personnel advocated in some
domestic quarters. These easily degenerate into a Western kind of Commu-

---

[14] Gunnar Myrdal has also played an important part in moving this range of problems closer to the
center of world poverty thinking. See *Asian Drama: An Inquiry into the Poverty of Nations* (3 vols.;
New York: Twentieth Century Fund, 1968). Myrdal's emphasis on corruption may be the international
equivalent of Patrick Moynihan's emphasis on the frailty of Negro family life. We are more aware of
these factors now and more willing to talk about them but, by and large, we have yet to evolve any
useful way of coping with them.

[15] "Foreign Assistance Act of 1966," in *U.S. Statutes at Large,* Vol. 80 (1966), Part 1 (Washington:
U.S. Government Printing Office, 1967), p. 800.

[16] Max F. Millikan, "The United States and Low-Income Countries," in Gordon (ed.), p. 525.

nist self-criticism complete with breast-beating, false humility, heightened
tension, and a certain irrelevance to the immediate problem. But they underline the need for change on *both* sides of the rich-poor relationship and are
probably healthy transitional devices. In addition they underline the relevance
of style and vocabulary. Walter Goodman reports on the participation of three
representatives of the New Politics in a seminar of older liberals at Princeton
University last year:

> They complained repeatedly of a lack of passion . . . not enough people there
> in fatigues and berets . . . and when they rose it was less to advance the course
> of argument, than to exhibit themselves to the dispassionate middle-aged as
> avatars of righteous indignation. They were constantly bearing witness. . . .
> They seem to have fallen into the belief that all international difficulties are
> susceptible to marches and slogans . . . . [Their] strong suit was the large ges-
> ture. . . . Their reiterated suspicion of reason when it is not adorned with
> emotion's trappings came out . . . clearly.[17]

Anyone familiar with non-Western, particularly African, participation in
United Nations debates will find much to recognize in this description. And
many will find much to deplore.

But marches and slogans undermined an American president and a French
one. The large gesture of the 1960 Declaration on the Granting of Independence to Colonial Countries and Peoples[18] and related resolutions has undoubtedly occasioned a radical reinterpretation of the United Nations Charter and
international law. "Irresponsible" pressures have undoubtedly made the UN
General Assembly more responsive to the concerns of the emerging nations
not only in economic and social fields but also in the matter of politics and
racial discrimination. Acceptance of the validity of other styles and other
vocabularies changes the way we see real problems which in turn changes
the kinds of solutions proposed. The reality behind the rhetoric of the international have-nots has been too easily dismissed by the policymakers of the
rich countries.

Political Unwisdom

Another facet of the war on domestic poverty has been the willingness of
its theorists to contemplate fundamental, radical programs that seemed to have
little real prospect of being translated into action in the near future. As recently as the early 1960's a few economists began working out the implications of various income maintenance schemes. The idea of guaranteed work
schemes and the possibility of wholesale grants to state and local governments
are now receiving similar attention.

[17] Walter Goodman, "The Liberal Establishment Faces the Blacks, the Young, the New Left," *The
New York Times Magazine* (section 6), December 29, 1968, passim.
[18] General Assembly Resolution 1514 (XV), December 14, 1960.

Our international poverty programs have for too long concentrated on gimmickry: a change of name (TCA to FOA to MSA to ICA to AID to ---, for example[19]); a shaking up of administrative tables of organization (cycles of functional and geographical orientation go back to the beginning of aid history both in the United States and in the UN); a provision of an aid patina for programs basically designed to meet other problems (food surpluses, support for military allies, etc.); a lumping of diverse transfers under the heading of "aid" to make programs seem bigger or, alternatively, a shifting of aid programs to other agencies to make them seem smaller; and so on.

The most constructive development specialists have concentrated on short-term problems: how to improve development lending, technical assistance, etc.; how to get more aid money out of the United States Congress; how to reverse trends toward protectionism in trade; how to give donor consortia and consultative groups more substantive responsibility; and so on. These are important concerns, but too little attention is being paid to elaborating the possibilities of more fundamental reforms. What, for example, might an international progressive income tax on rich nations look like? What structural changes in the *donor* economies would be required by a serious effort to encourage imports from developing countries? How might we devise a new regime to make international business more accountable to the community at large? What other aspects of international law need revision? What are the options for basic international monetary reform? Might we agree on a wholesale review of the burgeoning problem of debt among poor nations? How might international poverty programs be made independent of annual parliamentary appropriations without becoming the exclusive province of a group of technocrats? How can the special needs of small, unviable territories be met without compromising their right to independence? How might rich-country immigration policies mitigate the problems of both overpopulation and skill shortages in poor countries? How can we all work together on such universal problems as urban squalor, environmental pollution, youthful alienation? The stimulus of such exercises is, at the very least, considerable; and the example of the seriousness with which politicians now take schemes for income or work guarantees should prove that such exercises may not be so unwise politically after all.

Accommodation

Institutionalizing participation of the poor in policymaking may be the most important contribution of domestic poverty programs. This aspect of the domestic program is lately more honored in the breach since those who supply

[19] In this capsulated history of institutional name-changing the Technical Cooperation Administration was followed by the Foreign Operations Administration which in turn became the Mutual Security Administration. MSA was succeeded by the International Cooperation Administration which later evolved into AID.

finance and administrative support always seem tempted to opt for greater standardization, greater "efficiency," greater control. But the strategy continues to make sense. It minimizes many of the difficulties inherent in any donor-donee relationship: the donor's condescension and insistence on gratitude, the recipient's loss of confidence and self-respect, and so on. Furthermore, it makes the not unreasonable assumption that the poor have a right to participate in policymaking which affects their own future and an obligation to take some responsibility for the result. (Institutionalizing the participation of the poor in policymaking is not the same thing as is currently meant by "self-help" in aid jargon; the latter usually signifies changes in recipient-government policy recommended—nay, insisted on—by donors.)

At the international level Geiger points out that

> the eagerness and manifest ability of the donors to carry on [development] functions for the recipients inhibit the latter from developing their own capacity for initiative, decisionmaking, administration, and self-responsibility.[20]

He advocates that, much in the manner of the domestic model cities program or the postwar European Recovery Program (ERP), the United States

> limit itself to responding to the initiatives of the recipient countries, specifying in advance, if it wishes, the general kinds of programs and projects it is prepared to finance and the terms and conditions of its aid.[21]

While it may not be possible to make such a wholesale reversal of international aid policy, surely the thrust of this line of thinking has much to commend it.

The lack of meaningful participation in aid policymaking by recipient governments has been one of the greatest problems in rich-poor relations. Individually, recipients have to a greater or lesser extent made development plans (with a greater or lesser admixture of foreign advice) and have had, presumably, some influence on the way aid is used in their countries. Some have learned to play donors against one another to obtain more aid, more advantageous terms, etc. But, with rare exceptions, they have had little individual or collective part in determining how and in what form, much less in what amount, external transfers should flow to the developing world, and they have not had to accept responsibility for those aspects either.

The inter-American system has made the most serious attempt to incorporate the poor into policymaking machinery, perhaps in part because Latin insistence on taking responsibility, expressed first through the Economic Commission for Latin America (ECLA), meshed in time with United States perception of a Cuban threat to its security. The culmination of a drive to adapt the system to the economic and social needs of its poorer members was the

---

[20] Theodore Geiger, "The Lessons of the Marshall Plan for Development Aid Today," *Looking Ahead* (Washington, National Planning Association), May 1967 (Vol. 15, No. 4), p. 3.

[21] *Ibid.*

establishment in 1964 of the Inter-American Committee on the Alliance for Progress (CIAP) as the permanent executive committee of the Inter-American Economic and Social Council (IA-ECOSOC), itself a relatively recent innovation. CIAP has been called "perhaps the most interesting and potentially significant innovation in the OAS structure in recent years."[22] As originally envisioned, it was to have had wide powers of decision as to the form and allocation of *Alianza* funds, powers which would be complemented by the technical evaluation of a committee of independent experts. In the event, the Panel of Experts of the Alliance for Progress, the "Nine Wise Men" has been discontinued, and the "principle . . . [of] submitting aid decisions to an independent and functional organ . . . [has] received . . . less and less lip-service."[23] Evidently, lingering mistrust and perceptions of risk both in United States and Latin American governments have led to second thoughts. Nevertheless, CIAP's potential remains, as does the precedent for other international organizations. The important point is less the attempt to establish a kind of hemispheric brain trust in the Committee of Wise Men[24] than the attempt to give the political system real responsibility for the welfare of its members.

It is with respect to this last point that universal international organizations may play their greatest role. For in these institutions the issues of concern to the poor countries can be brought together, traded off, and discussed in a broad context. Is the effort involved in pressing for more aid worth the cost of countenancing continued inaction on lowering trade barriers, for example? Is a militant General Assembly resolution on Rhodesia worth the risk of scaring off potential investors from Africa? Can disarmament be advanced to the point where American promises of increased aid from the savings can be tested? In the complex of organs associated with the United Nations and in regional institutions organized along similar lines it should be possible to find arrangements that would not, as in UNCTAD, pit the poor majority against the massed antagonism of the rich but which would also not, as in the donor's Development Assistance Committee (DAC),[25] imply that the voices of the poor are irrelevant.

Furthermore, the possibilities for other forms and other forums have yet to be thoroughly explored. Frank Coffin sensibly points out, for example, that parliamentarians have "no forum . . . where economic questions . . . are systematically discussed with preparation and in depth" although their concur-

[22] John C. Dreier, "New Wine and Old Bottles: The Changing Inter-American System," *International Organization*, Spring 1968 (Vol. 22, No. 2), p. 483.

[23] Paul Rosenstein-Rodan, "La marcha de la Alianza para el Progreso," cited and translated by Raúl Sáez S., "The Nine Wise Men and the Alliance for Progress," *International Organization*, Winter 1968 (Vol. 22, No. 1), p. 254.

[24] See UN Document E/AC.54/L.28 for a proposal by Max Millikan to establish a similar organization on a worldwide basis.

[25] DAC is a part of OECD but encompasses a broader membership and has an independent chairman.

rence in economic policy is vital. He suggests that such a forum be devised to
include lawmakers from both rich and poor countries.

> The benefits would be twofold: There would be a recognition that countries
> other than one's own were deeply involved in the assistance effort; and the
> exchange between . . . the rich and the poor ought to be healthy and humbling
> for both sides. There is, of course, the risk that the net result might be to pro-
> voke a destructive confrontation and to reenforce existing prejudices. That
> risk is well worth taking, for it is inconceivable that the task . . . can be accom-
> plished without more influential, knowledgeable, and committed parliamen-
> tarians.[26]

The major drawbacks of the universal international organizations as vehicles for welfare programs have been the tendency to spread available funds
too thin in an attempt to satisfy all members, the related inclination to political timidity, the tendency to spawn new organizations for each new program
element (with consequent weaknesses of administration), and the inability
to command large amounts of money. One may also argue that the tendency
for all issues to be debated in the context of their meaning for the poor is unhealthy in the long run. Nevertheless, the relationship between the haves and
the have-nots may well be the most fundamental long-term problem of international relations today, one to which international organizations could make
a unique contribution. Ruth Russell emphasizes a slightly different, perhaps
even more important aspect:

> Any plan [that] . . . would help create . . . improved relations between the
> West and the Third World . . . would also meaningfully "strengthen" the
> United Nations in the only way in which that can be done—through using it.[27]

If this is to be tried, however, much greater effort will have to be put into
restructuring the machinery to make it better able to organize effective programs to meet the needs of the poor. This does not mean simply, or necessarily, the United Nations Capital Development Fund for which the poor have
been pressing since the 1949 General Assembly session. Nor does it mean the
obsolescence of bilateral programs. Rather, it means evolving machinery to
take account of both equity and political reality in the field of international
welfare policy. It means resolving questions of priority both as to function
and geographic distribution of funds. It means finding a way to include states
and territories presently excluded. It means clearing away some of the under-
brush of postcolonial inequities. It means curbing the vested interests of the
functional specialized agencies and integrating the World Bank group and
the International Monetary Fund (IMF) much closer into the international

---

[26] Frank M. Coffin, "Multilateral Assistance: Possibilities and Prospects," *International Organization,*
Winter 1968 (Vol. 22, No. 1), p. 284.

[27] Ruth B. Russell, *The United Nations and United States Security Policy* (Washington: Brookings
Institution, 1968), pp. 413–414.

network. It means considering seriously, and improving on, some of the existing quasi-automatic proposals for increasing monetary transfers and relating them to other aspects of the poor's economic needs.[28] It means evolving machinery and techniques for conciliation of differences before they can lend themselves to a kind of international confrontation politics. In short, it means creating a new basis, through the international mechanism, for intercourse between rich and poor.

THE CURRENT DEBATE

The approach taken above is quite different from that currently fashionable in the United States in favor of increased multilateralism in aid-giving. Those pressing for this reform today seem largely motivated by the desire to escape Congressional antagonism to foreign aid and the annual scrutiny that gives vent to that antagonism. The virtues claimed for multilateral aid are that it stimulates "a fair sharing of the burden by other countries" and that it "eliminates unhealthy political engangements [sic] from the aid process."[29] But the main advantage is presumed to be a relative insulation from the Congressional axe. "In the five years that I was presenting these [multilateral] programs to hard-nosed Appropriations Committees," remembers Harlan Cleveland, former Assistant Secretary of State for International Organization Affairs, "I was astonished to find we almost never lost a dime from the President's request to Congress."[30]

Aside from the question of how soon multilateral agencies could handle greatly increased funds this rationale begs some very important issues. First, it would be difficult to maintain the international character of multilateral institutions if the United States contribution were commensurate with its wealth. Millikan estimates that the United States "should" be supplying perhaps 60 percent to 70 percent of total aid funds. If American funding for multilateral agencies were to reach these proportions, as he points out, "the alleged advantages [of multilateralism] . . . in host-country receptivity to influence and in improvements in the U.S. image would be open to serious question."[31] The United States would still be blamed by others for too much activism and by Congress for things that went wrong. Furthermore, neither Congress nor the

---

[28] One of the most useful proposals is that of Maxwell Stamp, the British economist, for adding to the financing available to developing countries by reserving for their use a special portion of the new liquidity that will be created if the proposed special drawing rights (SDR's) are activated. Another proposal, by David Horowitz, Director of the Bank of Israel, would ask rich governments to subsidize the interest rates on monies raised by IDA in their private capital markets.

[29] Arthur J. Goldberg, "A New Foreign Policy for America—VII," *The Washington Post*, September 14, 1968.

[30] Cleveland, p. 8.

[31] Millikan in Gordon (ed.), p. 546.

State Department has proved averse to injecting domestic policy into inter-national aid programs.[32]

As to burden sharing, when measured by such tests of "sacrifice" as percent of gross national product or per capita contribution, the United States has for several years been carrying *less* than its "fair share" of the development-trans-fer burden. Among donor governments

> the U.S. now ranks seventh in percent of national income devoted to official aid. We rank tenth in terms of official and private aid combined. We now provide a smaller share of national income as aid than the average. And this is before taking into account this year's [FY 1969] drastic aid cuts.[33]

International organizations have historically required relatively small appro-priations which have been acceptable as "conscience money." When larger sums are involved, however, the attractions of multilateral agencies seem to diminish rapidly. In fiscal year 1969 Congress failed to vote the laboriously negotiated American share of either IDA replenishment or the Asian Devel-opment Bank's Special Fund, though strong support from the new Adminis-tration ultimately saved the former. It may well be that one result of multi-lateralizing aid would be a sharp reduction in total aid funds.

Two other objections to multilateralizing aid as presently conceived are perhaps more serious. First, the usual assumption is that funds would be channeled largely through the World Bank group whose reputation for pro-bity and efficiency is extremely high in the United States. The international agencies with a greater admixture of recipient control—the United Nations Development Program (UNDP) and related technical assistance programs, the newer regional banks, UNCTAD, etc.—rank considerably lower in public esteem. Little consideration has been given to how much support these would get under a multilateral policy though the delay in American funding for the Asian Development Bank does not augur well.

From the United States point of view making the World Bank Group the chief dispenser of development funds would be a "safe" solution, a way of simultaneously having one's cake and eating it. In line with the size of its financial contribution the United States presently has 25 percent of the voting power in IBRD, 64 percent with its DAC partners. Indeed, in most of the world the Bank is already considered far too sensitive to American policy positions. Significantly, most of our fellow *donors* are considerably more re-luctant than we are to contemplate enhancing the Bank's role. Insofar as multilateralization through the World Bank and its affiliates is seen by them

---

[32] See, for example, objections of both to approving UN Special Fund projects in Cuba. (Russell, pp. 341–342.) Perhaps the most notable example is Congressional insistence that American representatives to international organizations oppose aid to any country that has expropriated property of United States citizens without "adequate" compensation.

[33] William S. Gaud, "Development—A Balance Sheet," address to the International Development Con-ference, November 1968, p. 9. (Mimeographed.)

or the recipients as a subterfuge for maintaining United States control, therefore, it will be less acceptable.

Perhaps even more basic is the fact that proposals to increase the Bank's responsibilities—in effect, to ask it to take charge of world development strategy —assume (though this is rarely spelled out) that the problem of eradicating world poverty is primarily technical. While a certain consensus on economic strategy does appear to be developing, there is some question whether the Bank could gear itself to tackle the aspects of *economic* growth whose short-term returns are less visible, to say nothing of the social and civic aspects of modernization, much less the matter of inherited inequities.[34] It has been argued that part of the Bank's success is due to its ability to skim the economically productive projects off the top of development needs precisely because bilateral programs existed to take on the messier jobs.

PROBLEMS OF ACCOMMODATION

International aid programs, under any auspices, are only one aspect of the attack on world poverty even when the problem is narrowly defined in economic terms. Just as the American poor, the international poor may well suspect that the international order is designed to confine them to the bottom of the economic heap. The fear that their destiny may be to supply primary products under steadily worsening terms of trade—or worse yet, to depend permanently on "crumbles" (in the words of Gunnar Myrdal) from the rich —dies hard. It is not abated by the difficulty of reaching agreements to stabilize the prices of the commodities in which the poor countries are most interested, to say nothing of the apparent political impossibility of getting even serious discussion of more general schemes to compensate for swings in export income from primary products. It is not abated by the continuing unwillingness of the rich to go beyond vague generalizations (themselves an advance over prior rhetoric) on the desirability of preferences for exports of manufactures from developing countries while subsidizing exports of their own manufactures through institutions like the Export-Import Bank and devices like aid tying. It is not abated by the priority given by the rich to enlarging their own monetary reserves through such schemes as special drawing rights (SDR's) while assuring developing countries of the "benefits . . . they will derive if *industrial* countries are [thereby] enabled . . . to maintain high levels of economic activity."[35] The advice of the rich that the poor make ever more concessions to obtain private investment (which is then included in "aid"

[34] McNamara's proposals to take the Bank into the deep waters of agriculture, education, and, especially, population policy are already meeting resistance; the question of large non-project loans for financing imports has hardly been raised.

[35] Pierre Schweitzer, Director-General of the IMF, in a speech before ECOSOC, December 5, 1968. See UN Document E/SR.1571, p. 7.

totals) is rather less appealing when one considers the difficulty of attracting investment into basic industry and the political impossibility of permitting it to make most infrastructure investments. This list of complaints has been made familiar through years of debate in the UN; through reports of the UN regional commissions, particularly ECLA; and recently, through two sessions of UNCTAD. John Pincus offers little hope that the international North will reproach itself over "the ethical failings of material gluttony." As he says, however, "I think it is important for the rich to be aware that they are in effect choosing to help keep the South poor."[36] Perhaps the major contribution of the recipient-oriented international organizations has been to underline the aid-trade-investment-foreign exchange continuum.

Too many commentators on rich-poor relations accept too easily the Pauline phrase that "development is another name for peace." Indeed, on a very long-term view development may promote peaceful relations between states insofar as it includes a more equitable distribution of economic benefits. But to assume that the relationship is direct is to overlook the well-known unsettling effects of modernization itself; the serious problems of maldistribution of income within most developing countries, the political effects of which may easily spill over internationally; and arguments over relative economic shares between developing countries themselves which are already evident within UNCTAD on such things as trade preferences, for example.

Most of all, such a view misses the main point that we cannot rely on economic growth to "solve" the problems of accommodating the international South. The question being asked by today's poor, especially in the international organization framework, is whether the North (mainly the richer West, but increasingly the East as well) will make room on the bench of power. Such an accommodation would require a whole range of adjustments. As I have suggested earlier, the problem of world poverty is also bound up with anger at racial injustice, with resentment of historical maltreatment, with a "conflicted relationship"[37] of ambivalence and mutual mistrust. These difficulties cannot be dismissed as merely psychological problems, important as the latter are.

The sorry predicament of many poor states today is in good part of their own making, of course. We have seen entirely too much irresponsibility, too much corruption, too much outright venality from some leaders of these states. The trouble with irrationality is that it tends to become a way of life. Furthermore, the very faults that the poor nations lay at the door of the rich—arrogance, insensitivity, unwillingness to share power—are too often repeated by poor governments vis-à-vis their own people. But the fact is that the colonial legacy also has a good deal to do with the present state of affairs. The half-

[36] Pincus, p. 353.
[37] See Geiger, *The Conflicted Relationship*.

truths made familiar by the accusing poor are indeed half true. Lack of perfection in the poor does not absolve us of the need to reconsider policies when international institutions *do* work to their disadvantage.

If the rich can bring themselves to accept the dimensions of the problem, it is barely possible that gradual adjustment can, or can be made to, keep the world from polarizing into permanent hostility between rich and poor. The poor have had to realize that they are still largely dependent on the rich for capital, trade, and security and that they invite an international backlash by making too many demands. As with the domestic poor, this seems to be having a sobering effect.[38] Many of the leaders of earlier efforts to shout the rich into concessions have been forced from power at home—Kwame Nkrumah, Sukarno, Modibo Keita, Mohammed Ben Bella, João Goulart, etc. Problems of implementation have been seen by the developing countries themselves to be more intractable than previously thought, and time horizons have had to be lengthened. The governments of the poor are coming to see their own responsibilities more clearly. But the danger of emphasizing the developing countries' responsibilities is to forget our own.

Like its domestic equivalent, confrontation as a political style has merely receded, not vanished. It revealed the dimensions of the problem of poverty and reminded us all of the ugliness inherent in aroused masses, thereby spurring action that would not otherwise have occurred. Now continuation of more "responsible" leadership clearly depends on progress toward accommodation.

Internationally, this has been a period of reevaluation of past efforts, at least on the aid and development side. Hopefully, the reports now beginning to reach the public—the UN committees preparing for the second United Nations Development Decade (UNDD), the Commission on International Development, chaired by Lester Pearson and sponsored by IBRD, the Raúl Prebisch review of Latin American development, and Sir Robert Jackson's review of UNDP for the UN Secretary-General are the most important—will offer some useful suggestions. If they lead to action, they may help to reinvigorate the aid dimension of the attack on world poverty. But they cannot substitute for a realization of the interdependence of all the economic policies relating to world poverty. And most of all, they do not speak to the political and social dimensions of the problem.[39]

[38] UNCTAD II was noticeably lower key—to the point of inaction—than its predecessor. The General Assembly debate on Portuguese territories in 1968 was marginally more temperate and the resolution more conciliatory than in the past. Assembly Resolution 2461 (XXIII) of December 20, 1968, on international monetary reform is notably cautious in suggesting that the requirements of the poor should be taken into consideration. Examples can be multiplied.

[39] See Stanley Johnson, "Kicking a Sacred Cow: A Proposal for the Second Development Decade," *Vista*, January–February 1969 (Vol. 4, No. 4), pp. 34–44, for a suggestion that the UN "rethink" its economic and social role.

THE AMERICAN OPPORTUNITY

The United States, as the richest of the rich, will inevitably be the main target of the poor. At the same time, paradoxically, our present mood of withdrawal from international activism may result in a larger role for the international poor. An unwillingness to be the world's policeman forecloses the option of repressing with force the instability that follows from self-conscious poverty. If repression is unacceptable, inaction will merely hasten deterioration.

The rationalization that the international poor must wait on abolition of domestic poverty is also unsatisfactory. In a certain sense the two are in conflict. Both require substantial amounts of money which is always hard to mobilize. Both draw on similar kinds of personnel that have historically been in short supply. Both require inordinate expenditure of political capital on the part of the President to gain acceptance. A reduction of barriers against developing countries' exports would fall most heavily on labor-intensive, low-wage industries in which the domestic poor are disproportionately represented. These considerations account in part for the lack of enthusiasm for international poverty programs on the part of the domestic poor; American blacks, for example, have not constituted themselves for aid to black Africa, much less aid to the colored continents in general.

The problems raised by these conflicts seem less persuasive than the forces that work to link them in a common effort, however. The Congressmen who argue against international aid on the ground that charity begins at home tend to be those who oppose domestic poverty programs, too. Time and experience are enlarging the pool of skilled personnel for both kinds of programs and deepening the sensitivities of practitioners in both. Attempting to solve the problem of hard-core unemployment in the United States through subsidizing obsolete industry is likely to be a blind alley. Sooner or later the United States must face the fact of the extent to which it is already subsidizing uneconomic industries; programs to ease the necessary adjustments for both workers and entrepreneurs will be required.

Two key disabilities are shared by domestic and international poverty programs. Proponents of the latter have long bemoaned their "lack of constituency." Chileans and Pakistanis do not vote in United States elections; the domestic benefits of international aid programs to the steel and fertilizer industries, shipping interests, the universities, among others, have not been sufficiently clear-cut or dramatic to generate interest-group support. Domestic programs are discovering that they, too, have constituency problems. The poor are a minority in the United States, and they neither vote nor pay taxes in proportion to their numbers. As a result legislatures find it easier to oppose programs favoring them than to raise taxes or reduce benefits to others.

Both domestic and international poverty funds come out of the "tail end" of the federal budget. After defense expenditures and "fixed" costs like interest on the federal debt, social security, and statutory farm supports are paid, only 25 percent of the budget remains to cover *all* other federal activities. Domestic welfare programs, exclusive of social security, account for about 10 percent of the total budget; various international aid components for 1.6 percent. The political problem is how to enlarge that share of the economic pie. The question is not whether the United States can "afford" domestic and/or international poverty programs. It is, rather, whether we are willing to revise our sense of priorities to take greater account of the dimension of poverty. "Ultimately," as John Pincus points out, "any substantial increase in concessions must come from changing perceptions of the issues."[40] Richard Goodwin's comments with regard to the domestic scene are applicable internationally, too:

> We can easily command the resources to meet the immediate needs and demands of black Americans. But we cannot do this until white Americans are persuaded of their responsibility to act.[41]

The generation gap should help to strengthen the possibility of commitment. Today, even "responsible" youth—here represented by a junior Foreign Service Officer—believe that

> the United States' greatest strength is not its wealth, its military strength, or its technological superiority, but its generosity of spirit . . . the spirit of accommodation.[42]

If we can keep our newfound "cool," we may be able to accept a more modest place in the international order without abdicating our sense of responsibility to those less fortunate.

The immediate price of revising the way we think about the international poor may be a diminution in the number of dollars labeled "aid." This may well happen under any circumstance. As Jacob Kaplan notes, the tactic of selling international aid to Congress as a program to promote American security, particularly against Communist expansion, has been counterproductive:

> Hindsight suggests that . . . the interests of less developed and developed countries alike would probably have been furthered had a forthright campaign been launched [early on] to persuade the Congress and the public to assume greater responsibility for helping poorer countries. Lesser appropriations might well have resulted in the beginning, but it would probably have been easier to obtain larger ones currently and in the years to come.[43]

[40] Pincus, p. 351.

[41] Richard Goodwin, "Reflections: Sources of the Public Unhappiness," *New Yorker*, January 4, 1969, p. 52.

[42] Elizabeth A. Bean, "Down in Generation Gap: The Junior Foreign Service Officer Looks at the System," *Annals of the American Academy of Political and Social Science*, November 1968 (Vol. 380), p. 80.

[43] Jacob J. Kaplan, *The Challenge of Foreign Aid: Policies, Problems, and Possibilities* (New York: Frederick A. Praeger, 1967), p. 61.

Short-run reductions in "aid" might be a worthwhile price to pay, therefore. In any event, as this article tries to show, aid has been nowhere near as large in the past as it has been made out to be. A concentration on improving the "quality" of the remaining aid[44] and making adjustments in trade and investment policy might produce more net transfer of resources to developing countries than an equivalent expenditure of political effort to obtain increased aid appropriations. This would be particularly true if it was coupled with radical initiatives on debt remission.

From the developing countries' point of view the price of reduced aid levels may be a lower rate of economic growth, real or statistical, though I am inclined to think this is not inevitable. As noted earlier, the developing countries are already carrying 80 percent of the investment burden themselves. Furthermore, recent events in Pakistan underline the fragility of relying on economic growth to maintain internal stability when distributional goals are neglected.

The experience of our war on domestic poverty is already helping to change the atmosphere in the United States. It is giving us a better understanding of the many-sided nature of this problem and prompting us to look seriously at how we, the haves, must change to meet it. As Cleveland points out, "whatever we learn at home we will be expected to share overseas."[45] Too little attention has been paid to the hard questions of what domestic structural changes will be required if developing countries are to play a substantial part in world trade. We still underestimate the factor of race relations in world politics.[46] We have only begun to see how important the quality of the environment is to any civilization.

The dangers for a renewed international commitment will be the same as for the domestic one: discouragement because the process is so slow and failures so frequent; irritation with the different life-styles and imperfections of the poor; frustration because complexity will defy administrative neatness; dismay with the inevitable scandals; and backlash if the legitimate problems of those who are displaced are not attended to. These are dangers because they can lead to a failure of the will to pursue the goal, even to a belief that the goal itself is improper. But if we can sustain the political will to see us through both our domestic and international transitions, we may indeed "complete the creation of the world."[47]

---

[44] Through progressive untying of aid restricted to specific goods, through simplified procedures, through a broader definition of the uses to which aid can be put, etc.

[45] Cleveland, p. 10.

[46] For a first attempt to explore this question see Gunnar Myrdal, "The Role and Reality of Race," speech to the Foreign Policy Association, New York, May 28, 1968. (Mimeographed.)

[47] Michael Harrington, *Toward a Democratic Left: A Radical Program for a New Majority* (New York: Macmillan, 1968), p. 171.

The International Position of the Dollar in a Changing World

PETER B. KENEN

INTERDEPENDENCE IN FINANCIAL POLICY

PEACEABLE relations between states require that each nation affected by another's acts be induced to acquiesce in all those acts, but this acquiescence may take many forms. It may be quite positive, involving affirmation and, at times, concerted action, or it may be negative, involving mere silence or *pro forma* protest and, most importantly, total abstinence from countervailing acts. Economic and financial relations between states display all forms of acquiescence and too often demonstrate the sad results of failure to obtain consent. Their history, however, manifests gradual progress from an erratic reliance on tacit consent to a wide-ranging reliance on positive, explicit undertakings frequently accompanied by concerted action. Increasingly, moreover, that concerted action has been multilateral, not just bilateral. The tariff warfare of the twenties and earlier decades has now given way to the formal regulation of tariff policies, and the bilateral trade agreements of the 1930's, covering exclusively tariff reductions, have been replaced by a single comprehensive multilateral arrangement, the General Agreement on Tariffs and Trade (GATT) dealing with all aspects of commercial policy. The competitive exchange-rate depreciations of the thirties have likewise given way to formal regulation, beginning with the Tripartite Declaration of 1936 involving the United Kingdom, France, and the United States and culminating in the Articles of Agreement adopted by the Bretton Woods Conference of 1944 establishing the International Monetary Fund (IMF).

The domain of acquiescence is as yet incomplete, and the evolution of

PETER KENEN is Professor of Economics at Columbia University, New York. The author is indebted to the Editors of *International Organization* and to the members of his graduate seminar for comments on an earlier draft of this article. He is also indebted to several former students, especially Richard Meyer and Christopher Beauman, for some of the thoughts developed here.

foreign trade and investment has thrust contentious new issues to the fore more rapidly than nations have devised the instruments required to resolve them. The recent appearance and startling growth of multinational corporations has generated controversy over jurisdiction in matters of exchange control, taxation, and trade policy. More importantly, the practice of accommodation is as yet imperfect. A nation claiming to be injured when another raises tariffs will ordinarily come to GATT, but failing an agreed solution, GATT has no recourse but to authorize limited retaliation. In international monetary matters, moreover, frequent acquiescence in other countries' policies and less frequent but important acts of active cooperation have been punctuated by disruptive challenges to concerted action, and that action, when taken, has too often been limited to the provision of large-scale credits to deficit countries. Despite very frank discussions of policies in the Organization for Economic Cooperation and Development (OECD) and the Bank for International Settlements (BIS) active cooperation has rarely extended to the most important realm—mutually agreed alterations in national monetary and fiscal policies or in the exchange rates.

One can, indeed, contend that monetary cooperation between the major countries has not advanced much beyond the better moments of the twenties. Then, as now, central banks readily gave large amounts of credit to one another or organized consortia of private lenders. Now, as then, however, those credits are too often the visible confessions of failure to agree on changes in exchange rates or on other measures to end the imbalances that credits can merely finance. It is widely argued, for example, that United States leadership in organizing aid to sterling early in the sixties was born of Washington's belief that the alternative—devaluation of the pound—would weaken the American balance of payments. Sterling was regarded as the first line of defense for the United States dollar. Eventually, of course, the pound was devalued without disastrous consequences for the United States dollar, and the long delay before devaluation served merely to prolong the painful austerity which must go with devaluation without also allowing Britain to enjoy the gains from devaluation. The United Kingdom, moreover, incurred large external debts to protect the pound (and dollar) so that its present payments target cannot be mere balance but has instead to be a surplus large enough to pay those debts. Most recently, in 1968, the major central banks advanced some $2 billion in credits to France but did so to stave off the crisis created by the refusal of the Federal Republic of Germany to revalue the mark and France's refusal to devalue the franc (alternating with the French threat to devalue hugely). International monetary history from the Tripartite Declaration of 1936 through Bretton Woods and on to the crisis of the sixties can be described as acquiescence purchased by commitments to defend the status quo—to maintain virtually rigid exchange rates.

One could live with this regime if acquiescence were achieved in another realm. If nations could agree that some would run surpluses and others would run deficits and each would lend or borrow—gain or lose reserves—accordingly, no country would be forced to seek acquiescence in policies to alter its balance of payments. Any such agreement, however, has also to include consensus on components, not just on totals, and on the whole array of national policies required to evoke the proper patterns. All countries might agree, for instance, that continental Europe should reduce its surplus and that the United States should reduce its deficit, but any such agreement must come unstuck if the United States tries to bolster exports by, say, tax incentives while Europe seeks a decrease of American direct investment. Despite a decade of continuous consultation in OECD, BIS, and other institutions no such detailed consensus on targets or instruments has as yet emerged.

It is not hard to understand why full acquiescence has been so elusive in monetary matters. Many acts by governments affect other countries, but trade and payments policies are perceived to have a peculiar, symmetrical gain-loss effect, and international monetary policy has the further feature that explicit collaboration, not simple consent, is required to implement the most important measures.

One normally encounters this sense of gain-loss symmetry because decisions on international economic policies affect transactions between individuals in two or more countries altering the balance of advantage between them. Even here, however, explicit collaboration is not always needed to implement a policy. Tacit consent— failure to retaliate—may sometimes suffice. The United States can raise its tariffs unilaterally. Doing so, it aids its import-competing producers and injures foreign suppliers; this is perceived as gain-loss symmetry.[1] It can do so, however, without the assistance of other governments; its policy will be effective as long as other countries refrain from explicit countervailing acts. The United States can also declare a reduction in the gold value of the dollar, seeking thereby to devalue the dollar in terms of foreign currencies. If successful, it would make American goods more attractive than foreign goods, aiding its import-competing producers and export industries and injuring competitors throughout the world; devaluation would be gain-loss symmetrical. Under present institutional arrangements, however, the United States cannot devalue the dollar in terms of foreign currencies without the collaboration of all other governments. The foreign-currency price of the dollar is determined by foreign central banks which buy and sell dollars against their own currencies in the foreign-exchange markets. If they refuse to change the

---

[1] An increase of United States tariffs could, of course, injure American consumers and might also injure foreign consumers. Unfortunately, this more important effect is rarely perceived; it is the direct gain-loss effect on home and foreign output that too often dominates tariff policy (and exchange-rate policy, discussed below).

currency prices at which they intervene to stabilize exchange rates, they will completely frustrate American policy.[2]

The financing of long-lasting payments imbalances—deficits and surpluses resulting from the failure to adjust exchange rates or change other policies—is likewise symmetrical and calls for collaboration. No deficit country can maintain a fixed exchange rate unless it possesses a stock of foreign currencies to use for market intervention; it must buy up its own currency with foreign currency to prevent the excess supply of its currency from depressing its market exchange rate. A change in its holdings or borrowings, however, involves a symmetrical change in the asset position of a foreign country, and one country's operations in the foreign-exchange markets may also call for active help from a foreign central bank.

Even the majestic neutrality of gold does not solve the problem. No country can count upon financing a deficit by selling gold unless some other country is committed to buy gold, performing a positive act. Gold transfers, moreover, involve symmetrical changes in national balance sheets. Active collaboration and gain-loss symmetry were a vital part of the old gold standard.

Unfortunately, the full, mutual interdependence of financial policies was not clearly recognized in the days of the gold standard. Prior to 1914 each central bank pegged its own currency to gold and regarded the maintenance of that gold parity as its chief obligation. Taken together, the system of gold parities implied a network of national exchange rates—a full set of foreign-currency prices for each nation's money. But because the central banks maintained those exchange rates by dealing in gold bullion, not by intervening in the foreign-exchange markets, they looked upon a change in the gold value of a nation's currency as that nation's sovereign right despite its effect on exchange rates. Such a change was deemed damaging to national prestige and to financial stability but was nonetheless regarded as a unilateral, practicable act.

This view carried over into the twenties. In 1925, for instance, the United Kingdom hitched the pound to gold at its prewar parity. Economists, including John Maynard Keynes, criticized the move, warning that the old gold parity would put sterling out of line with other currencies—that the exchange rates would be all wrong. The critics, however, spoke to ears deafened by repeated assertions that the gold parity mattered most, not the exchange rates implied by that parity. Full understanding of gain-loss symmetry and the need for active collaboration did not dawn until the thirties, following the forced de-

[2] There has been much confusion on this point generated by a loose use of words. The United States defines the international value of the dollar in terms of gold (at $35 an ounce) and can change that valuation unilaterally. A change in the declared gold price of the dollar, however, is not devaluation in the strict sense of the term. The United States cannot alter the foreign-currency price of the dollar if foreign central banks continue to stabilize their own currencies in terms of the dollar (tacitly altering their currencies' gold values). More on this matter later.

valuation of the pound in 1931 and the not-so-forced devaluation of the United States dollar in 1933. Having cut the ties to gold, London and Washington each faced two options—to let exchange rates fluctuate freely in the markets or to intervene directly in those markets to stabilize exchange rates by dealing in currencies. Drifting toward the second course, they came soon to understand that their intervention had to be coordinated; the dollar price of sterling could easily be fixed by the British Exchange Equalization Account or by the American Exchange Stabilization Fund, but both could not be in the market at the same time unless they were agreed on aims and tactics.

The Final Act of Bretton Woods gave formal recognition to these facts, establishing a basis for consistent market operations in a new, ingenious way. Under that agreement, as put into practice, all major central banks undertook to stabilize their currencies by purchasing and selling United States dollars. Doing so, of course, they also undertook to stabilize the price of the dollar in terms of their own currencies. There was to be no need for market intervention by the United States. To carry out their operations, however, foreign central banks must hold or have access to the necessary dollars, and it was to be the special function of the United States to satisfy their needs. Some central banks have long held some of their reserves in dollars, but others, mainly European, prefer to hold gold, for a mixture of motives that need not be recited here. This second group of countries, however, was promised access to the dollars they would need for intervention; the United States Treasury promised to buy gold for dollars and also to sell gold to countries that had taken dollars from the foreign-exchange markets. A working division of labor was established between the United States and all other countries. The others undertook to stabilize exchange rates; the United States, in turn, undertook to accommodate the others' asset preferences by dealing in gold and dollars. A strict reading of the Final Act of Bretton Woods would make it seem that governments are still much concerned with gold; they may, in fact, declare their parities in terms of gold. In practice, however, these declared parities serve only to define the dollar prices of foreign currencies, thereby providing the benchmarks needed to govern market intervention.

The Passivity of Power

Whether in full knowledge of their implications or under a misapprehension, the United States agreed to these arrangements at Bretton Woods, surrendering direct control over the foreign-currency price of the dollar. Other countries can devalue or revalue their currencies vis-à-vis the dollar and can implement those acts by market intervention. The United States can therefore experience change in its exchange rate but only at the initiative of other countries. It has, in fact, experienced a substantial revaluation of the dollar since the Second World War in consequence of other countries' devaluations, a revaluation that has surely exacerbated its current payments problem.[3]

The importance of the problem, viewed prospectively, can best be illustrated by reciting the favorite scenario of those who argue for decisive unilateral action to end the United States payments deficit. The United States, it is suggested, should suspend the conversion of dollars into gold in order to produce two results. First, foreign central banks and governments could not buy gold with dollars they already hold and with those they might acquire in future exchange-market operations. Second, there would be no official gold price for the dollar—the convention that has helped other countries to stabilize their currencies in relation to the dollar. One cannot deny that this single step would solve the United States payments problem. The method by which it would be solved, however, would depend entirely upon the acts of other governments, not upon the American initiative. Other countries could follow one of two routes. They might continue to stabilize the prices of their currencies in terms of the dollar, buying additional dollars in the foreign-exchange markets as United States deficits fed dollars into the markets; they might solve the American payments problem by accumulating dollars that could not be converted into gold. They might instead abstain from intervention and allow the flow of dollars to raise the dollar prices of their own currencies rather than adding dollars to their reserves; they might permit the depreciation of the dollar required to increase American exports, decrease American imports, and improve the United States balance of payments.

It is hard to know how many countries would follow each of these two routes as decisions in these matters are not independent. If many countries go one way initially, others are quite apt to follow. It should be clear, however, that the United States cannot control the final outcome, save by exerting political pressures or throwing extraneous issues into a bargaining process, and that either solution would leave much to be desired. The need to accumulate inconvertible dollars rather than allow exchange rates to change would surely cause some governments to criticize and combat those United States policies they deemed to be the basic cause of the American deficit. Gaullist complaints about United States direct investments and overseas bases would echo in other quarters. But the alternative to open-ended involuntary lending,

---

[3] That revaluation amounts to some 375 percent since 1948, if measured by the weighted-average change in fourteen countries' exchange rates (Canada, Japan, Australia, India, the United Kingdom, France, West Germany, the Netherlands, Belgium, Italy, Spain, Brazil, Mexico, and Venezuela) but Brazil accounts for all but 39 percent. It amounts to some 485 percent if measured by the weighted average change in the exchange rates of all countries (except the Republic of Korea) accounting for more than 0.5 percent of United States exports. Notice, however, that most countries have suffered more rapid inflation than the United States so that a "purchasing-power-parity" computation based on changes in exchange rates and consumer prices would show a modest *devaluation* of the United States dollar: 59 percent for fourteen countries (and 17 percent without Brazil), or 113 percent for all major trading countries. Data from International Monetary Fund, *International Financial Statistics;* indexes weighted by United States exports in 1967. I am indebted to Miss Carol Gerstl for these computations.

a depreciation of the dollar, would shift the balance of competitive advantage toward the United States, leading to new demands for import restrictions and export subsidies, and these demands are already too loud in too many countries. Resort to these protective measures, it should be added, could not prevent solution of the United States payments problem. A free market in foreign exchange would respond to trade restrictions by forcing an additional compensatory depreciation of the United States dollar; if foreigners handicap American exports, the price of the dollar would fall further to make them more attractive. Those who impose restrictions, however, would succeed in shifting the burden of adjustment onto other countries, generating similar demands for more protection in those other countries and, generally, restricting world trade.

One should not preclude the better possibility of orderly adjustment in the key exchange rates. General agreement on a modest devaluation of the dollar, or, more to the point, a modest revaluation of the Deutschmark and certain other currencies, may not be out of sight. But experience in 1968, when France and West Germany declined to change their parities, suggests that agreement is still out of mind, and the universal acquiescence required to change the price of the dollar would be even more difficult to achieve. Whatever the practical prospects, moreover, one basic fact remains. Acquiescence is required and, in this particular case, the initiative lies abroad, not with the United States.

American initiative is constrained a second way, likewise a consequence of Bretton Woods. During the wartime consultations between Washington and London the British, led by Lord Keynes, proposed the creation of an institution quite different from the IMF. It would have been a global clearing union *cum* central bank operating on an overdraft principle. A country requiring dollars to stabilize its currency in the foreign-exchange market could have drawn on its credit line at the clearing union, transferring its drawing rights to the United States in exchange for dollars. The global supply of reserve assets could have been increased at will under this arrangement, merely by enlarging all countries' drawing rights. The very different IMF that emerged at Bretton Woods lacks this flexibility. It is, instead, a fixed pool of gold, dollars, and other currencies which countries can purchase against their own currencies. Those purchases, moreover, cannot be made freely; once a nation has purchased foreign currencies equal in value to its own gold subscription (one quarter of its total quota in the IMF) it must satisfy increasingly restrictive conditions to make additional purchases. In consequence, drawing rights beyond the so-called gold tranche are not perfect substitutes for national reserves (or for the automatic drawing rights envisaged in the Keynes plan). The Articles of Agreement do provide for a quinquennial review of quotas, and quotas have been enlarged on two occasions. An increase of quotas, however, does not provide an increase of reserves, nor does it substitute for larger reserves; automatic access to the IMF is enlarged by just one-fourth of any quota increase, and that same automatic access to the IMF is purchased by a further gold subscription—an exchange of one reserve asset for another.[4]

The Bretton Woods system then, did not provide ways to augment reserves in a regular, systematic way. It did not generate a new reserve asset under IMF control, as Keynes' clearing union would have done, but left the process of reserve creation to the vagaries of gold production and the willingness of individual central banks to hold foreign currencies as part of their reserves. Most importantly, central banks as a group could not increase their *net* reserves beyond the limits set by new gold supplies as the currency claims of one central bank are the liabilities of some other central bank. In effect, all countries but one could increase their reserves provided the remaining country willingly ran deficits in its balance of payments (and that its currency was regarded as a satisfactory reserve asset by other central banks).

The United States assumed this special role. From 1949 through 1957 United States payments deficits totaled $5.8 billion, of which a mere $0.5 billion was financed by gold and other reserve losses while $5.3 billion was financed by dollars transferred to foreign central banks and added to their reserves. From 1958 through 1968 United States deficits totaled $15.6 billion, of which $9.1 billion was transferred in gold and other reserve assets while $6.5 billion took the form of newly created dollar reserves.[5] At the end of 1968 United States reserves totaled $15.7 billion, of which $10.9 billion was gold, but dollar liabilities to foreign central banks totaled $15.2 billion.[6]

Some observers have suggested that the United States sought this special role,[7] which view would explain its opposition at Bretton Woods to the creation of a global central bank strong enough to do the job. My own reading of the record is quite different. The United States willingly ran deficits until the mid-fifties, seeking to establish a more balanced distribution of gold and other reserve assets, especially to restore the reserve positions of European countries. But it would have been quite willing to lose gold rather than accumulate dollar liabilities. The United States did not seek reserve-currency status for the dollar but allowed other countries to attach that status to the

---

[4] It should be pointed out that certain IMF transactions do increase reserves (automatic drawing rights) but only in an indirect, imperfect way. When one country buys another's currency, beyond its automatic (gold tranche) drawing rights, the other obtains additional automatic drawing rights known in the jargon as super-gold-tranche drawing rights. But the size and distribution of these extra drawing rights depends haphazardly on the size and currency distribution of conditional drawings at any point in time.

[5] Deficit computed on the "official settlements" basis.

[6] Data from Board of Governors, Federal Reserve System, *Federal Reserve Bulletin,* and International Monetary Fund, *International Financial Statistics.* Figures for early years approximate.

[7] See, e.g., John R. Karlik, "The Costs and Benefits of Being a Reserve-Currency Country" (unpublished Ph.D. dissertation, Columbia University, 1966), Chapter III.

dollar as they took on dollar assets through the middle fifties.[8] Forswearing regulation of its own reserve position by agreeing to trade gold for dollars, the United States foreclosed the choice between holding reserve assets (gold and foreign currencies) and incurring reserve debts (dollar liabilities to foreign central banks). It left the composition of its reserve balance sheet to other countries' asset choices and, more importantly, assumed a special obligation for the stability of the entire system. Decisions concerning its own balance of payments became, perforce, decisions to regulate the growth rate of global reserves, and as its liabilities grew through time, its policies affected the quality of those reserves. Growth in foreign dollar holdings relative to United States gold, necessary to enlarge total reserves by more than global gold accretions, impaired foreign confidence in the convertibility of existing dollar balances. To make matters worse the United States could not enforce decisions regarding the growth of reserves. Conscious American decisions to increase reserves by running deficits—if such decisions were ever made—could be vetoed by conversions of dollars into gold.

Why did the United States accept these constraints on its initiative in exchange-rate policy and its independence in managing its own reserves? One need not extract explicit answers from the record. One has merely to recall the unique economic and political position of the United States in the mid-forties—a position of enormous strength but also of special vulnerability. The then-accepted reading of interwar experience blamed the United States for most of the disasters of the thirties. Its enormous net creditor position, representing interallied debts and United States lending in the twenties, gave the United States a decisive role in interwar negotiations on financial matters. More importantly, the sensitivity of American imports to the domestic business cycle and their very large share in total world trade caused all other nations to share the fortunes of the American economy. Conversely, United States exports, while very large absolutely, were not a large share of domestic output so that the American economy was thoroughly insulated from disturbances arising abroad. Looking back upon the thirties, economists could justly say: "Whenever the United States sneezes, the rest of the world catches pneumonia." Finally, most observers feared that the postwar world would not be too different and that, in particular, the overwhelming economic problem after reconstruction would be another enormous American depression.

Hints of this consensus can be found in Keynes' proposal for a clearing union. It was explicitly designed to give other countries a blank check on the United States in case the American economy should take ill again, reducing

---

[8] The United States decision to buy and sell gold, reaffirmed at Bretton Woods, is sometimes cited as contrary evidence—that the United States sought to make the dollar a more attractive reserve asset. This is to miss the point. The decision was designed to make gold more attractive. Nations needing dollars for intervention would not have dared to hold gold as a reserve asset without the American pledge to buy gold for dollars.

American imports and driving other countries into payments deficit. The IMF's Articles of Agreement rejected this device but proffered an alternative to serve the same aim. If the United States slid into another depression, causing other countries to use up their reserves (and their dollar drawing rights at the IMF) the dollar could be declared a "scarce currency," and other countries could discriminate against American exports, thereby balancing their external accounts without resorting to deflation or devaluation.

The United States forswore the initiative in monetary matters because the postwar world looked to have a single economic center—one to which all other countries had to forge their separate links. It was not to be bipolar, let alone polycentral. The overwhelming size and apparent instability of the United States made it seem as though other countries would need the initiative in monetary matters. That same size, moreover, seemed to preclude unilateral acts by the United States, for anything it did would so much affect all other countries that they would have usually and collectively to neutralize its acts.

By now, of course, this country is not the sole center of economic strength. The other industrial countries, taken together or in subgroups, come near to matching its production and surpass its trade. Indeed, one can discern several emerging centers, including the European Economic Community (EEC) and, by itself, Japan. Significantly, the slowdown of European economic expansion after 1965 affected third-world trade no less severely than the United States recession of 1960–1961. What may be more important, the overseas activities of major American firms, including their trade and overseas production, account for a large share of their total output and their total profits. Compared to most other industrial countries, the United States remains relatively insulated from external disturbances, but that isolation is much less complete than it was in the interwar period. Changes in other countries' economic policies can have profound effects on vital American interests.

The United States retains enormous power, and changes in the international economy, underway or undetected, are quite apt to give it more. The overseas activities of United States firms, mentioned several times, cause decisions made in Washington, Detroit, and Pittsburgh greatly to influence the economic life of other countries. The emergence of the Eurodollar market has given the United States dollar new uses and prestige and created new channels to transmit the impact of domestic policy. Even as American monetary policies and, to less extent, fiscal policies have now to be attuned to the balance of payments, so too those same policies have come to affect credit conditions in other countries and cannot be conducted without this fact in mind. In 1968–1969, for instance, United States banks sought to escape the stricter policies of the Federal Reserve by borrowing billions of Eurodollars, thereby driving interest rates to new highs in the Eurodollar market and putting upward pressure on the home interest rates of other countries. Finally, the enormous political influence of the United States gives Washington considerable leverage in international financial affairs. It is not surprising that West Germany, the country most concerned to preserve the American military presence in Western Europe, has been the most willing to finance the United States payments deficit by buying American Treasury securities rather than acquiring ordinary short-term dollar claims or buying additional gold.

But the continued influence of United States policies, specific and general, is at once a source of strength and a constraint. Other countries cannot be entirely passive in the face of credit-market trends that undermine their aims. Further, United States efforts to combat inflation or to attract capital may have long-term consequences adverse to basic American aims, slowing economic growth throughout the world and curtailing world trade. More importantly, the use of political influence to accomplish short-term financial objectives can be counterproductive. Having played on German fears to finance its deficit, Washington is now constrained by its own success. It cannot think of pulling troops out of Western Europe without also asking whether West Germany would not turn its dollars in for gold.

As at Bretton Woods, though in different ways, the massive impact of the United States economy and of American policy continues to limit American autonomy. Though largest in size and power, even now, the United States must continue to behave as though it were but slightly more than one among equals.

Toward a Better System

The special role of the United States, defined at Bretton Woods, has to be perpetuated. The United States must still forswear full freedom in financial policy if only because autonomous acts may be self-defeating. Nevertheless, self-imposed parity with other countries, accomplished by accepting certain policy constraints, should earn full equality for the United States in certain critical domains. The United States must require the right to demand the acquiescence presently accorded acts of other major countries and, *a fortiori,* of weaker countries. It must press for three important changes in the international monetary system.

Acknowledging, at once, that there is just one exchange rate connecting any pair of national currencies, one has also to acknowledge that this same exchange rate cannot be decided by one of two governments. The Bretton Woods regime must give way to one of two new systems. On the one hand, governments may concur in total abstention from stabilization, leaving private markets to determine the exchange rates. This is the option favored by many economists, if only for want of workable alternatives. Abstention, however, would not be enough. Nations would have still to concert many vital policies in order to prevent wide movements in exchange rates adverse to their common interests and to the working of free-market rates, and they would have to abstain from using trade taxes and controls to offset any change in the free exchange rates. On the other hand, governments could agree on a set of rules to govern intervention and, in particular, to introduce needed changes in otherwise fixed rates when movements in reserves or other indexes argue for such changes. History suggests that it will be difficult to work out those rules, but it may not be impossible if governments will work to write *general* rules governing all future changes in rates rather than, as now, *ad hoc* agreements concerning a specific rate. A system of general rules would probably call for early changes as imbalances appeared and, therefore, modest changes, whereas *ad hoc* consultation (and, too often, deadlock) over specific changes tends now to take place too late, when large changes may be needed and, correspondingly, are more bitterly resisted.[9]

Noneconomists concerned with the development of general rules to govern relations between states may properly prefer this second option—regulated rates with rules for change. But if that is their choice, they must bring their influence and argument to bear against those of the economists, as we too often tend to favor the rule of markets over that of men.

Next, prompt action must be taken to remedy the major defect of the Articles of Agreement of the IMF. Adequate reserve-creating machinery must be started up in order to supply reserves at a regular rate and to reconcile national policy objectives. It will always be impossible to obtain consistent, comprehensive agreements on financial policies if nations are competing for a fixed or slow-growing stock of reserves. If global reserves do not increase to match the global total of desired surpluses, one country or another will fail to achieve its aims and may then adopt economic policies inconsistent with others' aims. Steady growth of reserves is not itself a sufficient condition for harmonizing policies, thereby to maintain stable exchange rates, but it is surely necessary. Here, of course, the basic reform has been accomplished; new machinery has been designed and is ready for use. Under an agreement reached a year ago the IMF is authorized to credit each member country with special drawing rights (SDR's) to be used in much the same way as Keynes' overdrafts. At the start of every five-year period the Managing Director of the IMF is authorized to propose the creation of SDR's in fixed annual amounts. If his proposal is adopted by the member governments, SDR's will be distributed among the countries in amounts proportionate to their IMF quotas. Each

---

[9] For a brief survey of current proposals for reform of the exchange-rate system, including formulas to regulate changes, see the *Economic Report of the President* (Washington: U.S. Government Printing Office, January 1969), pp. 145ff. See also J. R. Williamson, *The Crawling Peg* (Princeton Essays in International Finance, No. 50) (Princeton, N.J: International Finance Section, Department of Economics, Princeton University, 1965); and F. Modigliani and P. B. Kenen, "A Suggestion for Solving the International Liquidity Problem," *Quarterly Review* (Banca Nazionale del Lavoro), March 1966, pp. 3–17.

member, in turn, can transfer SDR's to another country in order to acquire that country's currency (or buy back its own currency held by the other country). Strict rules are proposed to prevent abuse of the new drawing rights. Any country can draw its account down to zero but may not remain there continuously. It need not reconstitute its total holdings (as with ordinary drawings on the IMF) but over any five-year period its holdings must equal at least 30 percent of its cumulative annual allotment. A country can use all its SDR's some of the time and some of its SDR's all of the time but cannot use all of them all of the time. Further, no member need accept SDR's from any other country if it has already accepted (from all sources) an amount twice as large as its own allotment. This last rule is designed to remedy one defect of the Keynes plan; SDR's cannot become a blank check on one member country. The new plan has been cast as a series of amendments to the IMF's Articles of Agreement and these have been ratified by a large number of countries. The machinery is ready for use as soon as governments are ready to begin.

Finally, there is urgent need for a consolidation of existing reserve holdings as these now comprise an untidy and unstable mixture of dollars, pounds, French francs, claims on the IMF, and national gold holdings. There is, in particular, a need to protect the monetary system against any massive switch from currencies to gold. Modest steps have been taken in this direction. The major central banks have now agreed to help the United Kingdom convert sterling into dollars by extending medium-term credits. No similar device, however, can be applied to the large number of dollars held by foreign governments. Central banks are willing to lend dollars to the United Kingdom but would not be as willing to lend gold to the United States. It would, indeed, be difficult to work out gold loans, if only because the countries holding the gold needed to meet a run on the United States gold stock are quite apt to join the run (if not, indeed, to start it). An increase in the price of gold could solve the problem by revaluing United States gold reserves sufficiently to repay foreign dollar holdings. But a higher gold price has several drawbacks. It would be inequitable in impact because it would reward the countries that have held gold relative to those that have held dollars. It would be uncertain in effect because we do not know how gold production would respond, and it is not at all clear that the increase in price needed to revalue existing gold holdings would thereafter evoke the "right" rate of increase through new gold production. Finally, it would be inefficient as it would draw additional real resources into the production of a commodity for purely monetary use; if central banks persist in the primitive belief that settlements between them must involve transfers of physical assets, one can surely find a cheaper poker chip than gold. There are, in short, better ways to forestall instability resulting from shifts between gold and dollars. Consider, for example, a simple plan proposed by several experts. Let all central banks deposit all their gold, dollars, and other reserve assets with the IMF, obtaining in exchange a new composite reserve asset backed by all the gold and other assets that had been held separately. Each nation would then have a *pro rata* claim on all the gold and dollars—and the dollars would no longer be a claim on United States gold. Some observers have objected that this consolidation would forever deny gold to those that had held dollars. These critics, however, ignore the fact that the American gold stock is by now too small to honor all the claims upon it—that no one has an undisputed claim to gold. Other critics argue that central banks already understand this simple fact and would not perpetrate a run on gold. This objection makes more sense but counts on rationality at moments of crisis. Rules that obtain in normal times tend often to break down amid uncertainty, political or economic. Consolidation is possible only when workable arrangements can be devised by reasoned argument. It will be impossible when it is most needed—when one can no longer appeal to reason and common interest.

United States Policy Toward Regional Organization

JOSEPH S. NYE

REGIONALISM has a long history as an important instrument of American foreign policy. Yet such a statement does not do justice to the variations in goals, means, and settings that have affected United States policy toward participation in and cooperation with regional organizations. These differences have been the cause of serious debate in the past and are becoming so again as we approach the 1970's.

REGIONALISM IN OUR PAST

One of the earliest strands of United States foreign policy, one that has persisted with varying strength to the present day, is the "western hemisphere idea," the notion of the uniqueness of the western hemisphere and its isolation from the rest of the world,[1] which was given form by James Monroe's disengagement of the western hemisphere republics from the Europe-centered international system. However, the United States did not demonstrate great interest in regional schemes such as the 1826 Panama conference proposed by Simón Bolívar. After 1890 the International Union of American Republics and its Commercial Bureau represented a pioneering example of a multipurpose regional organization, but it remained a weak and North American-dominated organization.[2]

It was not until the early twentieth century, in the aftermath of the United States intervention in response to the collapse of the European balance of power

JOSEPH S. NYE, a member of the Board of Editors of *International Organization*, is Associate Professor in the Department of Government, Harvard University, Cambridge, Mass.

[1] See Arthur P. Whitaker, *The Western Hemisphere Idea: Its Rise and Decline* (Ithaca, N.Y: Cornell University Press, 1954).

[2] According to William Manger when the Commercial Bureau was under the United States Secretary of State, it was more like an American agency than an international organization. See *Pan America in Crisis: The Future of the OAS* (Washington: Public Affairs Press, 1961), p. 33.

in World War I, that one finds in Woodrow Wilson's proposal of a policy of global collective security "the first instalment of the conflict between regionalist and globalist ideas."[3] It is ironic that the language of Article 21 of the Covenant of the League of Nations, stating that the global doctrine of collective security did not necessarily interfere with "regional arrangements" such as the Monroe Doctrine, was an insufficient bait to lure the United States Senate (for which it was written) into ratification of the Covenant but did become a convenient loophole for governments in the interwar period.[4] The United States, in any case, returned to its traditional policy of hemispheric regionalism as a counterpart to its isolationist European policy.

The major United States debate over policy toward regional organizations occurred during the latter part of World War II after the United States had been drawn once again out of "isolation" and beyond hemispheric regionalism. If the formal outcome of the debates as written into the United Nations Charter represented a globalist victory, it was in a large part because of the success of Secretary of State Cordell Hull who "represented a kind of residual Wilsonianism."[5] Arguments by writers like Walter Lippmann or statesmen like Winston Churchill abroad and Sumner Welles at home in favor of establishing organizations on the basis of explicit recognition of regional spheres of influence were rejected by Hull for fear that they "might lead to questions of balance of power" and provide a means for another retreat into isolationism.[6] Such globalist idealism seemed hypocritical to leaders of the United Kingdom who saw Latin America as a United States sphere of influence even if the United States did not call it such. However, by the time of the Quebec Conference of 1943 Churchill had lost faith in the possibility of creating a strong European regional council and decided that henceforth "the United States, rather than a revived and reorganized Europe, would have to counterbalance Russian power."[7]

Ironically, Churchill's decision was a harbinger of a coming change in the international system from a multistate balance of power to a bipolar structure that made Hull's victory a hollow one and greatly diminished the importance of the subsequent debate at the 1945 United Nations Conference on International Organization at San Francisco. One of the effects of United States hemispheric policy in the 1930's had been an increase in Latin American enthusiasm for hemispheric regional organization. Becoming aware of the high

---

[3] I. Claude, Jr., *European Organization in the Global Context* (Brussels: Institut d'Études Européennes, 1965), p. 8.

[4] See B. Boutros-Ghali, *Contribution á l'étude des ententes régionales* (Paris: A. Pédone, 1949), p. 8.

[5] Claude, p. 9.

[6] Cordell Hull, *The Memoirs of Cordell Hull* (2 vols; New York: Macmillan, 1948), Vol. II, p. 1646.

[7] William Hardy McNeill, *America, Britain and Russia* (London: OUP, 1953), p. 323. Subsequently, when out of power Churchill called for European unity, but it was never completely clear what he meant by "unity" or how he saw Britain's relation to it. Nor did his actions upon his return to power clarify the issue.

costs and low benefits of the past interventionist policy in Latin America and later faced by the threat of Axis powers' incursion into the area, the United States had gradually accommodated Latin pressures to use inter-American organization to introduce constraints on its freedom of action.[8] This experience of the 1930's and of close cooperation during the war, plus a reluctance on the part of some conservative Latin American elites to become too tightly enmeshed in an organization which the Union of Soviet Socialist Republics could use against them, led to Latin pressures at the 1945 Inter-American Conference on Problems of War and Peace at Chapultepec for revision of the Dumbarton Oaks proposals to protect regional organizations.

Thus at San Francisco, while resisting Egyptian efforts to define acceptable regional organizations in such a way that they would resemble the recently formed Arab League, Senator Arthur Vandenberg and America's Latin allies succeeded in amending the proposed charter to ensure that inter-American organization would not be jeopardized by the global organization.[9] Vandenberg argued that they had "infinitely strengthened the world organization by thus enlisting, with its overall supervision, the dynamic resources of these regional affinities"[10] while critics deprecated the resulting ambiguity in the language of the Charter. In fact, however, the formal outcome of the debate was far less important than the changes in the setting of international organization. After the onset of the Cold War and in response to Soviet support for UN involvement in western hemisphere crises American statesmen reinterpreted the relatively precise language of the Charter on "enforcement" action by regional organization just as easily as they did the relatively ambiguous language on "priority" for regional organizations. As Inis Claude so aptly describes, the Cold War prevailed over the Charter.[11]

In the decade following San Francisco American disillusionment with the United Nations as a security system led to the creation of a series of military alliances and organizations which came to be called "regional" although in some cases the degree of geographical proximity involved was very slight.[12] The first of these "regional" security pacts was the Inter-American Treaty of Reciprocal Assistance (Rio Treaty) of 1947; but like the Charter of the Organization of American States (OAS) of the following year this is best understood in terms of traditional hemispheric regionalism as a sort of epilogue

[8] See Bryce Wood, *The Making of the Good Neighbour Policy* (New York: Columbia University Press, 1961).

[9] See Ruth B. Russell, with Jeannette E. Muther, *A History of the United Nations Charter: The Role of the United States 1940–1945* (Washington: Brookings Institution, 1958), Chapter 27.

[10] Arthur H. Vandenberg, Jr., *The Private Papers of Senator Vandenberg* (Boston: Houghton-Mifflin, 1952).

[11] Inis L. Claude, Jr., "The OAS, the UN and the United States," *International Conciliation*, March 1964 (No. 547).

[12] For instance, the longest distance between the capitals of Southeast Asia Treaty Organization (SEATO) members (11,500 miles) is only slightly less than the longest distance between the capitals of UN Members (12,400 miles). We shall refer to such organizations as "quasi-regional."

to the 1930's or, in Arthur Whitaker's analogy, as a glacier that continued to move long after the snows that caused it had stopped.[13] The Rio Treaty helped serve as a model for the North Atlantic Treaty of 1949. However, the impetus for the creation of the North Atlantic Treaty Organization (NATO) and later of the establishment of the Southeast Asia Treaty Organization (SEATO) and the Central Treaty Organization (CENTO) was not the traditional United States regional policy but a growing involvement in the global politics of containment in a bipolar world. Along with its direct participation in the quasi-regional military pacts the United States also supported the economic reconstruction and regional integration of Western Europe through the Organization of European Economic Cooperation (OEEC) and the European Coal and Steel Community (ECSC). The United States also encouraged, or at least sympathized with, the Colombo Plan and made abortive efforts at the 1955 Simla Conference to stimulate similar regional organization in what it called "the arc of free Asia." In the mid-1950's the United States was likened to "a switchboard for most of the regional and joint efforts in the free world."[14]

By the 1960's the setting for regional organization had changed. The process of decolonization had greatly increased the number of third-world countries whose existence dramatized the "development problem" and whose slogans frequently stressed regional aspirations. This change was reflected in United States policy. In Walt Rostow's words it was

> one of the most important, if unnoticed, transitions in policy under President Johnson . . . that we are now actively supporting the building of regional institutions and regional co-operation in Latin America, Asia, and Africa as well as Europe.[15]

At the same time the degree of détente between the United States and the Soviet Union following the Cuban missile crisis of 1962 both eased the direct security threat in Europe and created a certain distrust of direct American dealings with the Soviets at potential European expense. This situation provided leeway for policies, including those of General Charles de Gaulle, which were less "Atlantic-oriented." Perhaps even more important than the announcement by France in 1966 that it would withdraw its forces from NATO assignment and command was the beginning by the Federal Republic of Germany (West Germany) in the same year of a new policy of contacts with the East which Pierre Hassner calls "the hour, so often falsely predicted, of a search for alternatives to the policy of integration in the West and reli-

---

[13] Whitaker, p. 155.

[14] Norman J. Padelford, "Regional Organizations and the United Nations," *International Organization*, May 1954 (Vol. 8, No. 2), p. 206.

[15] W. W. Rostow, "Regionalism and World Order," Department of State *Bulletin*, July 7, 1967 (Vol. 57, No. 1464), p. 69. (Originally a commencement address at Middlebury College, Middlebury, Vermont, June 12, 1967.)

ance on the United States."[16] At the same time United States European policy turned away from the "Atlanticist" schemes of the early 1960's, such as the creation of a multilateral force (MLF) for NATO, toward an emphasis on détente which sometimes appeared to Europeans to be at the expense of the Atlantic alliance. Whether the Soviet invasion of Czechoslovakia and the change of American administration have really altered these trends or, as seems more likely, have merely delayed them remains to be seen.

In any case, American policy toward regional organization was again under debate in the late 1960's. In the eyes of its critics the Administration of Lyndon Johnson was using the names of ephemeral Asian organizations to answer questions about its goals in Vietnam at the same time that it was neglecting regional organization in Europe. Thus critics charged that it had no overall policy toward regional organizations except at the declaratory level. Whatever the merit of this criticism, a number of critics, faintly echoing the debates of 1943, have advocated a more consistent policy of support for autonomous regional organizations without direct United States membership as a means to a new structure of world order.

Costs and Benefits of Continuing Past Policies

Before turning to the problems raised by the question of a policy of support for autonomous regional organization as a principle of world order, we must look in more detail at how the United States has used regional organizations in the past and at what the costs and benefits of extending such *"ad hoc"* policies into the 1970's would be. In general, one can identify four major clusters of interests that the United States has served through participation in and cooperation with regional organizations since World War II: 1) hemispheric influence; 2) containment; 3) economic development; and 4) conflict prevention and management.

Hemispheric Influence

One of the major United States policy interests that has been served through regional organization and certainly the most long-standing one has been the maintenance of a sphere of influence (exclusion of what *we* define as hostile external influence) in the western hemisphere, particularly in the Caribbean region. This is not to say that the only role of the OAS has been maintenance of a United States sphere of influence, but this has certainly been one of the roles as the United States use of the OAS in the cases of Guatemala in 1954, the Dominican Republic in 1965, and Cuba since Fidel Castro's takeover indicate.[17] It is instructive that at the time of the 1945 debates on the inclusion

[16] Pierre Hassner, *Change and Security in Europe.* Part I: *The Background* (Adelphi Paper, No. 46) (London: Institute for Strategic Studies, February 1968), p. 2.
[17] See Claude, *International Conciliation*, No. 547.

of a special clause in the UN Charter to protect the pan-American arrangements Vandenberg quotes Leo Pasvolsky, a staunch "globalist" opposed to the
inclusion of such a clause, as arguing that we would act despite a veto in a
Pan-American dispute requiring force.[18]

A regional organization offers the dominant power a basis for signaling
"hands off" to an external power and the means to achieve collective legitimization of actions it wishes to take in the region. A mistake by one superpower
in its estimates of the other superpower's intentions is a potential source of
nuclear holocaust. However, explicit agreements on spheres of influence that
might prevent such a mistake are taboo in the current system.[19] In these circumstances regional organizations such as the OAS or the Warsaw Treaty
Organization (WTO) can serve as salient points for tacit warnings between
the superpowers. Second, in cases in which the United States feels that its
security interests compel it to intervene to maintain its sphere of influence it
can turn *post hoc* to the OAS for at least partial collective legitimization, and
in the bargain over granting OAS approval the Latin states are given at least
a minor degree of leverage over the actual continued conduct of the intervention.[20]

There are several possible costs of using a regional organization for maintaining a sphere of influence. First, as occurred in the Dominican Republic
affair, intervention may appear to achieve legitimization primarily in the eyes
of United States elites and publics rather than in the eyes of elites and publics
abroad. If changing military technology in the 1970's reduces the military
security value of a sphere of influence[21] and increased polycentrism further
reduces the meaning of "Communism" and thus the psychological or political
loss we might incur from leftist revolutions in Latin America, the existence
of the OAS may lead to a considerable lag in the evolution of United States
domestic opinion behind the realities of the need for or the possibility of a
sphere of influence.

Second, spheres of influence tend to be unilateral impositions which may
be resented by smaller countries and some elites at home as well as abroad.
If the United States public believes in the legitimacy of OAS actions far more
than the Latin Americans do, this may mislead United States decisionmakers
and prevent them from making necessary responses and adjustments that

---

[18] Vandenberg, p. 189.

[19] See *International Herald Tribune*, September 14–15, 1968.

> Secretary of State Dean Rusk said last night that the Soviet Union, through military force, had
> established and maintained a "sphere of dominance" in Eastern Europe. He made the statement
> in categorically denying again that the U.S. government ever had any "spheres of influence"
> agreement or understanding with Moscow.

[20] See Jerome Slater, "The Limits of Legitimization in International Organizations: The Organization
of American States and the Dominican Crisis," *International Organization*, Winter 1969 (Vol. 23,
No. 1), pp. 48–72.

[21] For an argument that spheres of influence are becoming obsolete see Albert Wohlstetter, "Illusions
of Distance," *Foreign Affairs*, January 1968 (Vol. 46, No. 2), p. 250.

might alleviate such resentment short of costly violence. As evidence of such asymmetrical perceptions of legitimacy one can cite the difficulty with which the OAS has treated cases of alleged Communist threat in the hemisphere and the refusal of the Latin states to allow the Organization to develop any permanent or independent military capacity.[22] Nor is this situation likely to change in what will probably be a period of increasing nationalism as economic forces mobilize even greater proportions of the populations of Latin states in the 1970's.

Containment

A second major foreign policy objective which the United States has pursued through regional organizations has been the objective of "containment" —originally of Soviet power, later broadened to containment of "Communism." Both economic and military organizations have been used. Among the latter the United States created and participated in NATO—first the Treaty in 1949, then the highly developed Organization after the onset of the Korean War in 1950—as a means of establishing a credible commitment to defend Western Europe against the Soviet Union. With decolonization and increased focus on the power of the People's Republic of China (Communist China) in Asia Secretary of State John Foster Dulles promoted the quasi-regional Baghdad Pact (later CENTO) in which the United States was an observer and the quasi-regional SEATO of which the United States was a nonregional member as a means of completing the ring around "the Communists." It has been suggested that Dulles turned to these quasi-regional imitations of NATO because they were easy to sell to Congress, because they were expected to allow easier access to weak areas, and because they promised to limit American expense and responsibility.[23] In any event, the opposition of neutralist Asian countries and their refusal to join made the inadequacy of the quasi-regional pacts apparent even to Dulles who soon limited the United States commitment in SEATO.[24]

With the exception of NATO and the belated resurrection of SEATO for legitimization purposes after the United States had run into increasing criticism of its Vietnam policy quasi-regional military "pactomania" proved to be a very brief phase in United States policy. On the other hand, the objectives of containment have been pursued through other forms of regional organization.

In Europe the United States supported the economic integration of the Six while being cool to the ideas of a European Free Trade Association (EFTA)

[22] See John C. Dreier, "New Wine and Old Bottles: The Changing Inter-American System," *International Organization*, Spring 1968 (Vol. 22, No. 2), p. 485.

[23] Edgar S. Furniss, Jr., "A Re-examination of Regional Arrangements," *Journal of International Affairs*, 1955 (Vol. 9, No. 2), pp. 80–81.

[24] See Louis Halle, *The Cold War as History* (London: Chatto and Windus, 1967), p. 304.

in part at least because it was hoped that the former would lead to sufficient political integration to support a defense capability that could become an equal partner ("the other end of a dumbbell" in the image of the day) tied to the United States in the Atlantic alliance half of a bipolar world. In Asia after Dulles realized the failure of his pacts to attract neutral countries, which were then scheduled to meet at Bandung, the United States turned briefly to the idea of a regional economic organization supported by United States economic aid ("something like the OEEC") as a means of keeping Communist influence out of "the free arc of Asia." The regional organization aspect of the idea was dropped, however, after an unsuccessful conference in Simla, India, in May 1955 at which the smaller Asian states proved reluctant to accept a regional body interfering with their bilateral aid from the United States, particularly one that might be subject to Indian or Japanese leadership.[25]

More recently the Johnson Administration has turned to Asian regional organizations ranging in scope from the Asian Ministers of Education to the Asian and Pacific Council (ASPAC) as means of creating a sufficient sense of unity and common interest among the countries bordering Communist China so that they would no longer present a "vacuum of power" into which the United States might be drawn but could become strong "partners" instead.[26] The United States hoped to reduce the burden of containment by finding

> in regionalism a new relationship to the world community somewhere between the overwhelming responsibility we assumed in the early postwar years as we moved in to fill vacuums of power and to deal with war devastation and a return to isolationism.[27]

In assessing the benefits and costs of using regional organization as a tool for containment we cannot hope to settle differences of opinion over whether the goal of containing the power of Communist China, the Democratic People's Republic of Korea (North Korea), and the Democratic Republic of Vietnam (North Vietnam) in Asia and the goal of containing Soviet power in Europe are (or were) of equal (or any) merit. We can, however, discuss the suitability of regional organizations as means to those goals in the two settings.

The prime benefit of using military quasi-regional organizations for containment is that by institutionalizing and preparing defense projects in advance the credibility of the American commitment to the protection of an area is underlined or enhanced and thus so is the ultimate deterrent effect. However, United States membership in an organization alone is not a suffi-

---

[25] See Lalita Prasad Singh, *The Politics of Economic Cooperation in Asia: A Study of Asian International Organizations* (Columbia: University of Missouri Press, 1966), pp. 9–11. I am also indebted to Robert Denham for the research on this point.

[26] See Bruce M. Russett, "The Asia Rimland as a 'Region' for Containing China," in *Public Policy*, ed. by John D. Montgomery and Albert O. Hirschman, Vol. 16 (1967), pp. 226–249.

[27] Rostow, Department of State *Bulletin*, Vol. 57, No. 1464, p. 69.

cient guarantee of credibility. The quasi-regional and poorly organized SEATO seems to have lacked credibility. Even in the highly organized NATO, however, doubts about the credibility of the United States commitment, even reinforced by the stationing of American troops, arose in some circles in Europe, particularly after the Soviets obtained ballistic missiles capable of devastating American cities while (despite various efforts at institutional engineering) NATO's important nuclear retaliation capacity remained firmly in unilateral American hands. A second benefit of using the regional organization instrument is the creation of improved channels of communication both through regular conferences and through personal contacts that lead to "interpenetration of bureaucracies." A third benefit of the regional military alliance is the legitimization of "leverage" over partners' defense policies. Although this leverage has always been imperfect and depends on the need to control German power (independent of the Soviet threat) it also tends to vary with the degree of agreement in perception of the imminence and nature of the external threat. Consequently, to the extent that it does vary with the external threat and to the extent that détente progresses and the international system becomes less bipolar in the 1970's the benefits sought through regional military organization are less likely to be available.

The costs of the regional organization instrument are the obverse of its benefits. Influence is a double-edged weapon and the need to work through an organization may constrain America's freedom of policy. According to William and Annette Fox, United States membership in regional alliances

> has somewhat inhibited its policy from diverging radically from that of its partners, especially when their support was sought for American-defined purposes.[28]

On the other hand, in some cases, when the United States has changed its policy because of its perception of the security situation, the result has often been to exacerbate relations with our partners. Changes in NATO strategy have tended to be American led and have not always been well received in Europe.[29] It is instructive of the costs of this type of regional military organization in a period of diminished external threat that former Secretary of Defense Robert McNamara's flexible defense doctrine of 1962 led to concern among Europeans who feared that it might weaken the nuclear deterrent. Ironically, this United States doctrine was not officially accepted by the NATO Council until 1968 after the departure of France had contributed to its obsolescence.

The prime benefit of the nonmilitary regional organization as an instrument of containment has been the prospect of diminishing the burden on the

[28] William T. R. Fox and Annette B. Fox, *NATO and the Range of American Choice* (New York: Columbia University Press, 1967), p. 125.

[29] See Robert E. Osgood, *Alliances and American Foreign Policy* (Baltimore, Md: Johns Hopkins Press, 1968), p. 52.

United States both economically and in terms of American domestic political costs. The theme has been prominent since the early debates on United States support for European regional organization as well as in the more recent Asian policy statements of the Johnson Administration. There is the additional benefit that these economic and functional organizations may be the only means available for a containment policy in situations where local sentiment for nonalignment makes bilateral or regional military alliances with outside powers unpopular.[30]

The greatest cost of this policy is the risk of misperception of reality through the "telescoping of time"—a failure to take fully into account the length of the stages involved. The future image of a cohesive region capable of self-defense may be substituted for the divisive current reality, and the regional organization becomes a token or symbol that helps obscure a more accurate perception of reality. While it is true that political or cultural regional organizations may help establish a sense of regional identity, the type of integration or organizational structure that can be built on identity alone tends to be "token integration at the international level"—helpful but hardly sufficient as a basis for containment. It is also true that regional economic organizations can unleash a number of dynamic forces which can bring about a "spillover" into a higher level of integration in an area. There are difficulties with this, however, as a basis for containment policy. Although we are still at an early stage in our knowledge in integration theory, there are both theoretical reasons and practical evidence to cause one to be wary about the extent of these forces outside of the Western European context.[31] Moreover, even in Europe the rate at which economic integration might lead to a level of political integration that would entail a common defense capability seems to be much slower than was expected in the 1950's.

In short, the failure to see how very long the short run really is may obscure a full realization of the problems involved in using nonmilitary regional organizations as more than a minor instrument in containment; and this may lead to underestimation of the costs of continuing a containment policy in the international system of the 1970's.

Economic Development

A third major foreign policy objective for which the United States has used regional organizations as an instrument has been economic development, first in the reconstruction and expansion of the Western European economies, later

---

[30] There may be some areas where local regional military alliances will be politically acceptable and might gain legitimacy through formation of a regional organization. See, for example, recent discussions between Australia, New Zealand, and Malaysia. (*The Economist*, March 1, 1969 [Vol. 230, No. 6549], p. 28.)

[31] See Joseph S. Nye, "Comparative Regional Integration: Concept and Measurement," *International Organization*, Autumn 1968 (Vol. 22, No. 4), pp. 855–880; and Joseph S. Nye, (ed.), *International Regionalism* (Boston: Little, Brown, 1968).

in the various parts of the less developed world.[32] There were two distinct aspects of United States support for regional economic organizations in Europe.

First, American support for regional economic organization in Europe was partly out of belief in the greater economic efficiency, including greater competition in larger-sized markets than those typical of European states. Its willingness, however, to support regional protectionist abridgements of its universalist principle of most-favored-nation treatment in international trade and its readiness to suffer trade diversion were limited in Europe to "the Six" among which it was felt that the higher levels of economic integration would contribute toward political objectives as well.

The second aspect of United States support for regional economic organization in Europe had to do with the problems and tasks of allocating American economic aid. The desire to avoid being caught in the middle of constant disputes over allocation and a desire to avoid charges of domination were already reflected in the phrase in George Marshall's famous speech at Harvard University on June 5, 1947, that a unilateral plan would be "neither fitting nor efficacious." The result was the formation of the Organization for European Economic Cooperation charged with reaching agreements from a regional point of view on recommended distribution of American economic assistance.[33]

The United States was slow to extend this approach to less developed areas. Despite a rather beguiling remark by President Dwight D. Eisenhower that what was good for Europe might be good for Latin Americans, too, United States economic orthodoxy in the 1950's led to a cool reception for Latin American schemes for *Latin* regional economic organizations.[34] By the end of 1958, however, some United States leaders began to see the need to reappraise economic policy toward Latin America. (This perception was later enhanced by Castro's revolution but actually antedated it.)[35] In addition, the United States was faced with a concrete opportunity to assist the Central American Common Market (CACM) which, after careful cultivation by the

[32] In general, development has been conceived of primarily in its economic dimensions. For some evidence that regional organization can have an effect on "political development" as well see J. S. Nye, "Regional Integration and Political Development," *International Development Review,* September 1967 (Vol. 9, No. 3), pp. 17–19.

[33] For details see Ernst H. van der Beugel, *From Marshall Aid to Atlantic Partnership: European Integration as a Concern of American Foreign Policy* (Amsterdam: Elsevier Publishing Company, 1966).

[34] Eisenhower allegedly told a cabinet meeting in 1953,

> You know, we sit here and talk, all too rarely, about one commodity in one country, out of all the American republics. Yet when we speak of the affairs of Europe, we talk on a totally different level. Unity, unity, unity: we say it over and over. And we think back to Charlemagne. . . . But what is true for one continent should be just as true for another.

(Quoted in Emmet John Hughes, *The Ordeal of Power: A Political Memoir of the Eisenhower Years* [New York: Atheneum, 1963], p. 145.)

[35] See Robert Harrison Wagner, "Latin America and the Economic Policies of the United States" (Ph.D. dissertation, Harvard University, 1966), pp. 256–293.

UN Economic Commission for Latin America (ECLA) throughout the 1950's, had signed its first major trade integration treaty in 1958. The decision to break with former economic orthodoxy was dramatized by the particularly obvious necessity for a larger market among such tiny states and the alternative prospect of unending instability in an area of primary United States security concern. Subsequently, the United States Agency for International Development (AID) established a unique Regional Office for Central America and Panama (ROCAP) and by 1967 had granted some $100 million in support of regional projects.[36]

Support for regional economic integration became accepted verbal policy after the 1961 Charter of Punta del Este that launched the Alliance for Progress. As Miguel S. Wionczek has argued, however, its peripheral priority before the 1967 Punta del Este summit conference at which the United States committed itself to support a Latin American common market to be formed by 1985 meant that a variety of countervailing private and bureaucratic interests frequently prevailed in practice.[37]

In addition to support for Latin American economic integration the United States has experimented with and is a member of other forms of economic regional organization, such as: the Inter-American Development Bank (IDB) in which the staff is predominantly Latin American though the capital is North American; the Inter-American Committee on the Alliance for Progress (CIAP), based in part on the model of OEEC, which carries out multilateral studies of country programs designed (albeit somewhat imperfectly in practice) to be of assistance in the allocation of economic aid; and the Inter-American Economic and Social Council (IA-ECOSOC) which after the 1967 reforms of the OAS Charter which reoriented the OAS toward economic questions was raised to coequal status with the political Council.

In United States policy toward Africa a convergence of Congressional concern over the dangers of overcommitment which led to imposition of a legislated limit on the number of countries to which development assistance loans could be granted and a growing concern within the American administration with economic effects of the proliferation of tiny African states led to a redirection of the AID program toward promotion of regional economic organization. The catalyst for the change was the Korry Report,[38] commissioned

[36] See Joseph S. Nye, Jr., "Central American Regional Integration," *International Conciliation*, March 1967 (No. 562), pp. 50–57. Three-fourths of United States aid to the area remained bilateral. See also James D. Cochrane, "United States Attitudes Toward Central American Economic Integration," *Inter-American Economic Affairs*, Autumn 1964 (Vol. 18, No. 2), pp. 73–91.

[37] Miguel S. Wionczek, "Latin American Integration and United States Economic Policies," in Robert W. Gregg (ed.), *International Organization in the Western Hemisphere* (Syracuse, N.Y: Syracuse University Press, 1968), pp. 91–156. He cites United States resistance to regional shipping and payments schemes as examples. See also Christopher Mitchell, "Common Market—The Future of a Commitment: Punta del Este and After," *Inter-American Economic Affairs*, Winter 1967 (Vol. 21, No. 3), pp. 73–87.

[38] Edward M. Korry, former Ambassador to Ethiopia, was commissioned by President Johnson to recommend how AID could contribute more effectively to African development.

and received by President Johnson in 1966, which will lead to some 40 percent of United States aid to Africa for regional purposes.[39]

In Asia renewed emphasis on regional economic projects, in particular United States support since 1965 for the Asian Development Bank, was stimulated originally by the political difficulties that America encountered over its Vietnam policy[40] (witness President Johnson's 1965 speech at Johns Hopkins University, Baltimore, Maryland). Subsequently, however, the potential economic effects of the organization, as well as the prospect of getting Japan more involved in the region, have grown in importance.

A major benefit of supporting organizations involved in regional economic integration or regional services is simple economic efficiency. Some 90 less developed countries have populations under 15 million; 60 have markets under 5 million. At low levels of per capita income these population figures represent markets which can support only a limited range of efficient industry which the countries are bent on having for political reasons. Some such states are hard pressed to support a full panoply of services that go with sovereign status. The availability of this benefit is limited, of course, by the difficulty of promoting regional integration among less developed countries referred to above. In some cases at least, an outside catalyst or source of funds can increase the perception of regional economic cooperation as a non-zero sum game involving an expanding pie and thus may make a useful contribution.

A second benefit involves those regional economic organizations, including development banks, which are involved in the distribution of aid resources. As the giving of aid can sometimes appear demeaning and frequently involves considerable participation in domestic processes, the use of regional organizations may provide a means for recipient countries "to diminish their dependence and to increase the dignity of their position while accepting the international ties required."[41]

The potential costs of using regional economic organization for aid to economic development are the obverse of the benefits. Regional economic agreements may merely establish uneconomic industrial protection and only slightly reduce inefficiency; divert resources and attention away from other (e.g., agricultural) uses; and institutionalize the inefficiency in a way that may make it difficult to unscramble later. Thus far these costs are mainly hypothetical though there are some signs of them in Central America.[42] The costs of using

[39] See Anthony Astrachan, "AID Reslices the Pie," *Africa Report*, June 1967 (Vol. 12, No. 6), pp. 8–15. See also Robert S. Smith, "New AID Policies for Africa," *Foreign Service Journal*, February 1968 (Vol. 45, No. 2), pp. 16–19.

[40] Philip Geyelin, *Lyndon B. Johnson and the World* (New York: Frederick A. Praeger, 1966), pp. 276–278.

[41] W. W. Rostow, "The Role of Emerging Nations in World Politics," Department of State *Bulletin*, April 5, 1965, p. 495. (Address made at the University of Freiburg, Freiburg, West Germany, March 15, 1965.)

[42] See Roger Hansen, *Central American Regional Integration and Economic Development* (Studies in Development Progress, No. 1) (Washington: National Planning Association, 1967), Chapter V.

regional institutions in the allocation of aid may be a loss of efficiency by the donor as well as a diminution of leverage in return for gains in dignity and cooperation which prove to be only minimal, for, as John Montgomery remarks, in this field "it is doubtless easier to give than to receive."[43] The experience of CIAP thus far has not been wholly encouraging, and some African states have complained about United States regional aid policies.[44]

Whether the benefits of aiding economic development through regional organizations will exceed the costs will depend on levels of protection and capacity to cooperate in particular cases. Thus far the benefits seem far greater than the costs. Some difficulties may arise in the future, however, between the more protectionist Latin American vision and the generally liberal United States perception of a Latin American common market. On the other hand, the rationality of the policy in the 1970's will not be reduced if détente progresses and the need for political alignment leverage in the aid relationship decreases.

Conflict Prevention and Management

A fourth major foreign policy objective for which the United States has used regional organizations is the prevention and management of conflict. This policy includes two aspects: the use of regional organizations to promote "integrative solutions" in which parties are able to resolve an existing dispute by agreeing on upgrading a third or common interest; and "peacekeeping" in which no "common interest" is found but pressure is put on the parties by outside conciliators, or intervening forces, to cease fighting. In regard to the latter type of capacity the OAS, the Organization of African Unity (OAU), and the Arab League were relatively successful in playing an independent role in dampening conflicts between their members in eleven out of 21 cases, not counting ones they did not try to handle. Two-thirds of the successes, however, were achieved by the OAS where American leadership and logistic capacity played a crucial role.[45] Moreover, nearly all of the OAS cases concern the micro-states of the Caribbean area rather than the larger states of South America, and there are grounds to believe that future OAS capacity in this role may be more limited than it was in the past.[46] Outside the western hemisphere American policy has employed UN peacekeeping procedures with the

[43] John Montgomery, "Regionalism in U.S. Foreign Policy. The Case of Southeast Asia" (Paper prepared for the Wingspread Symposium on Southeast Asia, September 1965).

[44] See Raúl Sáez S., "The Nine Wise Men and the Alliance for Progress," *International Organization*, Winter 1968 (Vol. 22, No. 1), pp. 244–269. Also see *The New York Times*, May 14, 1967:

> The Guinean President made clear his opposition to multilateral or regional aid concepts. . . .
> He said this would subject him to economic neo-colonialism by the former colonial powers,
> particularly France.

[45] For details see Joseph S. Nye, *International Regional Organizations* (Boston: Little, Brown, forthcoming).

[46] See Dreier, *International Organization*, Vol. 22, No. 2.

exception of a futile effort to use NATO in the Cyprus dispute. Although former Secretary of State Dean Rusk has applauded the performance of the OAU and testified to Congress that United States support for regional institutions in Africa "has to do with their ability to settle disputes among themselves,"[47] it is almost impossible to detect this concern as an operational criterion among AID officials involved in implementing the policy.

On the other hand, the United States has frequently turned to regional organization in hopes of providing "integrative solutions" to disputes in several areas. A strong and consistent motive for American support for "small Europe" of the Six has been the concern with "integrating" Germany and France and providing a context for successful resolution of traditional conflicts such as the Saar dispute settled in 1955. United States support of the Central American Common Market is an example of another successful case.[48] On the other hand, attempts at promoting regional organizations as a means to an integrative solution of the Middle Eastern situation have been unsuccessful.[49] Similarly, President Johnson's 1965 announcement of support for the Asian Development Bank, a regional aid program, and the ensuing increased attention to the Committee for Coordination of Investigations of the Lower Mekong Basin seemed motivated in large part by the futile search for an integrative solution to the Vietnam imbroglio.

The benefits of a policy promoting either of the two types of use of regional organization for resolution of local conflicts are quite obvious. The more easily a dispute can be contained or resolved intraregionally, the less the likelihood of involving the superpowers and the less the burden on the United Nations system.

The costs are of several types. First, there is the possibility that a regional organization of which the United States is not a member might impose a solution intolerable to an American ally or in the case of the OAU or the Arab League might use any increments to its "peacekeeping capacity" for peacebreaking against what it considers intolerable regional enemies such as South Africa or Israel. Alternatively, the price of effective and acceptable regional peacekeeping action by the OAS may be a degree of United States initiative which may lead to resentment among Latin countries.

Second, the aid given to promote an integrative solution may have a cost in terms of interference with other criteria for giving aid such as economic efficiency or political alignment. If the probabilities of an integrative solution are very low, these costs may outweigh the benefits.

[47] U.S. Congress, House, Committee on Foreign Affairs, *Hearings, on H.R. 7099, Foreign Assistance Act of 1967,* 90th Congress, 1st Session, May 4, 1967, p. 855.

[48] Witness, for example, the 1968 resolution of the Honduras/El Salvador border incident. See *Visión,* August 2, 1968.

[49] Although an ironic sequel to the United States proposal in 1957 of a Middle Eastern development bank was that the United States finally gave in on its resistance to creation of a similar instrument in this hemisphere. See John C. Dreier, *The Organization of American States* and the *Hemisphere Crisis* (New York: Harper & Row [for the Council on Foreign Relations], 1962).

The prospect in the 1970's of achieving success in enhancing the "peace-keeping" capacity of regional organizations, particularly outside the western hemisphere, might depend on continued détente and the capacity of the super-powers to agree to limit their involvement in the regions concerned. On the other hand, the rationality of a policy of promotion of regional integrative solution would be unlikely to be affected by changes in the international sys-tem, except perhaps if there should be a return to tight bipolarity in which case alignment might become an important criterion for aid.

PROJECTING THE FUTURE

As we enter the 1970's, there is a fifth major interest that the United States could pursue through regional organization that is of a different order of mag-nitude: encouragement of change in the structure of the international system in accord with a new vision of world order. One can claim to see hints of this in past policy. For instance, in some versions of the "Atlanticist" regional vision the creation of a unified Europe was desired as a means to change rather than preserve the bipolar structure of power.[50] More recently, there were signs that the Johnson Administration was attempting to develop a doctrine of re-gionalism as a means of reconciling global involvement with a need to reduce "the burden that America has had to bear this generation."[51] This might be interpreted as a policy of creating regional balances of power from which the United States as the stronger superpower could stand back. Analogous to the United Kingdom's nineteenth-century European policy, the United States would intervene only occasionally to right the scales. Critics have pointed out that such a role is excluded in fact; for as long as containment in the ideo-logical sense has priority, America could only intervene on one side of the scales.[52] Many of the same critics, however, agree with the idea of supporting autonomous regional organization as a means of encouraging change in the international system.

Though the names and detailed descriptions of the current international system vary,[53] there seems to be general agreement that it is characterized by bipolarity in the basic structure of military power but by much looser struc-

[50] See Karl Kaiser, "The U.S. and the EEC in the Atlantic System: The Problem of Theory," *Journal of Common Market Studies*, June 1967 (Vol. 5, No. 3), p. 413; also George W. Ball, *The Discipline of Power: Essentials of a Modern World Structure* (Boston: Little, Brown, 1968), Chapter XV.

[51] President Johnson, "Four Fundamental Facts of our Foreign Policy," *Department of State Bulletin*, September 26, 1966 (Vol. 55, No. 1422), p. 453. (Address made at Lancaster, Ohio, September 5, 1966.)

[52] Stanley Hoffmann, *Gulliver's Troubles, or the Setting of American Foreign Policy* (Atlantic Policy Studies) (New York: McGraw-Hill [for the Council on Foreign Relations], 1968), p. 67.

[53] See for example Wolfram F. Hanreider, "The International System: Bipolar or Multibloc?," *Journal of Conflict Resolution*, September 1965 (Vol. 9, No. 3), pp. 299–308; R. N. Rosecrance, "Bipolarity, Multipolarity, and the Future," *ibid.*, September 1966 (Vol. 10, No. 3), pp. 314–327; Oran R. Young, "Political Discontinuities in the International System," *World Politics*, April 1968 (Vol. 20, No. 3), pp. 369–392; Hoffmann.

tures in the various functional and geographic subsystems. A particularly interesting model that spells out the political characteristics of the current system is the one constructed by Stanley Hoffmann. In Hoffmann's view the consecration of the nation-state (with UN membership as a prime source of legitimacy) and the change in the role of force both because of the potential self-defeating costliness of an actual use of nuclear weapons and because of the cost of ruling mobilized alien populations have led to an "inflationary" type of international system in which the maneuvers of small powers in the dominant polycentric layer are divorced from the ultimate (but muscle-bound) realities of military nuclear power in the basic bipolar layer; and a possible multipolar layer has only begun to emerge. In such a system milieu goals (the environment of the international system) are more important than possession goals (direct territorial, economic, or other concrete interests); world politics becomes "internalized" as domestic problems are linked with international forces, and the sources and types of power become more diverse. "As the physics of power decline, the psychology of power rises."[54] Considerations of prestige, informal penetration, and capacity to communicate effectively take on added importance.

In Hoffmann's view of the future of this system the possible proliferation of small, vulnerable, and thus unstable nuclear forces may present the superpowers with a choice between costly policing or a retreat that would let the world disintegrate into a series of jungles. The alleged benefits of certainty and control in a bipolar system[55] have already been greatly eroded by polycentrism and are likely to vanish completely if there should be creeping nuclear proliferation. As a Great Power the United States has an interest in preserving a degree of hierarchy in the system and in reducing the current separation between the capacity of states to participate in world politics and the responsibilities for world order which they are willing to undertake. The inflationary system that allows weak states more freedom of action to use their power than superpowers will likely lead to nuclear proliferation of the most dangerous kind. At the same time the United States has an interest in increasing diversity, particularly the emergence of China and the creation of an independent European power, for multipolarity would increase diplomatic flexibility and allow the Great Powers to devote more attention to each other rather than to policing their ideological "camps" and being drawn by bipolarity into marginal conflicts. To help keep the international system moderate and responsible the United States should encourage the creation of separate hierarchies in the various functional areas of international relations; the formation of an autonomous European power in world affairs; and the estab-

[54] Hoffmann, p. 65.
[55] See Kenneth Waltz, "The Stability of a Bipolar World," Daedalus, Summer 1964 (Vol. 93, No. 3), pp. 881–909.

lishment of autonomous regional organizations of the types that would involve
local regional powers in responsible leadership positions in economic, scientific, and peacekeeping tasks in the rest of the world—all under the ultimate
nuclear umbrella of two or three superpowers and within the normative structure of the United Nations and the various global economic and functional
agencies.

A possible objection to such a policy of support for regional organization
as a means of changing the structure of the international system might be
made on the ground that the setting of world politics of the 1970's will not
be favorable to regionalism. In fact, one's vision of the future of the international system depends upon the means one chooses for projecting it. If we
sketch the setting of the 1970's by projecting current technological trends and
their effects on defense considerations and economic transactions, the setting
may be uncongenial to regional organization. In Wohlstetter's view

> the revolution in transport and communications casts doubt not only on the
> new isolationism of a growing minority but also on the more respectable but
> rather mechanical regionalism that may frequently be found in both the Dem-
> ocratic and Republican establishments: the grand designs for Latin American
> common markets, Asian common markets, African unions, economic unities
> spanning the Middle East from Morocco to Afghanistan, and others.[56]

More generally, one could argue that as the tight bipolar system of the
1950's has loosened, some of the newly important subsystems have not had a
regional basis. For example, the recently politically important monetary subsystem with its Group of Ten is nonregional, and the inclusion of Japan in the
"Atlantic" Organization for Economic Cooperation and Development (OECD)
in 1964 may be typical of the future. In a world of jumbo air freighters, giant
supertankers, and large-scale data processing that facilitates capital movements
and multinational corporations, geographically remote trading partners such
as Japan and the United States should be able to increase mutual trade at least
as rapidly as the regional European Economic Community (EEC). In the
defense field nuclear and missile technology has already reduced the role of
geographical distance in military security, and similar changes can be expected
to result from satellite technology.[57] In the view of Thomas Schelling a new
type of global geography may be taking over in which gravity, earth spin,
and cloud cover may become as important in the world of satellites as Suez or
Gibraltar were for seapower.[58] In Wohlstetter's words, "the upshot of these
considerations of technology in the 1970's is that basic interests in safety will
extend further out than they ever have before."[59]

[56] Wohlstetter, *Foreign Affairs*, Vol. 46, No. 2, p. 250.
[57] See *The Implications of Military Technology in the 1970's* (Adelphi Paper, No. 46) (London:
Institute for Strategic Studies, March 1968).
[58] Speech to Foreign Policy Association, New York, May 1968.
[59] Wohlstetter, *Foreign Affairs*, Vol. 46, No. 2, p. 252.

Thus one could conclude that a foreign policy for the 1970's that places heavy emphasis on the promotion of regional organizations will be mistaken because technological trends indicate that the most important international systems of interaction—whether economic or military—will not be regionally based. Such a conclusion would be somewhat premature, however, for the early 1970's. Despite falling transport costs geography will still have an impact on price. Despite missile and satellite technology local and conventional defense techniques will remain relevant. Moreover, some technological changes may encourage regional organization. Communications technology may make possible direct and inexpensive regional communications in areas like Latin America or Africa where intraregional communications now often have to go through New York, London, or Paris. In addition, inexpensive breeder reactors may lead to nuclear proliferation of a type that encourages disengagement by distant powers eager to minimize their risks, as Hoffmann argues.

If, instead of projecting the setting of the 1970's on the basis of technological effects on transactions and the geography of defense we predict the continuation of a number of the political features of the current system, we get a very different picture of the potential favorableness of the setting for regional organizations. We can extrapolate from Hoffmann's model of the current system a number of the political characteristics that could provide statesmen with incentives to turn to regional organizations as useful tools for a variety of purposes.

1) With the diversification of power the prestige of regional leadership can become a useful symbol of power as the foreign policies of France, Ethiopia, and the United Arab Republic indicate in the EEC, the OAU, and the Arab League.

2) With the increased importance of domestic populations in world politics, yet the enhanced legitimacy of national sovereignty, regional organizations may provide an opportunity to appeal over the heads of governments to societal groups in other states (despite the sovereignty clauses often written in the charters) as the successful and unsuccessful efforts of the Ivory Coast and Ghana to influence their neighbors through the Conseil de l'Entente and the OAU demonstrate.

3) With the devaluation of military force traditional military alliances may be less attractive, but statesmen still feel the need to draw lines and introduce even a faint element of predictability into their search for security by political alliances under the guise of regional organization—witness ASPAC and the Association of Southeast Asian Nations.

4) With the predominance of milieu goals over possession goals regional organizations may be useful tools for shaping conditions beyond one's national boundaries, whether it be the creation of more favorable conditions for eco-

nomic development aid, the establishment of regional balances of power, or a group's assertion on the world scene of its collective identity.

5) Finally, with the increased importance of communications and signals regional organizations may be useful as "no trespassing" signs or "firebreaks" that will help to avert confrontations in a refragmented world, either between the superpowers (e.g., the OAS and the Warsaw Pact) or between the weak (e.g., the OAU) and the superpowers.

In short, as long as the international system of the 1970's maintains certain features of the current structure, there will be a number of political incentives for the use of regional organizations despite an ambiguous balance in the long-run technological trends. Thus regional organization appears to be neither the "automatic" trend of the 1970's as some enthusiasts suggest nor a relic of the 1950's as the skeptics seem to imply. At best the projected setting is ambiguous and thus enhances the room for policy choices.

Choices About the Future

Simplified debates over "regional vs. global organization" are not very enlightening. Not only are these not the only alternatives (there is also bilateralism) but most of the policy goals outlined above require a mixture of approaches. Choices must be made, however, about the proper mixture, and occasionally decisions must be made between regional and global organization or between types of regional organization. We have already mentioned the choice of the OAS over the UN in the field of hemispheric security.

In the field of trade policy the United States allowed the meaning of Article 24 of the General Agreement on Tariffs and Trade (GATT) to be compromised in the 1950's because of its belief in the beneficial political effects of European regionalism.[60] Similar conflicts might arise in the trade policy field over a large but partial European trade agreement if that appeared to be the only way to associate the EFTA countries with the EEC and over the question of special hemispheric trade preferences for Latin America if the global United Nations Conference on Trade and Development (UNCTAD) scheme fails.[61]

In the security field conflicts may arise between the pursuit of détente and the maintenance of NATO or over the value of autonomous European organization, such as occurred in the recent dispute over whether the European Atomic Energy Community (EURATOM) or the International Atomic Energy Agency (IAEA) should be responsible for inspection in Europe under a nonproliferation treaty.

[60] See Gerard Curzon, *Multilateral Commerical Diplomacy: The General Agreement on Tariffs and Trade and its Impact on National Commercial Policies and Techniques* (London: Michael Joseph, 1965), Chapter IX.

[61] For examples of the latter type of demand see J. W. Clark, *Economic Regionalism and the Americas* (New Orleans, La: Hauser Press, 1966).

The outcome of such decisions will depend on the extent to which one decides to promote autonomous regional organizations as a part of a long-run vision of world order. This in turn depends on the probabilities involved in creating such an order. We have argued above that on the basis of technological and political projections the probabilities are ambiguous. In these circumstances a sense of timing becomes the crucial factor for policy. While it is useful to have a clear vision at a high level of abstraction, a policy of promoting autonomous regional organizations must not be applied in doctrinaire fashion to all regions at all times in the same way.

Even if the creation of autonomous regional organizations without United States membership or control is an appropriate goal for the end of the 1970's, too rapid an implementation (e.g., an early American withdrawal from NATO or the OAS) or too premature an implementation (e.g., "an Asian common market" modeled on the EEC) could have opposite effects from those intended. Future organizational potential must not be mistaken for current capacity. The important question is whether in the early 1970's the various types of autonomous regional organizations (with the possible exception of Western European organizations) can become sufficiently strong to bear the burden that is expected of them. As we have argued above, the peacekeeping record of organizations other than the OAS (in which the United States' membership seems to make what difference there is) has not been impressive to date. The capacity of less developed countries to cooperate successfully in economic regional organizations with a scope broad enough to make a significant difference to economic development or the promotion of integrative solutions has been limited thus far to two somewhat shaky cases, the East African Common Market and the Central American Common Market. The management of regional balances of power under conditions of proliferation of vulnerable nuclear forces (e.g., potentially the Middle East) involves a complexity of considerable and possibly dangerous dimension. In short, policymakers may wish to encourage regional organization in accord with a long-run vision when the costs are low but should not necessarily opt for the regional alternative when the costs in terms of other goals are high.

Not only must an American policy on regional organization in the 1970's take account of problems of timing; it should also be based on a clear perception of potential conflicts between goals. The five foreign policy goals examined above are not always complementary. Unless this problem is clearly perceived and priorities are deliberately chosen, one goal may have costs in terms of another that nullify its benefits. We have already noted the conflict between regionalism for ideological containment and regionalism for the creation of a series of autonomous balances of power. In some ways the regional organizations we have created in Asia seem designed to prevent a Chinese sphere of influence. Containment may also conflict with a policy of support for regional organization for economic development or for integrative solutions—witness the 1967 American *volte-face* on a Mekong Committee commitment after it was felt that Cambodia had become too close to Hanoi.[62] "Containment" in the ideological sense might also make it difficult for the United States to continue regional aid to an East African or Latin American common market if one of the members underwent a "Communist coup." A policy of regionalism for local peacekeeping might have costs in terms of regionalism for economic development if, for example, United States financial aid to the OAU or United States training of African army units for OAU peacekeeping led to an expensive guerrilla campaign against Portugal and South Africa.

In conclusion, the setting for regional organization in the 1970's will be neither as clearly favorable as the enthusiasts nor as unfavorable as the skeptics predict. There will be scope for choice in our policy. In such circumstances a long-run vision is important if we are to escape the mere perpetuation of past policies which are beginning to lose their relevance. It is mildly ironic that the vision of a more flexible and moderate international system toward which regional organization would contribute might make the debates of 1945 over Chapter VIII[63] of the UN Charter relevant again. The United States might well wish to "un-rewrite" the Charter and go back to a system of Security Council approval (and potential United States veto) of regional organization enforcement actions before the United States embarked on a policy of giving peacekeeping aid to the OAU or the Arab League. And the United States might be willing to pay the price that would have been unthinkable at the height of the Cold War, i.e., Security Council approval (and possible Soviet veto) of enforcement actions in the American sphere of influence in the western hemisphere.

Long-run visions, however, are not sufficient basis for short-run policy, and a doctrinaire support for certain types of regional organization that would ignore problems of timing and fail to make distinctions between different areas would be mistaken. We cannot, in the early 1970's at least, escape the frustrations and expense of attempting to provide leadership in organizations like NATO and the OAS until other security systems evolve for those areas. Similarly, though we may wish to promote autonomous regional organizations for economic development and conflict prevention and management, the promotion of effective organizations of which we are not a member is only in small part within our control. United States policy toward regional organization in the 1970's should be informed by a long-term vision of an improved world order, but we must be careful not to mistake organizational symbols and future hopes for current reality.

[62] See John D. Montgomery, "The Political Decay of Foreign Aid," *Yale Review*, Autumn 1967 (Vol. 57, No. 1), pp. 1–15.

[63] Chapter VIII of the Charter is entitled "Regional Arrangements."

Unilateral and Multilateral Options
in the Execution of Foreign Policy

RFD

I

THE argument whether the United States in the conduct of foreign policy should lean toward multilateral or unilateral action tends to revolve in the stratosphere. Proponents of each course cite the conspicuous failures of the other and submit wishful designs varying from triumphant world government to uninhibited national sovereignty. Unfortunately, the range of real choices confronting the policymaker is very much narrower. Constraints on decisionmaking in a democracy, even in a dictatorship, are very strict and nowhere more so than on issues having to do with sharing among nations decisions affecting major national interests.

This article will examine, first, the pressures and impulses which drive the directors of foreign policy toward the widest feasible measure of unilateral action; second, the countervailing influences which sometimes move them to resort to multilateral instruments; third, practical problems which arise in working through and with some of the most significant of the latter; and finally, the range of real choices which may exist in this field during the coming decade.

II

Obviously, proponents of international organization and action are laboring under serious handicaps. Despite the lessons of two world wars this is still an age of exuberant and passionate nationalism. Not only have more than 60 new nations emerged since 1945 but the older ones in Europe and the Americas are resisting, with an obstinacy which Charles de Gaulle epitomizes but does not monopolize, efforts either to federate them or to restrict the political aspects of their sovereignty. Even the United Nations Charter was

RFD is an authoritative observer on the matters discussed in this article. He wishes to preserve his anonymity.

diluted at its inception with the famous Article 2 (7) which unblushingly states:

> Nothing contained in the present Charter shall authorize the United Nations to intervene in matters which are essentially within the domestic jurisdiction of any state or shall require the Members to submit such matters to settlement under the present Charter; but this principle shall not prejudice the application of enforcement measures under Chapter VII.

Since enforcement measures have extremely rarely been applied, this proviso has not yet significantly impaired the restriction.

The traditional doctrine of the overriding authority of the nation-state vis-à-vis both its citizens and its peers remains the conventional and the popular guide to the conduct of government. Any deviations from this norm are held by many to smack of unpatriotism, even treason. The slogan, "my country right or wrong," is still the natural first reaction of the average citizen of the United States, France, or Tanzania. This sentiment is, therefore, a central postulate of domestic politics of which every statesman must take account before he presumes to place any aspect of his nation's interest in the hands of an international organization.

In a very real sense this traditional constraint parallels the personal inclination of most national policymakers. Every wielder of power, big or little, likes to have as free a hand as he can. Few politicians are eager to add to domestic inhibitions either the complications of extracting unanimity from a dozen or more allied governments or the risks of giving free rein to "galloping majorities" in quasi-universal organizations. A President or a Secretary of State is likely instinctively to prefer the simplicity of unilateral action when he can get away with it and, where the sanction of an international organization is necessary or highly desirable, to do his best to see to it that American decisions are ratified there with as little change as possible. Needless to say, other governments and statesmen behave in the same way.

On the legislative side members of Congress, responding to their constituents and their prejudices, are even less likely, if they can help it, to let decisions they consider theirs pass to international bodies. They are particularly sensitive about their exclusive right to appropriate funds without which of course international, like national, agencies cannot exist. Thus, even if limited powers are theoretically granted to international organizations, the latter are often prevented from using them effectively by denial of the wherewithal. We saw how the remarkably successful UN peacekeeping operation in the Democratic Republic of the Congo came to an inglorious conclusion in the Article 19 controversy though in this case it was as much the exaggerated nervousness of the United States Department of State as the tightfistedness of the legislators which was responsible for the fiasco.

Perhaps most allergic of all to letting any significant element of decisionmaking on matters it conceives to be its concern slip into the unreliable hands of international organization is the fourth branch of the American government, the military. The military was as determined as was the Union of Soviet Socialist Republics to embed the veto in the UN Charter in order that American troops could not be ordered into action without United States consent. The only occasions on which military men have been happy with international operations have been when they have been able to dominate them, as in the North Atlantic Treaty Organization (NATO), the UN operation in Korea, or the Organization of American States (OAS) intervention in the Dominican Republic in 1965, or when they perceive only a minimal United States interest, as in the Congo. Otherwise, they have strongly preferred substantially unilateral American action even when, as in Vietnam, it has meant a very large United States commitment of forces.

The predisposition to unilateral action of the executive, legislative, and military policymakers is backed by a substantial majority of American public opinion. In the United States there is still a strong current of old-fashioned patriotism which considers its most cherished tenets infringed if the government consorts with, not to mention relies on, international organizations which are assumed to be dominated either by Communists or by Afro-Asians. There are, moreover, many unreconstructed economic interests which seek out the slightest excuse to revert to protectionism and to unravel the network of multilateral agreements and associations in the trade and monetary fields. There is a growing reaction to economic aid and trade benefits to developing countries which have seemed to foster neither gratitude, democracy, nor stability. On the whole, the majority of the electorate, insofar as it concerns itself with these matters, is skeptical of all supranational enterprises and was inclined, at least until Vietnam, to put faith in the omniscience and omnipotence of Uncle Sam.

Finally, under this rubric it is only fair to note that very few of the multilateral instrumentalities created since 1945—NATO, the International Monetary Fund (IMF), and the UN Development Program (UNDP) would be exceptions—have as yet demonstrated consistent and impressive effectiveness. Those who generally distrust them all, particularly the underdeveloped countries, have therefore ample ammunition with which to justify their criticism. We shall go into this point more fully later.

III

On the other hand, there are obviously some strong pressures in American society working in favor of international cooperation. Otherwise, international organization would not have proliferated to the extent it has during the last 25 years, for the most part under American sponsorship.

There is no doubt that the disastrous consequences to the United States both of events in other continents and of our failure to concern ourselves with them in time created a deep impression on American leadership and opinion during and after World War II. It became nakedly clear that isolationism was both impracticable and dangerous, that even our great strength was insufficient to assure our security, and that international interdependence was in many respects an inescapable fact of life. The more enlightened elements of American public opinion during the first postwar decade led the United States into a whole series of international commitments which over subsequent years created ties, habits, and feedbacks profoundly influencing our foreign policy.

It is worth listing some of these involvements in order to illustrate their variety: the United Nations, the Organization of American States, the International Monetary Fund, the International Bank for Reconstruction and Development (IBRD), the Food and Agriculture Organization (FAO), the North Atlantic Treaty Organization, the Organization for European Economic Cooperation (OEEC), the ANZUS Pacific Security Pact, the Southeast Asia Treaty Organization (SEATO), the General Agreement on Tariffs and Trade (GATT), the Development Assistance Committee (DAC) of the Organization for Economic Cooperation and Development (OECD), the International Development Association (IDA), the International Atomic Energy Agency (IAEA), the UN Conference on Trade and Development (UNCTAD), and the Alliance for Progress. In addition, there was of course a series of bilateral security treaties with such countries as Japan, the Republic of China (Nationalist China), the Republic of Korea (South Korea), and the Philippines.

Association with each of these organizations inevitably involved some deflection of the United States foreign affairs community from its accustomed course. Thinking about foreign affairs in and out of Washington became conditioned to the existence of these new entities and our involvement in them. A new environment was gradually created which was resented but necessarily tolerated, which in differing respects both restricted and enlarged the options open to those responsible for the conduct of foreign policy.

New organs of the bureaucracy were created for dealing with each multilateral body, and each of these organs acquired in time a life and vested interests of its own. There came to be in the government dedicated UN, NATO, SEATO, GATT, and OAS constituencies, each emotionally as well as bureaucratically attached to its multilateral client. Each served to feed back the views and interests of the client organization and of the nations which composed it into the national bureaucracy where they competed with the views and interests of the unilateralists and of other multilateralists. These new bureaucracies were often inclined to elaborate doctrines and devices relevant to their particular problems but not always as widely applicable as they believed. Some were carried to disastrous extremes like the doctrine woven around Article 19 of the UN Charter, some were lifted indiscriminately from one part of the world to another like the "lessons of Munich," and some were built out of plausible fantasy like the proposed NATO multilateral force (MLF).

Of course, this involvement of the United States in international commitments and associations would not have been possible without considerable changes in American public opinion, for the most part so resolutely isolationist even up to 1941. Each of the new associations created and relied on a new public as well as a new bureaucratic constituency, minorities in each case but articulate, persistent, and often well-heeled. Such institutions as the World Affairs Councils, the Foreign Policy Association, the Council on Foreign Relations, a large number of specialized university centers and schools, the Atlantic Council, the Middle East Institute, the World Federalists, the United Nations Association, and a host of other nongovernmental organizations concerned to a greater or lesser degree with foreign affairs all combined to educate on these matters a growing segment of the electorate and to create on behalf of most of the multilateral institutions or pacts to which the United States belonged pressure groups of varying degrees of strength and effectiveness.

Another capital factor in gradually building support for multilateral pursuit of American foreign policy objectives was the unhappy result of some of our more recent and ambitious unilateral ventures. The Dominican intervention, even though it was relatively brief and was masked by an OAS cloak, aroused considerable complaint in Latin America and some at home. It was, however, most of all the war in Vietnam, with its involvement of half a million American troops, mostly draftees, its 30,000 deaths in battle, its absorption of 40 percent of the defense budget and 14 percent of the whole federal budget, and its damaging impact on poverty programs and student morale at home, on balance of payments and on aid programs and the United States political image abroad, which more and more convinced the American people that they could no longer play so preponderant and so independent a role either as the world's policeman or as the world's banker. While the exploration of multilateral alternatives is still ill-formed and halfhearted, the climate may be more favorable to them than it has been at any time in the past fifteen years.

Before proceeding, however, to forecasts for the future it may be useful to examine in somewhat more detail how certain of these multilateral institutions have been used during the past two decades, how decisions when and how to use them are taken in Washington, and how diplomacy conducted and realities encountered in them play back and constrain decisionmaking by Americans. We shall look briefly at the conduct of business with and through NATO, the OAS, and SEATO and then turn at a little more length to the United Nations.

IV

The North Atlantic Treaty Organization is undoubtedly the favorite with United States policymakers of all the international political and security institutions of which the United States is a member. Its relevance to United States security is incontestable because it confronts our chief rival for world power and because the opulent area in which it is centered is the chief prize of that rivalry. Its members are congenial and relatively easy to work with because we have a common ancestry and share the same threat and the same stage of economic development. The degree of military integration under United States auspices has been remarkable. For all these reasons few of the qualms which usually inhibit American policymakers from wholehearted cooperation with international institutions trouble our participation in NATO.

Nevertheless, even with this preferred institution all is not smooth sailing nor is de Gaulle the only cause of rough weather. Our European partners have never made either the military or the financial contribution to the Organization that the United States thought necessary or that they originally agreed to make. On the other hand, the United States has irked the Europeans by failing, in their estimation, to take sufficient account of their views on a wide range of issues inside and outside Europe, from the level and manner of détente through the 1968 Treaty on the Nonproliferation of Nuclear Weapons to the war in Vietnam. A recurring problem exists in regard to United States leadership: There is complaint when it seems too insistent and domineering; there is almost equal complaint when it seems to slacken because the United States is preoccupied elsewhere.

Another partial exception to United States reservations about multinational structures is the Organization of American States. It represents the institutionalization and modernization of the Monroe Doctrine. In this respect it is almost as precious to American policymakers as NATO though the fact that the threat to its area has been on the whole less immediate than that to Europe has meant that attention to it has been more sporadic. However, when Cuba or the Dominican Republic became or seemed likely to become centers of hostile presence in the hemisphere, the OAS was promptly moved to the center of the stage.

The United States would no doubt like to see it, at least on the military side, more regularly and effectively organized to deal with both external and internal threats. Many of the other members, however, acutely conscious of the degree to which "the colossus of the North" dominates the machinery and its forces when assembled, are reluctant to give it wide powers or a permanent force structure. Their suspicions are sharpened by controversies between the

United States and themselves: friction over coups d'état, military regimes, and costly expenditures for sophisticated arms; the dwindling level of American aid; and, contrariwise, the "domination" of United States private investments.

The fact is that the discrepancy in power, interests, and objectives between the United States and its OAS partners is so great that an international institution embracing them all is so likely to seem an instrument for imposing United States policy on the others that they will rarely permit it to play a predominant role in hemisphere affairs.

A much less satisfactory regional organization, from the viewpoint both of the United States and of its other members, is the Southeast Asia Treaty Organization. Patterned after NATO and ostensibly copying much of its machinery, SEATO was at the outset entered with *arrières pensées* by some of its members: France, the United Kingdom, and Pakistan. The Organization was thereafter only tenuously held together by the United States and its other Asian members. While disillusionment with the Vietnam experience disposes many Americans to transfer Asian responsibilities to a regional security organization, it is clear that SEATO is no longer fitted to play that role except as the flimsiest sort of cover for United States power. It has failed therefore to meet the test of effectiveness either as a viable multilateral organization or as a useful vehicle for United States unilateral action.

The only international organization in either the security or the development field which is at the same time quasi-universal and impartial, unattached to either East or West, North or South, is the United Nations. Its very universality and impartiality, however, make it suspect to the Great Powers. Even in 1945 the United States envisaged for it a role carefully circumscribed to fit the national interests of its strongest Members. During its first decade and a half, however, the interests of a majority of Members, mostly European and Latin American, were close enough to those of the United States so that it was possible for it to be used for peacekeeping purposes in Korea, the Middle East, Kashmir, etc., despite the veto and without too much regard for the Soviet Union.

With the great additional influx of Asians and Africans in and after 1960 the composition of the General Assembly and the specialized agencies, even to some degree of the Security Council, was transformed. The Western "mechanical majorities" of which the Soviets had so long complained were replaced by Afro-Asian "nonaligned" majorities which, on the one hand, for the most part refused to endorse any action to which either the United States or the Soviet Union strongly objected and, on the other, showed an increasing disposition to recommend far-reaching measures in certain fields of primary concern to themselves—southern Africa, human rights, development, and trade—even if they lacked the authority or the resources actually to carry out these measures.

The United States therefore found itself after 1960 increasingly confronted by a situation in the United Nations which made that Organization less available for carrying out or reenforcing American policy and indeed more apt on occasion to put forward policies which were felt to be contrary to United States interests. The traditional dichotomy between unilateral and multilateral execution of foreign policy which had been partially veiled and diluted by the earlier composition of the United Nations now reemerged though in shifting and ambiguous forms. To make clear the options, obstacles, frustrations, and ambiguities which confronted the executors of United States foreign policy in the 1960's in this respect it will be useful to glance briefly at the multilateral exercise which best exemplified them all, the Congo operation and its Article 19 aftermath.

V

Crisis arose in the Congo in July 1960 a few days after independence when the Belgian community seemed threatened; Belgian troops were dispatched to protect this community; the alleged consequent threat to international peace and security was brought to the United Nations; and the Congolese government under Prime Minister Patrice Lumumba appealed to other governments, including the United States, for aid and support to replace that of Belgium. The Administration of Dwight D. Eisenhower, having in mind that the Congo was not an area of primary American interest and perceiving that United States intervention would be likely to provoke or aggravate intervention by Communist and radical African states, wisely chose a primarily multilateral rather than unilateral course in dealing with the problem.

This choice was facilitated by the fact that since one of the new African nations had appealed to the United Nations for help against an "imperialist" power, Belgium, the Soviet Union was at the outset disposed to cooperate and initial action to set up a peacekeeping force was taken without difficulty by the Security Council. As the Secretary-General and his representatives in the Congo subsequently used their authority to check interference by the Communists and radical Africans, consensus at the United Nations soon began to fray and steps had to be taken by the General Assembly. By early the next year, however, when the central issue had become secession in Katanga which the African states unanimously opposed, Soviet cooperation in the Security Council was once more resumed, though henceforward, particularly when the application of force by the United Nations against the secessionists became the question, the United Kingdom, France, and Belgium strongly objected and were only brought along with great difficulty.

United States decisionmakers were obliged during this classical four-year exercise in multilateral diplomacy to maneuver with great adroitness and flexibility between a wide variety of conflicting interests and their protagonists.

There were our close allies—the United Kingdom, France, and Belgium—which were skeptical in varying degrees of the UN involvement and would have preferred to handle the whole business through a Western caucus or consortium; indeed they sometimes sought to mobilize NATO against United States policy in the UN, calling in the Old World to redress the balance of the New. There were the African states unanimously desirous of preventing the disintegration of the Congo or a revival of Belgian domination but split between radicals and moderates as to the character of government they wished to see in Leopoldville and the foreign influences they were prepared to tolerate. There were the Soviet Union and its allies endeavoring to strengthen their hand in the Congo and throughout Africa, to discredit all Western states, and hence to support the radicals in and out of the Congo. There were the nations from all parts of the world contributing troops to the UN force—India, Indonesia, Ethiopia, Nigeria, Sweden, Ireland, Canada, Brazil—which were mainly concerned with doing a workmanlike job without political interference. There were the Secretary-General—first Dag Hammarskjöld and then U Thant—and his principal aides—Andrew Cordier, Ralph Bunche, Rajeshwar Dayal, and many others—interested in dealing effectively with the problem and thereby demonstrating the peacekeeping capabilities of the United Nations.

Domestically, decisionmakers were also subjected to a variety of pressures. Inside the State Department itself there was sometimes almost internecine warfare between the European Bureau, which supported the Belgians, British, and French, and the African and International Organization Bureaus, which advocated firm support of the Secretary-General and the United Nations. Consistent with the original United States decision, the three Presidents and two Secretaries of State involved, while often vacillating and hedging, came around in the end to backing the United Nations. The United States military, both because it had no desire to see American forces involved in the Congo and because it was providing substantial logistic support to the UN force, in this case consistently backed the multilateral option. On the other hand, some members of Congress, misled by adroit European and Katangese propaganda, repeatedly demanded that the executive branch prevent the United Nations from using force against the rebellious but anti-Communist Moise Tshombe. For the most part, however, the Congress was most concerned with limiting the mounting costs of the operation to which the United States was contributing about 50 percent. They did approve a generous United States purchase of a UN bond issue for this purpose but in the process so emphasized their feeling that the Soviet Union and France should share the costs that the State Department subsequently decided, probably mistakenly, that it had no choice but to provoke the fatal Article 19 confrontation.

The history of the Congo operation did demonstrate that despite powerful impediments from many quarters and the much less favorable composition of the United Nations the United States government was capable both of prompt resort to the UN in an unforeseen crisis and of persistent support of it in a peacekeeping operation lasting over a four-year period. Neither the opposition of its principal allies or its principal adversaries, the harassment of vociferous domestic pressure groups reflected in Congress, nor its own internal biases and frictions prevented it, when the conditions were appropriate, from providing indispensable support to this multilateral action. On the other hand, the internal and external oppositions were sufficiently strong to block an early decisive exercise of UN power which had been quite feasible and which could have brought the operation to a successful conclusion in two years instead of four.

This unnecessary prolongation was disastrous in that it greatly increased the financial cost, strained the tempers of American legislators and executives, hardened the respective positions of the United States, the Soviet Union, and France, and thus paved the way for the Article 19 confrontation and the subsequent stalemate in UN peacekeeping. There is not space here to examine this crisis in any detail but it is pertinent to note that as far as United States behavior is concerned, it represented an anachronistic hangover from the happier days of the fifties when the United States and its allies had been able to dominate the United Nations and a failure to realize that both the changed composition of the Organization and the new temper of the times made a major East-West confrontation inside the United Nations in 1964 inappropriate, self-defeating, and tragically damaging to the institution.

VI

We will conclude with a brief survey of choices and prospects in this field in the 1970's.

Despite the logic and the need for more powerful regional organizations we cannot be sanguine about the early development of new capabilities by such organizations in ways which would significantly relieve the United States of its present international responsibilities.

Unless the Soviet Union behaves in a particularly aggressive fashion, NATO is unlikely to take on significant new strength and function. It will remain primarily military, marginally political, and restricted to the European continent and its environs. It will continue to be troubled by controversies over appropriate sharing of military deployments and financial costs. Most of the constraints which inhibit wholehearted United States participation in other multilateral organizations of a political character will not apply to NATO, but none of its members seems likely to show more interest in the future than in the past in breaking it loose from its military framework. As a footnote, however, it is safe to say that the members of NATO and other developed nations are almost certain to involve themselves over the next decade in much more intimate forms of economic cooperation having both regional and global application. This imperceptibly tightening nexus may do much more than formal alliances to foster multilateral and limit unilateral options in international affairs.

As suggested above, the OAS, the second most significant regional organization in which the United States participates, suffers from two serious inhibitions: First, the Latin members find the disproportionate power of their North American partner alarming unless steadily circumscribed; second, they see little real value in a military and political association which does not bring them larger and more consistent economic benefits than the United States in its present mood seems likely to bestow. A broadening and deepening of the capabilities of the OAS depends on a very substantial reinforcement of the Alliance for Progress or other United States aid programs for Latin America which would incorporate firmer hemispheric political and security cooperation in a matrix of urgently needed economic support so substantial and reliable that it would be too tempting to resist. In other words, since the military threat is far less immediate and perceptible, an effective joint military structure or security apparatus would have to be bought by the United States at an even higher price than it paid in Europe.

The natural craving for multilateral company and cover which the United States feels in East Asia after Vietnam is unlikely to be satisfied in the way it wishes. There is and will be growing economic and at least symbolic political cooperation between East Asian nations but, while American economic support will be ardently sought, explicit United States membership in East Asian associations will usually not be. Individual Asian nations will continue to want unequivocal security guarantees from the United States, but no substantial multilateral security framework is likely to emerge to replace an obsolescent SEATO. The only significant multilateral options which the United States is likely to have anywhere in Asia will be economic. This is equally true for the Middle East and even more true for Africa except as the Organization of African Unity (OAU) may be marginally able to relieve the UN of some burdens which would otherwise, through the UN, involve the United States.

The principal multilateral option which the United States will have at its disposal in the near future, the only significant one in the security field except NATO, one of potentially growing importance also in the economic development field, is the United Nations. In this respect the United States government will be faced with a choice whether in the coming decade either 1) to rely on NATO in Europe, on a skeptical and reluctant OAS in the western hemisphere, and on such unilateral force as it is willing to supply and with such bilateral support as it is able here and there to muster in all the rest of the world; or 2) to run the risks and uncertainties of cooperation with the Soviet Union in the UN Security Council and/or the Afro-Asian majority in the UN General Assembly in working toward international peace and security.

As appears from our earlier analysis, the natural inclination of United States decisionmakers, reenforced by traditional Congressional and popular attitudes, has been and will be to lean heavily toward the first alternative. On the other hand, decisionmakers will be confronting Congressional and popular revulsion, arising from Vietnam and other recent experience, against unilateral American expenditure of blood, treasure, and prestige for international objectives. To some degree, therefore, though this is unlikely to be so absolute as some now fear, the choice may be between a relative United States withdrawal from international concerns, at least outside Europe and the western hemisphere, and a much greater reliance, if that should prove feasible, on the United Nations. Under these circumstances, responding to all the competing pressures we have just mentioned and coming out more or less as we have suggested, American administrations over the next decade might make a much more serious attempt than has been made since 1964 to revive and reenforce the peacekeeping capabilities of the UN and to expand massively the resources available to it for development.

For the first to succeed there would have to be either agreement with the Soviet Union, the United Kingdom, and France to make the Security Council an effective instrument of peacekeeping by negotiating Article 43 agreements or by reviving and elaborating the less formal procedures of the early 1960's; or there would have to be developed a renewed willingness on the part of two-thirds of the Members of the UN to apply the latter procedures through the General Assembly over the objections of one or more of the Great Powers. Since the latter alternative seems most unpromising, at least on any consistent and reliable basis, the real choice is whether or not to test the former and the real uncertainty is whether or not it would succeed.

If it fails, the multilateral option, outside NATO and marginally the OAS, will have little chance or scope in the security field though it will continue to be increasingly attractive in dealing with many aspects of economic interdependence. Even if the bid to the Soviets to restore the effectiveness of the Security Council succeeds, it will probably succeed only partially and inconclusively. Many years would no doubt lapse and many crises be lived through before one could have any solid reliance on the multilateral mechanism, even for dealing with turbulence in the third world, not to mention confrontation between superpowers. All the inclinations and ambivalences affecting decisionmakers in Washington in the choice between multilateral and unilateral action will continue to operate throughout the coming decade even under the most favorable circumstances.

Though an illusion in this sense has long existed and still persists, there is no magic formula for organization of the executive branch in Washington which would ensure that decisions in the field of foreign policy or any other field will be prompt, clear, and wise. Reorganization of the decisionmaking machinery in the White House, in the State Department, in the Pentagon, and among these and other agencies has been repeatedly undertaken, modified, reversed, and revived without more than marginal improvement in the character of the decisions.

This does not mean that machinery is negligible. There have to be effective procedures to ensure that critical problems are foreseen and soberly analyzed in time, that alternative initiatives and responses are devised and ready for use, and that clear unencumbered lines of authority are at all times available for approving, or rejecting, such initiatives and responses. That being said, it is the foresightedness, the sobriety, and the authority which are the elements necessary for success; the best of machinery can only provide an environment conducive to the exercise of these faculties.

An essential ingredient of decisionmaking must be an alert awareness of the pressures—personal, institutional, and popular—working in favor of unilateral national action and a steady resolution to resist these pressures when a broader view of the national interest so requires. This will often call for an avoidance of hallowed rhetoric by Presidents, of obsolete formulas and far-fetched analogies by Secretaries of State, and of facile reliance on weapons by Chiefs of Staff.

Even such exalted persons, however, do not exist in a vacuum. As suggested at the outset of this article, the pressures favoring unilateral national action are real and strong. The only way in which they can be over time surmounted and the policymaker freed to choose between multilateral and unilateral action on the basis of an impartial judgment of the national interest will be through a long process of education of American opinion in the realities of international affairs.

Of course that process has been going on since 1917 and more intensively since 1941. The participation of the United States in the United Nations, NATO, and many other multilateral organizations for more than twenty years bears witness to the progress made and is testimony to the wisdom and dedication both of some political leaders and of many private organizations and private citizens laboring in this vineyard. Still far more needs to be done particularly at a time when, as a result both of Vietnam and of compelling domestic concerns, an initially healthy tendency to look inward may, as is often characteristic of the American temper, be carried to a dangerous extreme.

The ultimate decision whether the United States during the coming decade takes the fullest possible advantage of multilateral options and organizations, both for the maintenance of peace and security in a nuclear age and for coping with population, famine, and rising expectations in Asia, Africa, and Latin

America, will be made by the American people and the American Congress. Whether that decision is an informed one will depend on the leadership and enlightenment which the administration in Washington and the opinion molders throughout the country provide. The first will have to be more candid, objective, and thorough in informing Congress and public than the previous Administration was, and the second will have to be more evenhanded and farsighted in balancing internal and external priorities than they have recently been.

A broad consensus of public support was built and maintained for the multilateral foreign policies of the first postwar decade. This consensus has been frittered away in the late sixties. A new popular consensus will have to be formed for the multilateral policies required in the seventies if they are to have both the political support and the ample resources they must have to achieve their purpose.

United States National Security Policy and International Organizations:

A Critical View of the Literature

DAVID A. KAY

THIS review essay will focus on four central questions which the author believes to be closely related to the problem of progress in the study of international organizations. These questions, narrowed to fit the scope of this essay, are the following: 1) What has been the role of international organizations in the national security strategy of the United States; 2) what has been the impact of the United States in the international organizations of which it is a member; 3) what has been the impact of participation in international organizations on the range of United States choices and methods in the foreign policy area; 4) what impact have changes in the shape of the international political system had upon United States participation in international organizations and upon those organizations' impact on the United States. This analysis will concentrate only on studies relevant to these themes.[1]

THE UNITED NATIONS AND QUESTIONS OF INTERNATIONAL PEACE AND SECURITY

Although United States foreign policy with regard to international organizations in general has not been a major focus of research interest in the past

DAVID A. KAY is Associate Professor of Political Science, Barnard College, Columbia University, New York.

[1] For thorough bibliographies see Alexander Rudzinski, *Selected Bibliography on International Organization* (New York: Carnegie Endowment for International Peace, 1953); G. P. Speeckaert, *Select Bibliography on International Organizations* (Brussels: Union of International Associations, 1965); and Ronald J. Yalem, "The Study of International Organization, 1920–1965; A Survey of the Literature," *Background*, May 1966 (Vol. 10, No. 1), pp. 1–56.

two and one-half decades, for reasons which this essay will attempt to make clear at a later stage, the role of the United Nations in United States security policy has been the subject of several searching examinations.[2] There are two major theoretical perspectives which dominate the literature dealing with the role of the United Nations in American foreign policy. One body of literature assumes or postulates that the international political system is developing in a particular direction and then proceeds to evaluate how well United States policy toward the organization conforms to the requirements of the postulated development of the system.[3] The second perspective makes a different assumption: That while the changing international political system can be characterized at any given point according to key variables, it is always in a process of transformation with a range of alternative outcomes. This perspective leads to use of a strategic-instrumental framework to evaluate the United Nations as an instrument of foreign policy given the current nature of the international system. The first perspective with its assurance that it knows the shape of international politics—past, present, and future—concentrates on the question: "How well has United States policy served the United Nations?" The second perspective, certain only of the shape of the past and present international system, concentrates on the question: "How well can the United Nations serve the United States?"

The distinction between these two perspectives and the implications for research of each can best be seen if we examine a major work in each category. For this purpose this essay will take the Russell and Bloomfield volumes.

In Russell's book the analysis of the United Nations and its relation to United States security policy is rooted in a perception of the international system dominated by the United States and the Union of Soviet Socialist Republics which are engaged in a relationship of contained conflict evolving in a unidimensional direction through coexistence and toward cooperation. The United States in this model of the system is required

> to maintain the deterring power of resistance to aggressive action, while seeking to influence the potential aggressors gradually out of their violent intentions through policies of constraint and collaboration.[4]

[2] The two most exhaustive accounts are: Lawrence D. Weiler and Anne Patricia Simons, *The United States and the United Nations: The Search for International Peace and Security* (New York: Manhattan, 1967); and Ruth B. Russell, *The United Nations and United States Security Policy* (Washington: Brookings Institution, 1968). Of special importance because of its conscious attempt to relate the United Nations to the wider arena of international politics and its use of a theoretical construct, the national interest, to explain and/or prescribe changes in United States policy is Lincoln P. Bloomfield, *The United Nations and U.S. Foreign Policy: A New Look at the National Interest* (rev. ed.; Boston: Little, Brown and Company, 1967). Also of importance because of its quasi-official character as an authorized statement of the Kennedy-Johnson view of United States policy toward the United Nations is Richard N. Gardner, *In Pursuit of World Order: U.S. Foreign Policy and International Organizations* (rev. ed.; New York: Frederick A. Praeger, 1966).

[3] A major example of this approach, and the one that this essay proposes to focus upon, is Russell.

[4] Russell, p. 11.

The development of the international system—and in Russell's model that is equated with the development of American-Soviet relations—is toward a broadly cooperative policy. In this cooperative policy context

> the Organization and its related group of specialized agencies still provide the best available means of expanding the areas of desired international cooperation on a global basis as the necessary will to cooperate is painfully cultivated. The relationship of the United States to the United Nations can therefore most usefully be viewed in a perspective of the best way to assist the Organization in overcoming the hazards that now prevent it from working as its Charter anticipates, as it would if its members carried out their Charter commitments. There is no other way to develop the kind of international system that remains the United States goal.[5]

The model fails to articulate explicitly the nature of the transformation force which is driving the system inevitably toward a duopoly of United States–Soviet cooperation, although there is the implicit argument that such a development is necessary if the United States and the Soviet Union are to continue to exist, e.g:

> There is no technical solution to the dilemma of decreasing security in the face of ever-increasing military power. Any successful political approach to the problem will have to be able to use the United Nations actively and constructively, if only because no other place exists where "all the varied interests and aspirations of the world [can] meet . . . upon the common ground of the Charter. . . ."[6]

The United States and the Soviet Union will either use the United Nations in the manner set forth in the Charter or the increasing insecurity spiral of the present system will force the two superpowers to destroy each other.

Given the stark alternatives of the Russell model, it is not surprising that she selects the survival option and proceeds to analyze United States policy in the United Nations from that perspective. "Strengthening" the Organization becomes in this analysis the dominant goal value against which policy is measured. United States policy which fails this litmus test is explained as "logical only in terms of a security policy that leads to using the world Organization as an instrument of the cold war."[7] Allies and alliances are seen as impediments to or drags on the development of enlightened United States policy, the necessity of maintaining strategic deterrence vis-à-vis the Soviets is acknowledged but the problems and complexities for the foreign policy process which flow from this necessity are largely ignored, and other channels and instrumentalities for conducting foreign policy are viewed as competitors of inferior value to the United Nations.

[5] Ibid., p. 23.
[6] Ibid., pp. 444–445.
[7] Ibid., p. 420.

Although the Russell volume yields a comprehensive description of United States policy in the United Nations,[8] the shortcomings of its perspective are serious and limit the contribution it makes to progress in understanding international organization. In selecting the United Nations as the exclusive unit of analysis the author omits all systematic analysis of the nature of the United States policymaking process. The reader is faced in this study with an exogenous variable called United States policy whose variation and interaction with other exogenous variables representing other national policies is described and to some extent evaluated according to its long-range impact on the Organization. No attempt is made to reveal, much less to analyze, the different actors in the United States foreign policy process with reference to the United Nations or to evaluate the impact of each on the dynamic process which produces national policy outputs. Having failed to focus on the interactive process which produces United States foreign policy, the author is also forced to ignore the feedback process through which participation in the United Nations may have affected both the methods of making and implementing foreign policy as well as the very nature of national security decisions.[9]

If it is true, as Russell accepts in several places, that the United Nations at its present stage of development is more an arena than an actor in international politics, then it would seem vital in a study of the national security policy in the Organization of one of the two superpowers to attempt to understand systematically the causal process which produces this policy. To ignore entirely as this work does the feedback process through which membership in an international organization modifies channels of foreign policy decision-making, and hence affects the shape of decisions, is to miss the real importance of national policy studies for progress in the field of international organization theory. Does attempting to achieve American national security objectives through United Nations procedures as opposed to non-UN channels result in a different distribution of influence in the American policymaking process? How has membership in the United Nations affected the ability of the United States to undertake unilateral, bilateral, or multilateral actions in the national security field outside of the United Nations? Has it created a new set of expectations internationally and/or domestically concerning the content or methods of American national security policy? Has it imposed new demands to which United States national security policy must address itself?

---

[8] This is obviously not intended to be the full-scale review which Ruth Russell's book deserves but an assessment of what its perspective contributes to the study of the role of national policy in international organization. Miss Russell has provided a detailed and accurate account of United States policy in the United Nations on a wide range of issues which is the task that she set out to accomplish.

[9] A superb example of this type of analysis as well as of what it can add to the understanding of national policy is to be found in Stanley Hoffmann, *Gulliver's Troubles, Or the Setting of American Foreign Policy* (Atlantic Policy Studies) (New York: McGraw-Hill [for the Council on Foreign Relations], 1968).

Has it provided procedures through which new and unknown demands can be made on the United States? These two intertwined dimensions, the internal decisionmaking process which produces American policy toward the United Nations and the feedback process through which participation in the United Nations affects American policy outputs, are ignored by Russell's exclusive focus on United States policy *at* the United Nations. The tunnel vision of this analytical scheme is particularly damaging because of the nature of the Organization which is heavily dominated by its environment—the major components of which are the nation-states that are Members of it.

At the systemic level in attempting to understand how changes in the structure of power and pattern of conflict in the world affect the role of the United Nations and its place in American national security strategy the Russell analysis is almost useless. The present state of the system is never fully developed and is largely categorized according to one variable, the relationship of the United States and the Soviet Union. This system is seen as developing in a unidimensional manner with only one stable outcome: United States–Soviet cooperation within a revitalized United Nations operating as envisaged in the Charter. This is a clearly inadequate conceptualization of the "alternative futures" faced by the international political system.[10]

Even if one grants Miss Russell's questionable belief that the only stable alternative to American-Soviet politico-military competition is a duopoly of cooperation, it certainly does not necessarily follow, as she seems to believe, that the two superpowers must then "use the United Nations actively and constructively."[11] If such a cooperative duopoly is to be the model of the international system in the future, its most immediate impact might well be to confine the role of the Organization to legitimizing authoritative pronouncements of the superpowers in the peace and security field in a manner similar to the role the United States and the Soviet Union apparently intended for the Organization in endorsing the 1968 Treaty on the Nonproliferation of Nuclear Weapons. If duopoly were to be extended to other matters, such as economic and social questions and peaceful change in the international distribution of political and welfare values, the modest role of the United Nations might as a result be constricted by the conserving bias of the duopoly.[12]

Most of Russell's problems at the systemic level flow from her failure to articulate systemic variables and to identify their dynamic relationship to the

---

[10] For a discussion of both the relationships between the state of the international system and the role of the United Nations and of a number of possible models of future systems see Oran R. Young, "The United Nations and the International System," *International Organization*, Autumn 1968 (Vol. 22, No. 4), pp. 902–922.

[11] Russell, p. 444.

[12] For a similar argument with reference to this type of model see Young, *International Organization*, Vol. 22, No. 4, pp. 917–918.

United Nations. This is particularly unfortunate in a study focused on one such variable, the national security policy of the United States.

If one is interested in understanding the meaning of national policy for the Organization as opposed to describing its vicissitudes, it is necessary to have at least some crude model or theory of organizational development. At the present time international organization theory does not have such a model except in the area of regional economic integration. However, to this writer at least, it is clear that regional integration has been the most stimulating area of international organization research for the last ten years precisely because of the conscious effort of the major theorists in this area to develop and test hypotheses concerning the dynamics of organizational development. Unfortunately, Miss Russell has limited herself to providing excellent descriptions of the rise and atrophy of various issues and the injection of new issues and their fate from 1945 through 1967 without asking or even guessing what the meaning is for the Organization of the issues that it has been asked to handle or that have bypassed it or the effect on the Organization of the alternative dispositions of issues. What, for example, are the implications for the development of the Organization of the various alternative means for dealing with political change that have developed in the United Nations, e.g., the UN Temporary Executive Authority (UNTEA), the UN Operation in the Congo (ONUC), or Indonesian independence?[13] In this case again the failure is one of not developing analytical categories as a basis for generalizing. It is in one sense the result of continuing to hew too closely to the canons of historiography and neglecting those of political science.

The second major perspective which dominates the literature concerning the role of the United Nations in American foreign policy uses a strategic-instrumental framework to evaluate the potential of the Organization as an instrument of foreign policy given the current pattern of world politics. This perspective is best represented in the literature by Lincoln P. Bloomfield's *The United Nations and U.S. Foreign Policy: A New Look at the National Interest* which was first published in 1960 and revised in 1967.

In Bloomfield's book the analysis of the relationship between United States foreign policy and the United Nations is rooted in a belief that

> the key to understanding U.S. policy toward the United Nations can be found only in the violently shifting world environment in which both must function. Profound changes have taken place in the equations of world power and in the atmospherics of the international climate. It is precisely because things have not stood still that there is an urgent need for reappraisals of strategies and policies which have served us reasonably well under different circumstances.[14]

[13] In this connection see the suggestive categories of Young in *ibid.*, p. 912.
[14] Bloomfield, p. 9.

Its immediate focus is the strategic-instrumental one of seeking to determine "how can the United States make the most effective use of the United Nations in achieving its paramount objectives in the years immediately ahead?"[15] For this purpose Bloomfield's model erects the national interest—defined as "the goals and objectives of American external policy"—as the standard

> against which to estimate the extent to which the use of U.N. machinery may advance or retard our cause. The utility of the United Nations, then, is tested in the light of what in political shorthand has come to be called the "National interest."[16]

Bloomfield then proceeds to identify what he sees as the fundamental national interest of the United States given the shape of the international political system of the mid-1960's. From this fundamental national interest which is

> to secure the kind of world environment in which our nation—and, by definition, other nations—can cultivate their societies without excessive insecurity and external threats of disruption.[17]

Bloomfield derives a set of interrelated United States policy goals and objectives under the categories of military security, political security, stability and welfare, and world order. The remainder of the book is a sensitive and often brilliant analysis of the potential offered by the United Nations for the attainment of these objectives.

For the development of international organization theory Bloomfield's analysis has one serious limitation. He has provided an excellent model of how to derive from the existing pattern of world politics the parameters of effectiveness of an international organization and of how to test policy objectives and alternatives against these. However, he has not provided us with any model of the sources or procedures through which United States policy is formulated.[18] This is in spite of the fact that in concluding his study Bloomfield asserts

> probably nothing is more important in determining the role of the United Nations on the world political stage than the nature of the U.N. image that leading statesmen hold in their minds. Whether or not those images are accurate or even rational, they define in broad terms national attitudes toward the United Nations. Moreover the process is a reciprocal one, with national attitudes in their turn affecting the prospects of the world organization.[19]

Both Bloomfield's analysis and certainly international organization theory could have greatly profited if in addition to examining the suitability of the

---

[15] *Ibid.*, p. 21.

[16] *Ibid.*, p. 27.

[17] *Ibid.*, p. 42.

[18] There is included in an appendix a brief description of "The Mechanics of U.S. Participation in the United Nations." But the appendix is not integrated into the structure of the analysis. (*Ibid.*, pp. 247–258.)

[19] *Ibid.*, p. 239.

United Nations as an instrument of foreign policy he had examined the context of the United States policymaking process for using the United Nations.
It should be emphasized that it is not that the policymaking context is important but probably properly the subject of a separate book; it is that policy analysis can rarely fruitfully be separated from the context from which it derives.
Bloomfield shares with many others the habit of discussing the United Nations as an instrument to affect the external environment which can perhaps
even ensnare other states into following the norms of the Charter. This is, of
course, correct, but there is a failure to recognize the existence of any feedback
into the United States policymaking process from the use of the Organization.
This feedback process will almost inevitably be ignored when the policymaking context is omitted from the framework of analysis. Yet all should realize
that in all human endeavors instruments not only shape the external environment but the very lives and cultures of those who wield the instruments.[20]
In international organization theory the linkage between the use and performance of an organization and national policy has been largely ignored.
If one is interested in the development of theoretical frameworks which contribute to an understanding of the dynamic interactions between international
organizations and their members this key linkage deserves concentrated attention.

UNITED STATES FOREIGN POLICY AND REGIONAL SECURITY ORGANIZATIONS

In the adjustment of the United States to its new role in international politics after the conclusion of the Second World War regional security organizations assumed a role of major importance. As Robert Osgood has written,

> not only have they [regional alliances] been a major means of projecting Amer-
> ican power; they have also been the most prominent instrumentality by which
> the nation has related itself to a vastly expanded role in the international arena.
> In addition to being calculated instruments of deterrence, alliances have ap-
> pealed to the American ideal of organizing order by means of collective insti-
> tutions.[21]

These regional security organizations and the policy of the United States within them have provided a major focus for research in the post-World War II
period far exceeding the United Nations or other international institutions as
topics of interest.[22] Among the regional security organizations the North At-

[20] For a fascinating discussion of this phenomenon from the perspective of cultural evolution see
Peter Farb, *Man's Rise to Civilization as Shown by the Indians of North America from Primeval Times
to the Coming of the Industrial State* (New York: E. P. Dutton & Co., 1968).

[21] Robert E. Osgood, *Alliances and American Foreign Policy* (Baltimore, Md: Johns Hopkins Press,
1968), pp. 1–2.

[22] For thorough bibliographies see Norman J. Padelford, "A Selected Bibliography on Regionalism
and Regional Arrangements," *International Organization*, November 1956 (Vol. 10, No. 4), pp. 575–
603; Yalem; and the selected bibliographies included in the quarterly issues of *International Organization* and *Foreign Affairs*.

lantic Treaty Organization (NATO) has commanded attention far exceeding that of any other such organization. Therefore, this part of the essay will concentrate on the literature concerning American participation in NATO.

If one were to analyze the six-foot shelf of books that has been produced since 1949 on NATO, it could be divided logically but unequally into two categories. The first, and by far the larger category, consists of policy prescriptions to deal with the periodic crises that have afflicted NATO. Reflecting the immediate symptoms of the crises that they are attempting to cure, these studies have generally focused on the problems of adjusting the realities of the alliance to the changing requirements of military strategy in a nuclear age.[23] In the form in which most of these studies have been prepared they are characterized by a generally brief relevance to the student of international organization. The constant tempo of crises in NATO quickly destroys the relevance of most policy prescriptions. The crisis of the Lisbon goals was succeeded by the problem of *MC-70* which was followed by the question of nuclear control and the flexible response, etc.

It is to the immense credit of those scholars who have centered their attention on the policy analysis of NATO-related problems that pat assumptions and patterns of action were frequently challenged and new courses frequently explored because of their writings. This having been recognized, however, how can one judge their contribution to the field of international organization? It is this writer's opinion that this body of policy prescription literature should be viewed as a huge lore of partially analyzed data demanding further analysis. As written, most of these studies provide excellent insights into the role at various points in time of regional security organizations in the American national security strategy; they contain a wealth of data on the extent and limits of the United States influence in such organizations as well as on the dynamic problems of managing an international subsystem including a preponderant power; they recognize, although they seldom analyze, the dependent variables behind changing national perspectives and policies and their interaction within the context of an international organization; they deal with the manifestations, if not the underlying phenomena, of the impact of changes in the international system on the role and tasks of international organizations. What these studies lack is a framework of analysis which could generate meaningful hypotheses about the development dynamics of such organizations, the impact of national participation in such organizations both

---

[23] In this category are included such works as the following: Alastair Buchan, *NATO in the 1960's* (New York: Frederick A. Praeger [for the Institute for Strategic Studies], 1963); William W. Kaufman (ed.), *Military Policy and National Security* (Princeton, N.J.: Princeton University Press, 1956); Henry A. Kissinger, *Nuclear Weapons and Foreign Policy* (New York: Harper & Row, 1957); Henry A. Kissinger, *The Troubled Partnership* (New York: McGraw-Hill, 1965); Klaus Knorr (ed.), *NATO and American Security* (Princeton, N.J.: Princeton University Press, 1959); Robert Osgood, *NATO: The Entangling Alliance* (Chicago: University of Chicago Press, 1961); Timothy W. Stanley, *NATO in Transition: The Future of the Atlantic Alliance* (New York: Frederick A. Praeger, 1965).

on the organization and more importantly on the members themselves, and the relationship between these subsystems and other component units of the international system.[24]

The second category, much smaller than the first, focuses explicitly on the policy process of American participation and the meaning for this process of such participation.[25] William T. R. Fox and Annette B. Fox have provided an exceptional demonstration of the potential for the study of regional security organization as well as other types of international organization of an approach which is rooted in a sensitivity to the concerns and constraints of the decisional process of an important member state. Their book provides a framework which integrates a vast amount of data about: elites' and policymakers' expectations and perceptions concerning NATO; the impact of participation in NATO on American foreign policy outlooks, objectives, and process; the actual and potential uses of NATO in the attainment of American foreign policy objectives; and the decisional process of NATO. This book provides a telling demonstration of the leverage that analysis of American policy and behavior with respect to international organizations gains when centered on the input and feedback process connecting the United States to an international organization.

IMPLICATIONS

What is the significance of the preceding analysis for future research concerning United States policy and behavior with respect to international institutions? One glaring need is to move toward hypotheses at least and hopefully frameworks of analysis which encourage comparative study of United States policy in different international organizations. The paucity of studies concerning United States policy in the United Nations is the result to a considerable extent of early disillusionment with the Organization in operation in the cold-war arena and a belief that the action was someplace else—in the regional security organizations. The process of superpower interaction with other states and the international system within the context of an international organization and the implication of such interaction for the superpower and the international system have not served as common denominators of analysis. Most research since 1945 on United States policy toward international organization has been parochially bound to the confines of one organization and has shown an almost compulsive fear of broader generalizations.

[24] One such approach which with some elaboration would provide a challenging framework for the reanalysis of much of the data of the policy prescription school is to be found in Stanley Hoffmann, "Discord in Community: The North Atlantic Area as a Partial International System," in Francis O. Wilcox and H. Field Haviland, Jr. (ed.), *The Atlantic Community: Progress and Prospects* (New York: Frederick A. Praeger, 1963), pp. 3–31.

[25] The major study in this category and the one that this review focuses upon is William T. R. Fox and Annette B. Fox, *NATO and the Range of American Choice* (New York: Columbia University Press, 1967). This essay, however, is not intended to be the thorough review which this significant work deserves.

Studies of United States policy with regard to both the United Nations and NATO have shown an extreme reluctance to recognize the nature of the dynamic connections between the shape of the international system and the role of international organizations. Not only are causal models lacking but so is causal reasoning concerning the process of transformation and change linking the international system, international organization, and national policy outputs. In studies focusing on the United Nations the connections are usually ignored while in NATO studies analysis is generally focused on change in one variable, i.e., the changing distribution and capabilities of weapons systems.

There are signs, however, that studies of United States policy toward international institutions are undergoing a transformation of their own which may have a far-reaching impact on international organization theory. The volume by Fox and Fox breaks with tradition by calling attention to the wider problem of how one is "to describe and assess the impact of participation in an international organization" before narrowing its focus to NATO.[26] Their basic framework of analysis is highly salient to other international organizations and hopefully will lead others to use a process-policy framework in analyzing United States policy in other organizations.

A second encouraging sign is Ernst Haas' new textbook *cum* theoretical framework *cum* policy analysis.[27] Haas in this short book sketches a suggested linkage between international systems, the American domestic systems, the United Nations, and regional security organizations in terms of strands of interdependence and then proceeds to draw policy conclusions. There is much to quarrel with in this book—terms are loosely defined and inconsistently used and the model of the American political process is primitive when contrasted with the Fox book, to mention two major points. However, Haas is to be applauded for at least sketching suggested linkages. The demonstration effect of this work should serve as a useful prod to others in the field.

If we are to move ahead in international organization theory in other than the regional economic sector there is much to be said for identifying United States policy and behavior as they relate to international organizations as the key bases from which that advance must begin. The immediate problems in this realm are challenging and important; the data concerning it is perhaps more easily available than for any other sector and because of the salient role of the United States in the international system as well as in individual international organizations the spillover potential of theory in this sector is greater than in any other.

[26] *Ibid.*, p. 77.
[27] Ernst B. Haas, *Tangle of Hopes: American Commitments and World Order* (New York: Prentice-Hall, 1969).